EDUCATION AND THE
QUEST FOR MODERNITY IN TURKEY

EDUCATION
AND
THE QUEST
FOR MODERNITY
IN TURKEY

by

ANDREAS M. KAZAMIAS

THE UNIVERSITY OF CHICAGO PRESS

Library of Congress Catalog Card Number: 66-20585

The University of Chicago Press, Chicago 60637
George Allen & Unwin Ltd, London W.C.1
The University of Toronto Press, Toronto 5, Canada

PRINTED IN GREAT BRITAIN

Dedicated to
Kappa Delta Pi Honor Society in Education
Comparative Education Center, The University of Chicago
George W. Angell, Jr.

213-3/

PREFACE

THE idea of embarking upon a study of Turkish education was conceived in 1961, when I joined the staff of the Comparative Education Center of the University of Chicago. One of the areas of research conducted by graduate students and members of the faculty focused on comparative studies involving schools and their relationship to the social, political, and economic institutions in a variety of societies and countries. It was felt that a similar undertaking concerning Turkish secondary schools would add to the knowledge that was being accumulated on what may be called the 'social dynamics' of education.

On September 29, 1962, my family and I arrived in Ankara and registered at a local hotel. In order to carry out the study I had planned, it was absolutely essential to secure permission from the Turkish National Ministry of Education to visit schools and to administer a questionnaire to the students. Very soon I discovered that the few letters of recommendation I carried were not sufficient credentials to gain access to the authorities; and rightly so, I may add. It was at a moment of frustrated expectations that I met George W. Angell, Jr., and Fred Weinfeld, both of whom were then in the service of the Agency for International Development and were attached as advisers to the Research and Measurement Bureau of the Turkish Ministry of Education. I explained my predicament to them and solicited their help. Their response was immediate and heartwarming. Without their understanding, co-operation, and advice, I could not possibly have completed my study, only part of which is reported in this volume, but which will occupy me for quite some time. For Bill Angell's and Fred Weinfeld's assistance, which included meetings with Turkish officials and professional advice on the construction of the questionnaire, the coding of the responses, and the transfer of the data on IBM cards, I am most grateful.

I wish also to express my thanks to many members of the Ministry of Education and the Research and Measurement Bureau, particularly to Messrs. Osman Ulkümen, Ibrahim Yurt, Abdurrahman Sh. Sanay, Shefik Uysal, and Ibrahim Ozgendash, all of whom gave freely of their time to help me at various stages of the project. For interminable discussions on Turkish history, culture, and education, as well as on some burning issues of the day, which provided indispensable information and insights for what is included here, I am especially indebted to Dr Selâhattin Ertürk, teacher, poet and philosopher.

Although I am grateful to all these people for materials, advice, and encouragement, they bear no responsibility for what is said here. I am sure that there are many points with which they would disagree, and they might well wish to disassociate themselves from the conclusions I have drawn.

On this side of the Atlantic, I should like to express my thanks and appreciation to several organizations, groups, and individuals. The Comparative Education Center and the University of Chicago granted me a year's leave of absence and sufficient supplementary financial support to enable me and my family to spend the academic year 1962–3 in Turkey; Kappa Delta Pi Honor Society in Education awarded me the Harold Benjamin Fellowship in International Education and has partly subsidized the publication of this book; and the Co-operative Research Branch of the U.S. Office of Education has supported the processing, tabulation and analysis of the data on the students in the *lise*. Among my former colleagues at the University of Chicago I should like to acknowledge the help of Professors C. Arnold Anderson, Charles E. Bidwell, Mary Jean Bowman and Philip J. Foster.

The instrument used to gather the empirical data on the lise students, the analysis of which constitutes most of Chapter X, was in part adapted from the questionnaire used by Foster in his research on secondary schools in Ghana and reported in his book *Education and Social Change in Ghana* (University of Chicago Press, 1965). The combination of the historical and sociological approach which pervades much of this study was also in part the result of stimulating and often heated discussions with all of the aforementioned Chicago colleagues. In many respects Foster's study of Ghanaian education and the present study on Turkish education illustrate two variations of the consequences of institutional transfer or 'borrowing': they involve the 'functional' adaptation of two Western models by two different traditional cultures. The two studies provide enough materials for a fruitful comparative educational study, although this was clearly beyond our purpose.

Here again although I profited from the counsel, insights, and work of these persons, they are in no way responsible for the outcome.

A.M.K.

University of Wisconsin

A NOTE ON TRANSLITERATION, SPELLING, AND PRONUNCIATION

THE rules of thumb described below were adopted in order to facilitate the printing of the manuscript and its reading by those not familiar with the Turkish language. Since it is not a difficult language to pronounce and generally conforms to certain phonetic rules, those who know Turkish will have no difficulty in recognizing the 'liberties' I have taken and the subtle distinctions I have omitted.

1. Most letters present no problems and are retained in their Turkish form. Their approximate pronunciation is as follows:
   - a — a (as in cut)
   - b — b (as in bed)
   - d — d (as in dog)
   - e — e (as in red)
   - f — f (as in fool)
   - g — g (as in good)
   - h — h (as in hell)
   - i — i (as in pit)
   - j — j (as the French je in jour)
   - k — k (as in king)
   - l — l (as in love)
   - m — m (as in mud)
   - n — n (as in nut)
   - o — o (as in doll)
   - ö — ö (as the French eu in deux)
   - p — p (as in pie)
   - r — r (as in red)
   - s — s (as in sing)
   - t — t (as in tell)
   - u — u (as in bull)
   - ü — ü (as the French u in tu)
   - v — v (as in vase)
   - y — y (as in yet)
   - z — z (as in zebra)

2. The following consonants are transliterated into approximate English sounds:
   c into j (as in jam)
   ç into ch (as in church)
   ş into sh (as in shop)

13

3. ğ and the dotless ı are changed into g and i.
4. All diacritical marks and circumflex accents over capital letters are omitted.
5. Where a Turkish word has been widely used in English, the English form is used (e.g., kismet, vizier, pasha).

CONTENTS

15

INTRODUCTION

TURKEY as we know it today is a relatively new state, although Turks appeared and entrenched themselves on the Anatolian peninsula, the heartland of present-day Turkey, early in the Middle Ages. As a nation-state Turkey came into being in 1923, after a struggle against foreign powers and an internal revolution which substituted a republican form of government for the existing Ottoman Islamic theocracy. The Turkish Revolution, however, was more than a political event; it was a social, cultural, and economic revolution as well. Its aim was not merely to overthrow a political system, but to transform the entire fabric of the society along modern Western lines.

Although social and cultural change through *inkilâp* ('reformism' or 'revolutionism') became a basic principle after the proclamation of the republic, the movement towards modernity predated the attainment of nationhood and had its roots in the Ottoman period of Turkish history. It began in the eighteenth century and culminated in the Young Turk and the Atatürk revolutions of 1908–9 and 1919–23 respectively. Any examination, therefore, of this historical process would be incomplete without a consideration of the pre-republican attempt at what is often referred to as *islahat* ('improvement').

The term 'modernization' as applied to Turkey refers to the process of transforming Ottoman Islamic institutions, concepts, and a way of life into those of a secular, constitutional republic. As such, modernization encompassed several specific aspects of change. Beginning with the introduction of European weapons and with reforms in military training, it gradually came to include changes in government institutions, in the bureaucracy, in education, in political ideologies, and in the broader culture of the society. Under the republic, modernization became an all-encompassing goal signifying total institutional and cultural change: a secular, national republic with authority vested in a popularly elected national assembly, instead of an Islamic theocratic empire based on the concept of the *millet* (a religious and ethnic group) and governed by a sultan-caliph; an industrialized and planned economy with an indigenous entrepreneurial group rather than a bureaucratic feudalism, foreign entrepreneurs, and primitive methods of cultivating the land; a state system of secular schools rather than the religious *mekteb* (primary school) and *medrese* (college); mobilization and utilization of all the manpower resources of the society, and full political participation by all members of the state rather than sharp bifurcations between rulers and ruled, urban and rural, educated and illiterate; knowledge and a scientific way of thinking rather than ignorance and superstition; loyalty to a clearly defined Turkish state rather than to an amorphous Ottoman Empire; an adapted Swiss civil code rather than the prescriptions of the *sheriat* (the Islamic Holy Law); a Roman alphabet rather than the Arabic script; a hat rather than a fez; and generally the adoption of new, mostly Western, ways of thinking and behaving.

This 'grand transformation' has aroused the interest of foreign observers and has been the subject of a spate of historical and sociological studies as well as of more journalistic and impressionistic enterprises. In the United States, an unusually large number of scholarly volumes has appeared within the past five years alone.[1] Scholars seem to have found a fertile ground in Turkey to test or expand their theories of social change and to examine variations in the interplay of traditional and modern forces, thus providing material for comparative analyses. The Turkish Revolution, with its emphasis upon secularism, industrialization, nationalism, democracy, and so on, has furnished the political scientist and the sociologist with interesting variations to compare the different countries of the Middle East which have emerged from a common traditional

---

[1] For the most comprehensive treatment of the subject, see Bernard Lewis, *The Emergence of Modern Turkey* (London: Oxford University Press, 1961). Recent studies in book form which focus on specific aspects of the modernization movement include: Roderic H. Davison, *Reform of the Ottoman Empire, 1856–1876* (Princeton: Princeton University Press, 1963); Sherif Mardin, *The Genesis of Young Ottoman Thought: A Study in the Modernization of Turkish Political Ideas* (Princeton: Princeton University Press, 1962); Kemal H. Karpat, *Turkey's Politics: The Transition to a Multi-Party System* (Princeton: Princeton University Press, 1959); Richard D. Robinson, *The First Turkish Republic: A Case Study in National Development* (Cambridge, Mass.: Harvard University Press, 1963); Nuri Eren, *Turkey Today and Tomorrow. An Experiment in Modernization* (New York: Frederick A. Praeger, 1963); and Niyazi Berkes, *The Development of Secularism in Turkey* (Montreal: McGill University Press, 1964).

background; namely, the Ottoman Islamic Empire. One recent study considered what light Turkey's development throws on the process of political modernization if it is examined in conjunction with Japan; that is with another country which embarked upon a programme of planned change and has had better results.[2] Others have written about Turkey because, as one author put it, 'I have gradually evolved a deep interest in the Turkish people for their own sake', and because Turkey 'throws the whole problem of accelerated development into bold relief'.[3] Because of Turkey's membership in Western alliances and America's involvement in Turkish development, some research may have also been stimulated by such questions as, 'Where does our money go?' or 'Can democracy work in Turkey?'

For one who is interested in research on education and schools, as the present writer is, Turkey's quest for modernity and the reforms associated with it are exceptionally rich. In a rather general sense, the entire modernization movement was an experiment in education: how to create new values, new ideologies, new human beings, or new Turks. In a more restricted sense, formal education or schools were considered crucial agents or vehicles for disseminating Western ideas and accomplishing the modernizing goals of both the Ottomans and the Turks. Students of the Turkish transformation have made references to the significance of education: how, for example, during the Ottoman period Western schooling was introduced and how this created more liberal ideologies and leaders who ultimately assumed power; and how under the republic the educational system was modernized and used as an instrument of nation-building. Although it is generally agreed that modernization in

[2] See Robert A. Ward and Dankwart A. Rustow (eds.), *Political Modernization in Japan and Turkey* (Princeton: Princeton University Press, 1964). For other examples of comparative analysis, see Lloyd Fallers 'Equality, Modernity, and Democracy in the New States,' in *Old Societies and New States*, ed. Clifford Geertz (Glencoe: The Free Press of Glencoe, 1963), pp. 158–219; Leonard Binder, *The Ideological Revolution in the Middle East* (New York: John Wiley & Sons, Inc., 1964); A. J. Meyer, *Middle Eastern Capitalism* (Cambridge, Mass.: Harvard University Press, 1959); and Lewis V. Thomas and Richard N. Frye, *The United States and Turkey and Iran* (Cambridge, Mass.: Harvard University Press, 1952).

[3] Robinson, *op. cit.*, p. viii.

its multifarious aspects was related to education, no study has yet appeared which treats the problem in any great detail or precisely shows the connections between education and social change.

In most available studies,[4] historical and otherwise, few attempts have been made to view education in relation to other characteristics of the society in which it functions, or to place it in the mainstream of Ottoman and Turkish development. Some sporadic attempts are made in that direction, but they are fragmentary and often based exclusively on anecdotal accounts. Studies that deal exclusively with education under the republic have relied largely on official documents (reports, guides, rules and regulations, curriculum outlines, etc.), which have often been assumed to correspond to reality. There has been a conspicuous absence of empirical research to find out what the schools actually do.[5] It is not uncommon, therefore, to find unqualified criticisms of the existing system: namely, that it is inappropriate for the 'needs' of the society, that it is too monolithic, too academic, and so on; or that what Turkey needs is more practical education, more technical and agricultural training, and the like. Such diagnoses may indeed be correct; but it is meaningless to characterize a system of education as 'inappropriate' unless one specifies in what respects and to what groups of people such characterizations apply. Before any attempts are made to evaluate an educational system, or

[4] The best source in Turkish is the five-volume history of education by Osman Ergin, *Türkiye Maarif Tarihi* (*History of Turkish Education* [Istanbul: Osmanbey Matbaasi, 1939-43]). Others include: Hasan Ali Yüjel, *Türkiyede Orta Ogretim* (*Secondary Education in Turkey* [Istanbul: Devlet Basimevi, 1938]); and Nevzad Ayas, *Türkiye Jumhuriyeti Milli Egitim* (*National Education of the Turkish Republic* [Ankara: Milli Egitim Basimevi, 1948]). For the best study in English, see Richard E. Maynard, 'The Lise and Its Curriculum in the Turkish Educational System' (Ph.D. dissertation, The University of Chicago, 1961).

[5] Empirical research on what the schools actually do is just beginning in Turkey. A survey conducted in 1959 of the values of secondary-school students sought to assess the impact of lise-level institutions on the political culture of the nation. So far only part of the findings have been published: see Frederick W. Frey, George W. Angell, Jr., and Abdurrahman Sh. Sanay, *Ogrencilerin Meslek Gruplarina Bagladiklari Degerler* (Ankara: Test ve Arashtirma Bürosu, 1962). A comprehensive study by Frederick W. Frey, *The Turkish Political Elite* (Cambridge, Mass.: M.I.T. Press, 1965), includes much information on the role of education in political elite formation. Some of the findings of this study are discussed in Chapter IX.

to suggest changes, it is necessary to establish as carefully as possible the actual operation of that system within the society; that is, its relation to the social, political, and value system of the society at large.

The purpose of the present study is to shed more light on the modernization movement in Turkey and on the present place of education in Turkish society, thus filling certain gaps in a fast-growing enterprise. Specifically, the focus here will be on two interrelated aspects of education: (a) the modernization of the legally sanctioned system of schooling; and (b) the relationship between education and the socio-political development of Turkey.

Since the modernization movement had its roots in the Ottoman period of Turkish history, the 'Ottoman Islamic Background' will be examined first. Part One of the study, sets the stage, so to speak, for the unfolding drama which reached a climax in the Kemalist-republican period. It pays particular attention to traditional educational institutions, ideas, and practices; to the introduction of schools like the Galatasaray *sultani* (secondary academic school) and the *mülkiye* (school for civil servants), as well as to new administrative measures such as the codes of 1869 and 1913; and to the effects of these innovations on the modernization movement prior to the 'total break' that took place under Atatürk. The approach in this part is essentially historical, and events are treated within certain demarcated historical periods.

Parts Two and Three cover the period since the proclamation of the republic. Each chapter deals with a specific topic: Part Two with the development and present structure of the educational system and curriculum, the nature and function of the schools, and the general growth of the educational enterprise; and Part Three with the relationship between education and certain aspects of Turkish society and culture—recruitment of elites, nationalism, secularization and laicization, the occupational structure, values, and so on. The approach in Parts Two and Three is both historical and sociological, and the sources include documentary materials as well as the results of field research conducted by the writer on academic secondary school (*lise*) students.

The story of the lise since 1869, when it was first established,

21

epitomizes some of the salient features of Turkish modernization. It represents a type of formal schooling considered necessary for the creation of a vital segment of modernizers; of that 'creative minority' which has always been a potent force in Turkish development and social change. It was felt that an empirical sociological investigation of the social functions of the present lise would provide additional material indispensable to an assessment of Turkey's quest for modernity. One of the main aims of the present book is to examine the reaction of a traditional Islamic society to Western ideas and institutions and their adaptation to local conditions. The lise has been such an institution and continues to occupy a pivotal position in this historical process.

This book is essentially a case study in educational modernization, which was itself an integral part of a broader historical movement with deep roots in the past. Although the study is limited to Turkey, it deals with a problem which finds parallels in other countries that have sought to build a new social order along modern Western lines. To be sure, in her approach towards modernity Turkey has had to contend with problems peculiar to herself; nevertheless, many of the processes at work are to be found in other emerging or transitional societies. It is hoped, therefore, that this study will contribute something to the accumulation of knowledge about education, and to the dynamics of social change.

PART ONE

THE OTTOMAN ISLAMIC BACKGROUND

CHAPTER I

EDUCATION AND
EARLY OTTOMAN MERITOCRACY

IN THE hundred years or so between the conquest of Constantinople and the death of Suleiman the Magnificent in 1566, the
Ottoman Empire reached its highest glory. It was a period of
unprecedented territorial expansion, and of consolidation and
regularization of social and political institutions. Firmly ensconced on three continents (Europe, Asia, and Africa) with
the centre of gravity on the site facing the Golden Horn and the
Sea of Marmara, the early sultans developed a system of government whose power structure was quite unusual—and paradoxical. This was the system of the *kapi kullari* (slaves of the
'Porte'), who formed part of the 'palace clique', the highest
ruling administrators and military leaders of the empire. It
was a daring experiment in government, similar in some respects to the ancient Chinese Mandarin system and to the
Mameluke system of Egypt, and it was the closest approxima-
tion to Plato's *Republic* in the Western tradition. It was paradoxical in the sense that slaves became rulers, and non-Turks
as well as non-Moslems in origin became the leaders in war and
in government of an Islamic society.

The system of the kapi kullari was also a daring experiment
in education. At a time when education was associated with
birth and social class, and reinforced social cleavages in Western Europe, the Ottomans shunned birth, wealth, and other
aristocratic accoutrements, deliberately making education an
important criterion for selection, social advancement and
occupational placement.

The education of the kapi kullari was partly provided by the *Enderun Mektebi* (Palace School) which was strategically situated inside the Grand Seraglio behind Ayia Sophia. This school is significant for another reason. It was primarily a secular institution under the control of the sultan or, in a rather loose sense, the state, in contrast to the other educational institutions, especially the mektebs and medreses. These establishments were religious in character and recruited their students exclusively from the Moslem population of the empire. The medreses trained the future jurists, priests, teachers, and learned men who constituted another elite pillar of the Ottoman society, the 'Moslem Institution of the Ottoman Empire'.[1] Thus the stage for the development of Ottoman 'secondary' education was set, so to speak, with a bifurcation in the upper elite strata of the society and in the schools. The lines of demarcation in both the elite group and the schools were clearly defined in terms of function and composition.

The distinguishing characteristics of the two elite groups and their schools were later (from the seventeenth to the nineteenth century) blurred, and the religious orientation of both the rulers and the schools predominated. But with the advent of modernization in the nineteenth and twentieth centuries they re-emerged for quite different reasons, and finally, after the Kemalist Revolution, secular tendencies gained complete control over both the elite groups and the schools. In view of this, a study of the Ottoman background of Turkish education must begin with the schools of the early period, the Golden Age of the Ottoman Empire.

THE PALACE SCHOOL

There is no conclusive evidence as to the ideological sources

---

[1] This study will use only one of the two categories used by Lybyer, namely, the 'Moslem Institution of the Ottoman Empire'. Where mention is made of his other category, 'the ruling institution,' it will mean only the highest ranking administrators and military leaders and will exclude the large numbers of the civil and military bureaucracy. For the twofold Lybyer classification, see A. E. Lybyer, *The Government of the Ottoman Empire in the Time of Suleiman the Magnificent* (Cambridge, Mass.: Harvard University Press, 1913), p. 367. For a critique of the Lybyer thesis, see Norman Itzkowitz, 'Eighteenth Century Ottoman Realities,' *Studia Islamica* (Larose-Paris, 1962), pp. 73–94.

of the Palace School, established soon after the conquest of Constantinople. Certainly several characteristics of the system of recruiting and selecting leaders and the process of educating them bore striking resemblance to Plato's system as presented in the *Republic*. But there is no indication that Sultan Mehmet II (the Conqueror) had the Platonic model in mind, although he knew Greek and he may have conceivably read Plato. But the idea of recruiting and training slaves for service in the palace and the state had empirical precedents in the Islamic world—the caliphs of Baghdad did it—even in the pre-conquest period of Ottoman history. Through *devshirme* (the Law of Draft), non-Moslem boys were recruited for service in the state as page boys attached to the palace and as members of the Janissaries, the elite branch of the Ottoman army. By the time of Murad II (1421–51), this system had evolved into a recruiting pattern for political leaders as well. During the reign of Mehmet II, it was systematized, and the Palace School emerged as a formal educative and selective agency for the choicest youth of the empire.

What, then, were the characteristic features of the school and how did it fit into the institutional framework of Ottoman society? Barnette Miller gives the following general description:

'Among the institutions within the palace gates, one was unique and remarkable in the originality and boldness of its conception, in the power and extent of its influence and in the long continuity of its history—the Palace School of the Grand Seraglio. A great military school of state, primarily secular in purpose and essentially so in character, it was without prototype in Islam . . . while in the comprehensiveness of its curriculum and in the length and severity of the training which it afforded, it appears to be equally without parallel in the general history of education.'[2]

The aim of the school was clear and simple: to train the ablest children for leadership positions in the Ottoman body politic, either as military leaders or as high administrators in the 'Sublime Porte' and the provinces of the empire. It was, one might say, a super-elite institution in the sense that only a few members of an already selected group, which exhibited

---

[2] See Barnette Miller, *Beyond the Sublime Porte: The Grand Seraglio of Stamboul* (New Haven: Yale University Press, 1931), p. 47.

outstanding excellence in body and mind, were allowed to enter it.

But perhaps the most intriguing and paradoxical feature of the school was the social composition of the student body. The recruits chosen were unmarried, non-Moslem, male slaves who were selected on the basis of physical and intellectual criteria rather than by blood or wealth. That a rather 'open' pattern of recruitment should take place in an Oriental absolutistic society is especially interesting, for Western European education was enmeshed in the aristocratic matrix of rigid social classes with few, if any, doors open for lowly people to rise in the social hierarchy. It was paradoxical that non-Moslems were being recruited and trained to become the guardians and rulers of a Moslem Empire. Plato would have been delighted that physical and intellectual aspects of human nature were regarded as the crucial determinants for admission into the ruling class; but the fact that recruitment was confined to slaves would have revolted him.

Equally interesting, but to modern moralists utterly exasperating, were the methods used to recruit and select the cadre of prospective 'slave rulers'. The youth were taken from their parents between the ages of ten and twenty, through tribute, gift, capture, and purchase. Detached from their homes, they were brought to Constantinople and reduced to the status of personal slaves of the sultan. They remained so all their life, even though they sometimes advanced to the post of grand vizier, the highest administrative office in the state below the sultan. In line with the Islamic religion, nearly all of them adopted Islam, although they were not forced to do so.[3] Selection

[3] According to the Moslem religion, the People of Scripture (Christians, Jews, and Zoroastrians) were to be tolerated rather than forced to accept Islam or die, as idolaters were. Thus devshirme 'slaves' fell within the People of Scripture category. But it should also be noted that unless the person recruited through the devshirme accepted Islam, he could not advance very far in the Ottoman hierarchy. Hence, there was a subtle sort of inducement to accept the Islamic faith. The acceptance of Islam becomes significant also in the Lybyer twofold classification of the elite group referred to previously. It is true that until the end of the reign of Seleiman the Magnificent, the criterion of religion was a determining factor in recruitment into the 'ruling institution', although even then there were some notable exceptions (see Itzkowitz, *op. cit.*, p. 82). But once a person entered the service of the sultan, either as a page or as a member of the administrative or military bureacracy, the religious criterion all but disappeared as a distinguishing feature.

at all stages before entering the school, and while in school, was done by highly trained officials.[4]

Once the very choicest of the recruits were selected (about two hundred annually or between twelve thousand and fifteen thousand in all), they entered the palace as *ich oglan* (inside boys). As such they were both students in the Palace School and pages in the service of the sultan, but the two roles were merely two parts of the same interrelated educational process. The school was organized into seven halls or grades, each of which constituted a step in an ascending ladder of difficulty. In addition to receiving instruction by special teachers in the arts of the courtier, the administrator, and the warrior, and to the learning of certain subjects, students performed menial tasks such as serving food and drink and taking care of the falcons. Instruction was broad in its scope: it included Turkish, Arabic, Persian, Moslem religion and culture, Turkish customs and rules of courtesy and etiquette, riding, archery, wrestling and sword practice, music, and apparently mathematics. In addition, each page was expected 'to work at something and work in earnest'. The teaching staff, primarily drawn from outside, consisted of members of the *ulema* (learned sages of Islamic thought and culture) and of lay scholars, scientists, musicians, artists, and poets. But in addition one must mention as teachers the *lâla* (tutor), who supervised and presided over each company of ten pages.[5]

The comprehensiveness of the school's curriculum and its cultivation of what has often been referred to as the liberal, the practical, and the vocational in education are most striking. Compared to the curriculum of Western schools during a comparable period, the Palace School was less intellectual in its

[4] For a more detailed treatment of this aspect of selection, see Sir Hamilton Gibb and Harold Bowen, *Islamic Society and the West: A Study of the Impact of Western Civilization on Moslem Culture in the Near East* (London: Oxford University Press, 1950), I, Part I, 43–4; Lybyer, *op. cit.*, pp. 48–9; L. S. Stavrianos (ed.), *The Ottoman Empire: Was It the Sick Man of Europe?* ('Source Problems in World Civilization' [New York: Rinehart and Company, Inc., 1957]), pp. 10–11.

[5] For the best Turkish source on the range of the curriculum, see Osman Ergin, *Türkiye Maarif Tarihi* (*History of Turkish Education* [Istanbul: Osmanbey Matbaasi, 1939–43]), I, 10–20. For sources in English on both the curriculum and the teaching staff, see Gibb and Bowen, *op. cit.*, pp. 56–7; Miller, *op. cit.*, pp. 62–9; Lybyer, *op. cit.*, pp. 75–6.

orientation, but more practical. The aim was to create the Ottoman ruler, the warrior statesman envisaged as a 'man of letters and a gentleman of polished speech, profound courtesy, and honest morals'.[6]

The Palace School functioned within the framework of an astonishing political structure. Both the school and the broad power structure within which it was encapsulated were based on the criterion of meritorious achievement and service. Promotion from one hall to another and occupational placement and advancement were based on merit rather than on birth or wealth, and the meritorious ruled the empire. Hence, what Michael Young has called 'meritocracy' at its best is found in the Ottoman Islamic society of the period. De Busbecq, the Imperial ambassador to Constantinople between 1554 and 1562, described the sultan's household as follows:

'The Sultan's hall was crowded with people among whom were several officers of high rank. Besides these there were troopers of the Imperial guard . . . and a large force of Janissaries; but there was not in all that great assembly a single man who owed his position to aught save valour and his merit. No distinction is attached to birth among the Turks; the deference to be paid to a man is measured by the position he holds in the public service. . . . In making his appointments the Sultan pays no regard to any pretensions on the score of wealth or rank . . . he considers each case on its own merits, and examines carefully into the character, ability, and disposition of the man whose promotion is in question. . . . Among the Turks, therefore, honours, high posts and judgeships are the rewards of great ability and good service. If a man be dishonest, or lazy, or careless, he remains at the bottom of the ladder, an object of contempt; for such qualities there are no honours in Turkey.'[7]

This meritocratic pattern of recruitment and career opportunities in the upper crust of the government contributed to a relative fluidity in the system and prevented concentration of power in the hands of a hereditary caste. It also seemed to serve adequately the interests of the Ottoman state, for it furnished a loyal cadre of well-trained warrior-statesmen who were ready and eager to carry out the wishes of the sultan and

---

[6] Miller, *op. cit.*, p. 63.
[7] Stavrianos, *op. cit.*, pp. 3-4.

to be the watchdogs of an expanding empire. And education was a *sine qua non* of its existence and stability.

But as De Busbecq observed, Ottoman meritocracy was not confined to the highest officials of the Ottoman civil bureaucracy and the military. It was also extended to the religious sphere, to what Lybyer has called the 'Moslem Institution of the Ottoman Empire'. Since the education of the members of this institution was in many respects different, it also needs to be examined separately.

RELIGION AND THE MEDRESE

The Palace School provided a special type of education for a special group of people. It was not a universal school, although the criteria for recruitment into it were universalistic. The responsibility of providing an education for the people was left to private initiative and to the religious agencies in the society. In addition, Ottoman society being Islamic, assigned major roles to religious functionaries in education, government, and the administration of justice. Ottoman Islam provided a popular education for the masses and a more specialized education for various members of the religious hierarchy, interpreters of the sheriat, and prospective teachers of the empire.

The Mekteb

In this early period of Ottoman history, popular education was provided in the mektebs, commonly known as *okumak yerleri* (reading places) or *tash mekteb* (stone schools), where instruction was essentially limited to teaching and learning the Koran. The first schools of this type were attached to the mosques, but gradually they spread and often existed separately. Supported by a *vakif* (special endowment), they were free but not compulsory. Although this level of education was not universal for all children, it was available in most places for any parent who wanted his child to profit by it.[8]

Thus popular education in Islamic Ottoman society was not the responsibility of the state. It was the function of the religious institutions and was essentially designed to induct the

[8] Lybyer, *op. cit.*, p. 204.

masses of the people into the Ottoman Islamic culture. With other agencies, such as the mosque, it performed a socializing function, and for the large masses of the people it was a terminal type of education.

For the non-Moslem, Christian members of the Ottoman Empire, education was provided by the respective ethnic and religious groups. This again was done mainly in connection with the churches and was largely a question of inducting the young into the religion, and often the tenets, of their culture. Thus, for example, Greek communities around Constantinople supported schools for Greek children out of special contributions given in churches, and aimed at inculcating Greek Orthodox religious beliefs and teaching the Greek language and culture. The wealthier families had special tutors for their children, as did the Ottoman Moslems. It was not, however, until the eighteenth century that the Greeks began to establish a wider network of schools at the primary and secondary levels.[9]

The mektebs constituted one of the most important avenues through which the values of Ottoman Islamic society were transmitted to the young. They lubricated, so to speak, the machinery for maintaining Ottoman Islamic ideology among the masses, and they formed the basis of a religious educational stratification under the control and direction of the sultan as caliph and of his highest-ranking religious dignitary, the *Sheyhülislâm*. Above the mekteb were the medreses, and at the top, the higher medreses or law schools, which were more of university rank.

The Medrese

The medrese provided a more advanced religious instruction than the mekteb. The course of study, especially in this early period, included a variety of other subjects (grammar, syntax, logic, metaphysics, rhetoric, geometry, arithmetic, tropics, stylistics), even medicine.[10] It was always attached to a mosque, and it was free. Students were even given free food and a small

[9] Tryphon, Evagelides, *He Paideia epi Tourkokratias: Hellelika Scholeia apo tes Haloseos Mechri Kapodistriou* (Athens: A. P. Chalkiopoulou, 1936), I, 24 ff.

[10] See *Encyclopedia of Islam*, III, 361–2; Lybyer, *op. cit.*, p. 203. See also Richard E. Maynard, 'The Lise and Its Curriculum in the Turkish Educational System' (Ph.D. dissertation, The University of Chicago, 1961), p. 8.

allowance. Instruction was graded, but also individualized, and each student could advance as he wished.

Like the Palace School, the medrese occupied a pivotal position in Ottoman society. It trained the teachers, including those in the Palace School, and all the ulema of Ottoman society. Insofar as the ulema performed functions other than purely religious ones in the judiciary, public administration, diplomacy, and politics, the role of the medrese was at least as important as that of the Enderun in the Ottoman body politic. As guardians of the laws, to which the Moslem population owed absolute obedience, the higher ulema occupied an influential position in the power structure of the Ottoman state; as educators of the whole society, they controlled most of the means of cultural and religious communication with the populace and were responsible for the stability of the empire and the conservation of its traditions.

As with the Palace School, recruitment into the medrese and promotion within it were based on merit rather than on family background, and ecclesiastical careers were assigned according to meritorious performance. Thus the principle of meritocracy held true not only in high civil and military positions but also in religious offices.

During the Golden Age of the Ottoman Empire (fifteenth and sixteenth centuries), the two types of career education for the elite corps (civil, military, and ecclesiastical), represented by the Enderun and the medrese, complemented each other and, as one historian put it, 'made possible the greatness and the permanence of the Ottoman nation'. Although the one aimed at creating soldiers and administrators and the other, judges and learned men, they interacted and contributed to each other's greatness.[11]

It appears, therefore, that education in the early Ottoman period (until the end of the sixteenth century) was a major factor in the social advancement of the individual and in his occupational placement. Careers were closely linked with educational background, and there was an open system of recruitment into the schools. The two types of schools discussed above performed clearly defined functions which were closely

[11] Lybyer, *op. cit.*, pp. 232–3.

interrelated with the political structure of the Ottoman state. It would, however, be a mistake to limit education to these two types of schools, unless one meant formal education in the strictest meaning of the term. A great many other educational activities were carried on outside the schools.

OTHER EDUCATIONAL AGENCIES

The Ottoman Village

The Enderun and the medrese educated the leaders of the society. But there were still the large masses of the people, the peasants of the empire, for whom education was largely a process of socialization, a process by which they were inducted into the values and mores of an Islamic society, and by which they were trained to combat the vicissitudes of their physical environment. Any account of Ottoman education, from the earliest time to the twentieth century, would be incomplete if it did not consider the informal educative agencies of the village, that perennial feature of Ottoman Empire and its successor, the Turkish Republic.

There is very little evidence concerning the structure and character of the village in the early Ottoman period, but it is known that they have remained substantially unchanged, especially in Anatolia. Hence, by looking at what is known in later periods, the original features of the village might be reconstructed with a reasonable degree of accuracy.

The typical Anatolian village was an isolated, closely knit community which derived its livelihood from agricultural pursuits and livestock breeding. It consisted of a small group of extended patrilineal family units within which there were clear-cut differentiations in roles between men and women and between the elders and the younger members of the group. The village society was an authoritarian patriarchal society, sustained by a subsistence economy and circumscribed by a limited set of loyalties which seldom extended beyond the family and the village. When loyalty did go beyond the immediate family and village, it was a loyalty to the sultan-caliph not as the political leader but as the religious head of the state. The sultan-caliph was, however, too far removed from the cultural and intellectual environs of the village. The ideology of the group—the values which lubricated the workings of the village system—was dictated by the Islamic religion and the sheriat, adapted in many respects to satisfy the needs of the villages. It was a 'folk Islam', which provided security and a minimum of conflict, and which, by its belief in *kismet* (fate), and its association with 'massive superstition', provided some sort of explanation for the hardships of life.[12]

Within this ideological and institutional framework, individual decision making was at a minimum, if not non-existent, and, to use McClelland's term, the 'need for achievement' was stunted. The predeterministic philosophy of life, the individual's concern with the welfare of his immediate groups, the limited loyalties, and the existing laws of inheritance—all nipped in the bud, as it were, any motivation to achieve. The individual was not an innovator or creator but a preserver; his outlook was not liberal but conservative. This had both its advantages and its disadvantages. On one hand, it provided for stability, security, and happiness in the individual.[13] Because inheritance laws stipulated that family property was to be divided among the heirs of the head of the household upon his death, amassing large land holdings was difficult, and the road from riches to rags was easily travelled. In this respect the openness of Ottoman society, discussed earlier, pertained to the villages as well. There was, in addition, no role or social conflict so characteristic of advanced societies, for an individual's social status was accepted. On the other hand, this social and ideological structure prevented an individual from breaking away from his immediate group and from embarking upon innovative pursuits. Moreover, it isolated him and the village community, preventing them from participating fully in the body politic. The distance between the rulers and the ruled was great, a gap which has been a persistent obstacle to political, social, and economic development in Ottoman, and later in Turkish, society. In Ottoman society, there was little sense of identity with a nation, no national consciousness or political consensus.

---

[12] For a good recent analysis of the structure and ideology of the Anatolian village, see Richard D. Robinson, *The First Turkish Republic: A Case Study in National Development* (Cambridge, Mass.: Harvard University Press, 1963), pp. 39–59.

[13] *Ibid.*, p. 44.

The empire was a conglomeration of religious and ethnic groups without political bonds; this was true even among the Turkish-speaking Moslems.

In terms of literacy skills (reading and writing), the Anatolian peasant was overwhelmingly illiterate. There were, as noted previously, many primary schools attached to mosques or set up by individual agencies, but even in them instruction consisted of memorizing the Koran. The Koran itself was written in Arabic, a language totally alien to the Ottoman Turkish-speaking peasant. In the mekteb the Ottoman child usually memorized passages from the Koran and could sometimes read the text, but this was done without any understanding of its meaning. As Gibb and Bowen wrote: 'A grasp of their [verses from the Koran] meaning seems, indeed to have been regarded as of less moment than an ability to recite the sacred words correctly, these being held by the vulgar to possess an almost magic power.'[14] Vestiges of this phenomenon are found even today among the oldest people in Turkey.

The mektebs were more like Sunday schools than schools where the rudiments of education were taught. Skills needed to perform the various tasks of peasant life were learned at home and on the job. As one modern writer put it, 'Children acquired an education of reality through the world of realities'; they learned 'how to hoe or to plough the fields, to care animals, even to construct a house, by watching their father, brother, in short, their relatives and neighbours in daily life'.[15]

The educational activities of the village strengthened the authoritarian, patriarchal character of the community. The young boy relied on the wisdom of the *imam* (religious leader), accumulated through a memorized type of education, and on the older members of his family group for the technical skills to carry out the ordinary activities assigned to him. The village boy was set apart from the cultural activity of the city and from the intelligentsia of Ottoman society. Romanticized

[14] Sir Hamilton Gibb and Harold Bowen, *Islamic Society and the West: A Study of the Impact of Western Civilization on Moslem Culture in the Near East* (London: Oxford University Press, 1950), I, Part II, 142.

[15] Nermin Erdendug, *A Study of the Social Structure of a Turkish Village* ('Publications of the Faculty of Language, History and Geography, University of Ankara,' No. 130 [Ankara: Ayyildiz Matbassi, 1959]), pp. 42–5.

Turkish folklore tells of instances where a bright boy would leave the village, go to a city, attach himself to a learned man, and finally join the ranks of the ulema group; but such instances were rather rare.

The Ottoman Bureaus

Educational functions were also performed by institutions which were set up for purposes other than educational. Of special importance in the Ottoman period was the *kalemiye* (bureaucracy) with its two principal sections: the financial administration under the *bash defterdar*, and the central administration under the *reis efendi*.[16] Usually a prospective *kâtib* (bureaucrat) began at a *kalem* (bureau) as an apprentice and gradually worked his way up the bureaucratic hierarchy to the position of scribe or perhaps of bureau chief. During his period of apprenticeship a bureaucrat learned not only how to keep books and accounts; he also learned how to read and write. In this sense the bureaucracy, as distinct from the palace group and the Palace School, was yet another agency for training a very important branch of the Ottoman body politic, one which became increasingly important in subsequent centuries.

SUMMARY AND EVALUATION

André Maurois once said that 'sharply defined periods are only historians' concepts'.[17] Hence, by starting with the fall of Constantinople, a rather arbitrary point of departure has been chosen. Nevertheless, the middle of the fifteenth century is a convenient demarcating point in a continuous historical evolution, marking the end of one epoch and the beginning of another. Institutional consolidation accompanied territorial expansion, and education reached its most accomplished form.

Three types of schools which constituted the formal aspect of education have been examined: the mekteb, the medrese, and the Enderun Mektebi, all of which had clearly defined functions and adequately fulfilled the purposes for which they

[16] Itzkowitz, *op. cit.*, pp. 86–7.
[17] André Maurois, *The Edwardian Era* (New York: D. Appleton-Century Company, 1933), p. 286.

were established. The mektebs supplied the universal basis for the Islamic religious structure; they were the schools of the people. To the large masses they symbolized education itself, the memorization of verses from the Arabic Koran. Although illiterate peasants may not have been able to grasp its meaning, this type of religious education provided the emotional substratum for the cohesiveness of an Islamic society and the means by which the universalist spirit of Islam was maintained. It was not an accident, therefore, that the mekteb and the mosque were so closely connected: the former was a necessary supplement to the latter; and where there was no special room for a mekteb, the mosque performed both religious and educational functions. Nor was it an accident that maintenance of mektebs was an important concern not only of ecclesiastical leaders but also of high-ranking state officials (including the sultan), and of persons of private means.

Equally significant, insofar as the religious foundations of the society were concerned, were the medreses. These schools were also attached to the mosques and trained both religious and civic leaders. The medreses and their alumni, some of whom entered the ulema group, provided spokesmen for the society's religious ideology. The ulema articulated the basic values of that society and acted as one of its most important reference groups. Possessing the necessary characteristics of book learning and writing, as well as erudition, which were denied the ordinary person of the mosque and the mekteb, the ulema set themselves apart from the illiterate masses. This may also have been a factor in the high prestige which was accorded the more learned of the ulema, and in the general respect which the Ottomans, and later the Turks, have had for education. But one point to bear in mind is that the ulema group was set apart from the rest of the populace, thereby creating a social and religious bifurcation which had important ramifications in the subsequent history of the Ottoman society —a bifurcation which was reinforced by the two types of schools.

Another important aspect of the mekteb and the medrese was that the educational functions they performed were more of a conserving than an innovating nature. This, to be sure, is a feature of education in general. Insofar as schools transmit the cultural heritage or induct the young into the culture of a society, they are more conservative than innovative. But in societies which are characterized by social and economic development, schools contribute to change as well: they prepare the youth for newly created positions in the society, and they train them in the skills needed to maintain the pace of change. Moreover, in societies which are not regulated by an absolutistic and predeterministic philosophy of life, but which view the individual as an important agent for change, education seeks to expand intellectual horizons and to free the individual from the cultural constraints of his immediate environment. None of these necessary elements for innovation were present in the traditional Ottoman religious setting, or in the religious schools which operated within it. The Ottoman child did not go to the mekteb to learn and to question, nor to be trained for any newly created social and occupational roles. Likewise, the student of the medrese looked forward to a place within an already established structure; he would merely interpret the Koran and the sheriat and see that its laws were carried out. There was not much opportunity in these Ottoman educational establishments for the free expression of human intellect or spirit of inquiry. This element becomes crucially important in the subsequent course of Ottoman history. Later, when new currents of thought and new practices impregnated the Ottoman society, the conservative nature of the religious institutions was a factor in the conflicts that characterized the process of modernization. But in the early stages of Ottoman history these educational institutions did adequately what was expected of them. The element of conflict that appeared later on was non-existent. As yet there were no external intrusions which would upset the existing equilibrium. Maintaining what existed was more important than changing it. Education reinforced a culture which was confident of its superiority over anything else, hence change was really an irrelevant factor.

The Palace School was far removed from the people, except those in the immediate service of the sultan's palace. It was, in a sense, a very private affair, but one, nonetheless, that trained people for posts which regulated and controlled the administrative and military wings of the empire. But unlike the mekteb and the medrese, the Enderun was an artificial contrivance; it was a tool invented and used by the sultans to create a cadre of faithful servants who would work for the expansion and maintenance of their authority over the vast domains of their empire. Under the strong leadership of the early sultans, and because of the demonstrated stability and military superiority of the Ottoman state, the Enderun and the broader institutional structure which it served proved solid and viable. They both retained their 'openness' in matters of recruitment, occupational placement and promotion, and functioned with surprisingly little friction with religious institutions. Indeed, there was an amazing hospitality between them. But this, as we shall later see, did not continue, for specific reasons peculiar to Ottoman historical development and because no meritocracy can continue for long and still maintain its original features unless it is one of the Platonic utopian kind. Sooner or later built-in mechanisms will develop and undermine it. Rulers, being men, will sooner or later seek to perpetuate themselves, whatever their original station in life; and once this occurs the system loses its fluidity and meritocratic purity. At least this is what historical experience has shown, and nothing indicates that it could be otherwise. And this is what happened in the Ottoman meritocracy.

The schools of the early Ottomans, especially the Enderun and the medrese, provided a formal type of education for 'talented' people. The mektebs gave a religious orientation to those among the masses who desired it. But much of the socializing aspect of education of the masses was done by 'non-school' agencies—generally the home, the elders, and the village. A child's training for participation in society was done by parents, relatives, friends, and imams. The relationship between the young and other members of the society was personal. As in the formal institutions, its purpose was to maintain the existing equilibrium rather than to upset it. The village was an isolated, self-sustained community, and the individual had no loyalties extending beyond the physical boundaries of the village. Any contact with outsiders was very limited. The individual was not a fully participating member of the body politic, nor did he have a sense of belonging to a nation. The bond that held the Moslem masses of the people and the rulers together was religious uniformity, not political consciousness.

The institutional and educational patterns described above set the stage, for the long-lasting, and indeed long-drawn-out, Ottoman drama which was marked by episodes of glory, internal corruption, withdrawal, reform, and final decay and defeat. In the early unfolding of the plot some of the chief actors emerged in a rather pure and uncorrupted form. They exhibited the virility and self-confidence of a pioneer race. The palace ruling clique was sustained by a unique and exacting education, and faithfully carried out its master's wishes in war and in peace. The religious institution was confident of the superiority of the Moslem faith and enjoyed the prestige that befitted it in an Islamic society. The peasants continued in the felicitous state to which they had been accustomed since the time of the Hittites and Sumerians. But the continued vitality of the system depended on how well it was able to adjust itself to changing circumstances, and how well it could meet the challenge of Western progress and innovation. This story constitutes another phase in the evolution of the Ottoman society and will be taken up in the chapter that follows.

CHAPTER II

EDUCATION AND
DEFENSIVE MODERNIZATION

CONTACT with the West began soon after the Turkish tribes implanted themselves on the Anatolian peninsula, but historians have taken the second half of the eighteenth century as the starting point of the systematic borrowing of techniques and institutions from Europe, and hence of Ottoman modernization. Even then, however, there is some doubt as to how deep such borrowings ran insofar as the general fabric of Ottoman society was concerned. It was not until the nineteenth and twentieth centuries that the process gained momentum and, if the bucolic and changeless life of the provinces is excluded, that the modernizing tendencies affected many of the more significant Ottoman institutions, including education. This chapter will examine early attempts at modernization, during the reigns of Sultan Selim III (1789–1807) and Sultan Mahmud II (1809–38), as a background to the major reforms of the nineteenth century known as the Tanzimat. But any examination of this phase of modernization presupposes a look at the character of the society which was going to be modernized.

THE CHANGING NATURE OF TRADITIONAL INSTITUTIONS

Institutions of Government

During the post-conquest period, the sultan managed to maintain a strong centralist type of administration with ultimate power and authority vested in his own hands. The basic meritocratic principle in recruitment and educational and

42

occupational placement functioned in a relatively pure form. But as new external and internal conditions were created in the seventeenth and eighteenth centuries, the institutional framework of the government underwent certain important transformations.

One major development was the change in the political power structure of the Ottoman state. As long as the empire enjoyed the fruits of military victories and its destiny was in the hands of a group of capable sultans, there was a relative equilibrium among the important branches of government, that is, the military, the bureaucratic, and the religious. But in the latter half of the eighteenth century there were already signs that the dizzy level of Ottoman power and internal consolidation would not continue for long. The Ottoman army, 'the terror of the world', was halted at Vienna. After two unsuccessful attempts to capture the coveted city, the Ottomans were forced to abandon the siege and to withdraw. A long period of intermittent wars with the European powers, of armistices and signing of treaties followed, the upshot of which was that the empire lost its expansive, dynamic, and self-confident character. In the ensuing centuries the primary aim was to preserve what had originally been attained. Even this defensive policy, however, was unsuccessful. From the eighteenth century on, the period was one of defeat and gradual chopping off of large chunks of Ottoman territory.

The gradual waning of the Ottoman military superiority was inextricably bound up with several other indications of a loss of Ottoman power and organic solidarity. Economically, the empire was beset with problems created by changes in the international commercial thoroughfares. The discovery of new sea routes by the Western maritime powers turned the whole Eastern Mediterranean 'into a backwater', and havoc was created in the monetary system of the empire. The need to maintain large military forces, and an ever increasing number of salaried personnel made more and more demands on the treasury and drained a steadily shrinking economy. Unlike the Western powers, the Ottoman economy continued to function on outmoded methods and techniques. As Bernard Lewis put it, 'while Europe swept forward in science and technology, the Ottomans were content to remain in their agriculture, their industry, and their transport, at the level of their medieval ancestors'.[1]

With the general weakening of the military and economic power there were concomitant shifts in the internal balance of political power. One such shift was the rise of the *dere-beyi* (provincial landlord) and the *ayân* (provincial notable), who had emerged by the eighteenth century as challengers of the hitherto strong central authority of the sultan. In a sense these local magnates formed a semi-feudal aristocracy, and they rose to such prominence that the representatives of the central government—the sultan's governors and the judges (*kadi*)—very often became tools in their hands. They were able to wield authority independent of the sultan, owned large estates, and founded local hereditary dynasties.[2]

Another shift in the internal balance of power was the growth of the power of the Janissaries, the sultan's standing army. The Janissaries, who were stationed at the 'Porte' and in the provinces, supported the central government less than previously. In many of the distant provinces they controlled the government; and in Istanbul they often demanded who should hold power. In addition, they became less of a solid fighting force and more of a disorganized band of marauders.

Likewise, the court and the religious institution underwent significant transformations, all of which tended to weaken the control of the central government and the general solidarity of the empire. The sultans, for example, gradually withdrew from active participation in the conduct of affairs into what Gibb and Bowen have called 'a majestic seclusion', and surrounded themselves with 'the traditional pomp of monarchy'. This cut them off from any populistic support they may have had and weakened the organization of the entire 'ruling corporation'. Although the void created by the retirement of the sultans

---

[1] For a fuller discussion of these effects, see Bernard Lewis, *The Emergence of Modern Turkey* (London: Oxford University Press, 1961), pp. 27–32.

[2] For the rise of the ayâns, see Halil Inaljik, 'The Nature of Traditional Society: Turkey,' in *Political Modernization in Japan and Turkey*, ed. Robert E. Ward and Dankwart A. Rustow (Princeton: Princeton University Press, 1964), pp. 45–8. On the rise of both the dere-beyis and the ayâns, see Sir Hamilton Gibb and Harold Bowen, *Islamic Society and the West: A Study of the Impact of Western Civilization on Moslem Culture in the Near East* (London: Oxford University Press, 1950), pp. 193–9.

could have been filled by the grand viziers—indeed attempts were made in that direction—this did not prove satisfactory. The grand viziers themselves were in constant fear of being dismissed, and they did not prove to be capable of assuming such leadership, except perhaps during the period when the vizierate was in the hands of the Köprülü family (at the end of the seventeenth century). The doors were thus opened for palace intrigues, and for flatterers and counsellors unfit to proffer sound advice to influence the decisions of the sultan.[3]

The ulema assumed more and more power which, in view of the changed character of the sultanate, could no longer be satisfactorily contained. The process by which they elevated themselves to a different level of authority is a fascinating study in the internal transformation of an institution and of the changes in its functions. Because the ulema had such a tremendous role in education and in Ottoman modernization, their transformation will be examined in somewhat greater detail.

The distinguishing feature of the ulema was their learnedness, for much of their authority rested on the educational functions they performed.[4] Although the ulema continued to be regarded as the learned men of the society—which indeed many of them were—as time passed learnedness or education ceased to be the sole determinant of a person's place in the hierarchy.

Previously, education was an important criterion of selection and occupational placement. Gradually, however, ascriptive criteria surpassed achievement criteria in importance—a shift which will be discussed later. Beginning with the seventeenth century, the power equilibrium changed: there was a waning of the ulema's power as a learned profession, and a strengthening of their power as a political and socio-economic force. By the eighteenth century a learned asistocracy emerged, consisting of the great *mollas* (judges, high ranking religious leaders), men who possessed wealth, rank, and a social position, unparalleled in the history of the ulema institution. Moreover, because they possessed certain privileges—exemption from taxation and freedom to impart their fortunes to their descendants or relatives—this new social class became almost hereditary. The

[3] Gibb and Bowen, *op. cit.*, pp. 174–7.
[4] *Ibid.*, Part II, p. 81.

weak central administration could not hold them at bay; graft, corruption, and the breakdown of clear-cut educational criteria for advancement and holding of office, opened the way for the establishment of a closed, powerful, hereditary class, suspicious of 'outsiders' and anxious to maintain its position. In order to accomplish this, they even allied themselves with the Janissaries, not because they approved of them, but rather because they were afraid that alienated Janissaries would be a threat to their position.[5]

Recruitment and Selection

An examination of the changes in the internal balance of power among the various constituent parts of the Ottoman government in the seventeenth and eighteenth centuries unavoidably includes an examination of the changes in recruitment and selection patterns. Indeed, historians have identified changes in recruitment and selection as major contributing factors in the 'decline' or 'decay' of the Ottoman institutions.

In the analysis of the earlier Ottoman governmental institutions (the palace, the bureaucracy, the military, and the religious institutions), the meritocratic principles of selection, advancement, and occupational placement were emphasized. It was also stated that education was important and that, insofar as original recruitment into the palace group and the religious institutions was concerned, religion played a major role. Indeed, according to Lybyer, and Gibb and Bowen, the religious criterion was the determining factor. This applied not only to the palace group and the religious institution, but also to the 'ruling institution' in general—the palace clique, the military, the administrators, and the bureaucrats of the empire. Gibb and Bowen have further maintained that with the abolition of the devshirme by the eighteenth century, freeborn Moslems replaced non-Moslems in the 'ruling institution', a change that proved disastrous to the cohesiveness and solidarity of the institution itself and the Ottoman government in general.[6]

Parts of this thesis have recently been questioned by Norman Itzkowitz, who has shown that in the seventeenth and eighteenth centuries, recruitment into the several branches of the

[5] *Ibid.*, pp. 106–8.
[6] *Ibid.*, Part I, pp. 81–3.

government was not based solely on the religious criterion. For example, many of the eighteenth century grand viziers were not born Moslem, and many of the sixteenth and seventeenth century men who occupied the office of bash defterdar ('head keeper of all documents relating to the holding of fiefs, or the chief register-keeper') were of Moslem, not Christian, origin. Likewise, people of non-Moslem origin even found themselves in the Moslem or religious institution.[7] The force of Itzkowitz's rebuttal applies more to the post-Suleiman period than to the heyday of Ottoman glory. It is also a criticism of the neat classification into 'ruling' and 'Moslem' institutions. The pillars of Ottoman government do not seem to lend themselves to such a simplistic categorization, for the so-called 'ruling institution' itself should be further broken down into the palace clique, the bureaucracy, and the military,[8] with varying patterns of recruitment and selection in each. If Itzkowitz's breakdown is accepted, the palace clique, which supplied most of the executive personnel for the civil administration and the military during the early period, is found to have been maintained by the system of devshirme, which did, in fact, rest partly on the religious criterion.

Whether or not the Gibb and Bowen thesis or Itzkowitz's rebuttal is accepted the fact remains that in the seventeenth and eighteenth centuries there were important changes in the patterns of recruitment and selection into the major government institutions. For one thing, the devshirme system was abolished, which changed the character and social composition of the Janissaries and the palace group; and for another, achievement and education had lost their original importance as basic criteria of selection and advancement. The Janissaries had ceased to be the disciplined, dedicated fighters whose *raison d'être* was the protection and expansion of the empire; instead, they developed into a self-perpetuating, self-seeking and dangerous group, and an added financial burden. Likewise, the open system of recruitment into the palace group, and thence into the highest careers in the administration, was marked

Norman Itzkowitz, 'Eighteenth Century Ottoman Realities,' *Studia Islamica* (Larose-Paris, 1962), pp. 81–3.

[8] Itzkowitz does not include the palace clique, although he recognizes that it formed a distinct part of the career patterns. *Ibid.*, p. 85.

by graft, corruption and favouritism; where previously merit and education were the basic desiderata for admission, promotion, and occupational placement, other factors such as wealth, bribery, and 'connections', or 'pull', now entered the picture.

Similar tendencies in the pattern of recruitment, advancement, and occupational placement were evident in ecclesiastical careers and in the bureaucracy. In the high posts of the ecclesiastical institution, diplomas and the distribution of offices were often purchased or granted to a very limited class of Moslems; ascriptive criteria and favouritism entered into the process of selection; and learnedness ceased to be the sole determining factor for entrance into the profession.[9] This tended to lead to a struggle for promotion within the ulema group and to a consequent loss of power.[10]

In addition to the palace group, the military, and the ecclesiastical officials, there was a large cadre of civilian officials who constituted the bulk of the *mülkiye* (bureaucratic institution). These bureaucrats, who staffed the chancery and the finance office, entered the bureaus as apprentices and, on the basis of meritorious service, could rise in the bureaucratic hierarchy to become full-fledged katibs; some of them might even become bureau chiefs, thus entering the upper ranks of the bureaucracy. Since posts in this institution were allocated largely to Moslem Turks, entrance into the bureaus was an important avenue for social mobility, for many of these people were excluded from entrance into other institutions. As the bureaucratic institution expanded, however, a quasi-hereditary bureaucratic structure and a rigidity in the pattern of recruitment developed. As time passed, these officials were recruited from the established bureaucratic families. Often a young man was placed in a government office by his father or relative or someone else of importance in the institution.[11]

On the eve of modernization, therefore, openness in the pat-

---

[9] Gibb and Bowen, *op. cit.*, Part II, pp. 154–5.

[10] Uriel Heyd, 'The Ottoman "*Ulema*" and Westernization in the Time of Selim III and Mahmud II,' *Scripta Hierosolymitana*, I (Studies in Islamic History and Civilization' [Jerusalem: Magnes Press, Hebrew University, 1961]), pp. 77–8.

[11] See Bernard Lewis, *Istanbul and the Civilization of the Ottoman Empire* (Norman: University of Oklahoma Press, 1963), pp. 91–2.

tern of recruitment and selection into the various government institutions was sullied, and in many cases positions and promotions were allocated on the basis of non-achievement and non-educational criteria. As early as 1630, Kochu Bey, himself a product of the devshirme system, complained to the then Sultan Murad IV that one of the reasons for the incipient decline of the Ottoman power lay in the appointment and promotion to government offices of incompetent and unworthy people. He pointed out particularly the entrance of 'Turcomans, gypsies, Tats, Kurds, foreigners, Lazes, nomads, muleteers and camel-drivers, porters, syrup venders, footpads and cutpurses' into the palace clique and the Janissaries.[12] Although Gibb and Bowen do not go to such extremes, they have attributed the decline of Ottoman power to similar reasons, especially the admission of Moslems into the 'ruling institution'. On the other hand, Turkish scholars have rejected such a theory. That a state, according to them, consisting mainly of people of Turkic ethnic origins and based essentially on the Moslem faith should decay because Moslems and Turks were admitted into the high institutions of its government, is not only absurd, it is also a contradiction in terms.[13] Osman Ergin seems to agree with Ahmet Hikmet Müftüoglu, the eminent historian and writer, who attributed the Ottoman decline to the selfishness and irresponsibility of the palace group and to the great gap which separated this group from the masses of the people. According to Müftüoglu, the palace clique constituted a separate caste dedicated to the sultan, but not to the people, whom they despised and exploited.[14]

Although Müftüoglu's explanation may have a nationalistic bias, it cannot be brushed aside lightly. The isolation of the sultan and his high officials in Istanbul from the rest of the people, and the formation of a sort of semi-hereditary caste could only have deleterious effects upon the solidarity and organization of the empire. In addition to Müftüoglu's and Itzkowitz's views, there are other considerations which would further weaken the Gibb and Bowen theory.

[12] *Ibid.*, pp. 174–5.
[13] See, for example, Osman Ergin, *Türkiye Maarif Tarihi* (*History of Turkish Education* [Istanbul: Osmanbey Matbaasi, 1939–1943]), pp. 14–15.
[14] *Ibid.*, pp. 15–16.

At the height of Ottoman glory, one of the necessary conditions for admission, placement, and promotion within the ranks of the rulers was an exacting and selective system of education. The background of the devshirmes was less important than their talents, performance, and level of education. The vigour of the ruling class came not so much from religious or ethnic origin, but from the system of education through which it was trained. When the criterion of merit and the exacting methods of training the young recruits became flaccid, there was a noticeable loss of vitality and a decay. Such a flaccidity could have occurred even if the rulers had continued to be recruited from people of non-Moslem and non-Turkish background, for it is quite unrealistic to expect any meritocracy to continue unsullied for long. Rulers would naturally, for example, establish a closed system of friendships and associations which would militate against the fluidity and openness of the selection and recruitment system.[15]

Be that as it may, when Sultan Selim III ascended the throne in 1789, the Ottoman Empire was no longer the great, powerful, cohesive entity of the Golden Era of the fifteenth and sixteenth centuries. Something had to be done to save it from the persistent threat of the European powers and from internal disintegration. In 1792 the new sultan sought advice from eminent Ottomans on how to meet the European challenge, and how to save the empire. Some of these men suggested reforms, thus ushering in the period of Westernization or modernization which paved the way for the ultimate transformation of the Ottoman Islamic state into the modern Turkish Republic.

DEFENSIVE MODERNIZATION UNDER SELIM III AND MAHMUD II

Several characteristics of the modernization movement in the Ottoman Empire are noteworthy. First ,the initiative for change came from within rather than from without, although the forces which impelled change were both external and internal; second, early modernization, or more appropriately, 'Westernization' or 'Europeanization', was conceived and en-

---

[15] For a more detailed examination of what could conceivably happen in a meritocracy, see Michael Young, *The Rise of the Meritocracy 1870–2033: The New Elite of Our Social Revolution* (New York: Random House, 1959).

gineered by an indigenous elite group consisting of sultans and their close followers; third, concrete manifestations of the reform movement began with changes in the military sector, although by a slow and compelling logic it spread to the social, political, and cultural sectors; fourth, the change was inspired by Europe, especially France; and finally, education in the broad meaning of the term was assigned a major role.

In issuing his imperial rescript called *Nizam-i Jedid* (New Order) in 1793, Selim III was motivated by a desire to strengthen the armed forces of the empire to combat the European threat more effectively. It was a large-scale plan intended to elevate the fighting capacity of the army by introducing new methods of training and a new military technology. In 1826, Sultan Mahmud II destroyed the Janissaries, thus eliminating an obstacle to the consolidation of Ottoman power and to the creation of an efficient and modern fighting force. The Janissaries were among the reactionary elements opposing Selim III's New Order and were responsible for the massacres during the revolt of 1807 and the deposition of the sultan.

In these efforts to modernize the army, the initial impulse and the guidance came mainly from France. The new military schools established during this time were based largely on French models; French officers, technicians, and military experts were brought over as teachers and instructors; and the French language was made compulsory for all students.[16]

The modernization of the army was part of a larger plan to Westernize or Europeanize the total institutional framework of the empire, including some of its cultural accoutrements. During the sultanate of Mahmud II (1809–39), changes were made in the structure and organization of the central government, in land ownership, in the control and disposition of *evkaf* (pious foundations), in the system of education and communications, in styles of dress, and so forth. Some of Mahmud II's reforms aimed at restoring the power of the sultan and the centralization of authority which had been weakened since the days of Suleiman the Magnificent. In addition to doing away with the Janissaries, Mahmud II curtailed the autonomy of the ayâns, abolished the *timar* (military fief)—thus destroying

[16] Lewis, *The Emergence of Modern Turkey, op. cit.*, p. 58.

the foundations of Ottoman feudalism—extended his authority over a reorganized Ministry of Evkaf, and established new ministries and advisory committees. Other reforms such as the change of nomenclature of ministries and departments and in the style of dress of government officials, aimed at making the state modern in appearance as well as in fact. Mere changes in names, however, did not bring about changes in the conduct of public affairs; nor did the new styles of dress (frock coats and the fez) and the new office equipment. Yet, as Lewis points out, all these changes 'did mark the first step towards the break-up of old, well-entrenched institutions and their replacement by others of foreign provenance'.[17]

What is highly significant, in view of subsequent developments, is the fact that the early phase of Ottoman modernization was also directed towards the education and training of civil officials to staff the various newly created or transformed ministries, and towards the establishment of a system of education based on the European models. Indeed, education was considered the prime agent for accomplishing the aims of Westernization. In reforming the army, attention was focused on the creation of a well trained and well educated officer class, on the establishment of different kinds of schools (military, naval, medical, engineering, music) for maintaining a more efficient fighting force, and on the teaching of foreign languages, especially French. Likewise, in reforming government institutions, attempts were made to eliminate favouritism, privilege, bribery, and the like in the recruitment and selection of officials and to restore the application of universalistic criteria. In 1833 Mahmud established a *Terjüme Odasi* (Translation Chamber) at the 'Sublime Porte' to train interpreters to fill the gap in government posts created by the dismissal of the Greek dragomans.[18] Also, beginning with Selim III the Ottoman embassies in Europe served both diplomatic and educational functions: those who were appointed to posts abroad utilized

[17] *Ibid.*, p. 967.

[18] *Ibid.*, pp. 865–8. For more details on the education and positions of some of the Greek dragomans, especially the Phanariotes (from Phanar or Fener, a section in Istanbul), see also Metropolites Helioupoleos Gennadios, *Historia tou Megalou Revmatos* (*Arnavutköy*) (Istanbul: Tsitoures Bros., 1949), pp. 158–207.

their stay not only to further the interests of the 'Porte', but also to increase their knowledge of foreign languages and culture.

It was also in Mahmud II's reign that the first attempts were made to establish education as a state responsibility and to build schools other than the traditional mektebs and medreses. In 1824 a *ferman* (imperial edict) decreed that popular education at the primary level was the responsibility of the state.[19] This had no immediate effect, however, and primary schools continued to be under the control and supervision of the sheyhülislâm. Yet it was quite a novel idea and a precedent for subsequent developments. Although the ferman of 1824 remained a dead letter insofar as reform of existing primary schools was concerned, the government decreed the opening of a new school and, for the first time in Ottoman history, appointed a Minister of Education. The new school was to be called *rüshdiye* (from *rüshd*, meaning 'adolescence' or 'maturity'). Its purpose was to provide a more advanced type of education than the *sübyan* (primary) schools in preparation for the various military, naval, and medical schools and for government offices. Originally it was envisaged as a sort of secondary school to fill the gap that existed between primary schools and higher institutions. In reality, however, it was something like a senior primary school, with a leaving age of approximately twelve.

Writers disagree as to the exact date of the establishment of the first rüshdiye. According to Nevzad Ayas, the first school which was actually called rüshdiye was not established until 1847. However, in 1838, the year in which a new Minister of Rüshdiye Schools was appointed, a school called *Mektebi Maarifi Adlî* (School for Justice Education) was opened in the Sultan Ahmet Mosque. This school, which was later divided into the *maarifi adliye* (justice education) and the *ulumu edebiye* (literary sciences), came under the supervision of the new minister. Hence, Ayas concludes, this institution could reasonably be accepted as the first rüshdiye.[20] Hasan Ali Yüjel, on the other hand, says that the Mektebi Maarifi Adlî, which he places

[19] Nevzad Ayas, *Türkiye Jumhuriyeti Milli Egitimi: Kurulushlar ve Tarihcheler* (Ankara: Milli Egitim Basimevi, 1948), pp. 199–200.
[20] *Ibid.*, p. 201.

on the rüshdiye level, was established in 1840.[21] Ubicini, a contemporary writer, does not include the Mektebi Maarifi Adlî among the rüshdiyes, but classifies it under 'special schools' which were founded by Mahmud II for young men 'intended for civil employments'.[22] The exact date of the appearance of these schools may, however, not be so significant as the fact that they represented a departure in the governance of education, a more secular orientation in the school curriculum, and the first step in the establishment of a graded system of schools (primary, secondary, and higher) along European lines.

The attempted reform of schools was only part of the reform movement in education and of the broader Westernization movement. Several features of this broader movement merit further comment. First, the most successful results were in the military and administrative spheres of the empire and, more significantly, in the upper echelons of these sectors. This meant that the impetus for change started in two strategically located elements in the Ottoman power structure. The masses of the people were untouched. Yet the very fact that change originated with the power elite was of vital significance: the chances for rapid modernization to occur are greater if the carrying element is already ensconced in the power structure than if it has to fight its way towards the attainment of a position of power.

Secondly, the introduction of new schools, with their rather secular orientation and with their emphasis on the acquisition of foreign languages and modes of thinking and behaving, laid the foundations for the creation of a different cadre of elites. Sooner or later, such a group would come into conflict with the traditional elites, who, mostly educated in the medreses, were imbued with traditional Ottoman Islamic values and beliefs. This, as will be shown later, was what indeed happened.

Significantly, France and the French language acquired a predominant place among the foreign influences in the Westernization or modernization movement. This meant that the French *savoir-faire* came to be associated with upper-class

---

[21] Hasan Ali Yüjel, *Türkiyede Orta Ogretim* (Istanbul: Devlet Basimevi, 1939), p. 4.

[22] M. A. Ubicini, *Letters from Turkey: An Account of the Religious, Political, Social, and Commercial Condition of the Ottoman Empire; The Reformed Institutions, Army, Navy, Etc.*, trans. Lady Easthope (London: John Murray, 1856), pp. 197–8.

Ottomanism, and the Ottoman leaders came into contact with the liberal thought of the French Revolution. In seeking to 'borrow' foreign institutions, French models were most highly esteemed. The following chapter will show the importance of this in the developing patterns of education and their underlying ideas.

CHAPTER III

EDUCATION AND
THE ERA OF THE TANZIMAT

THE road towards modernity, which was charted by Selim III and Mahmud II, was followed with accelerated speed by their successors. Four months after his accession to the sultanate in 1839, Abdul-Medjid and the new Ottoman ministers promulgated the famous *Hatt-i Sherif* (Noble Rescript) which was read aloud by Reshid Pasha, the Minister for Foreign Affairs, at an august gathering of dignitaries in the Gülhane (Rose Chamber) of the Royal Palace.[1] The proclamation of this rescript inaugurated a new era of reforms, known as the Tanzimat, which spanned the middle decades of the nineteenth century and stretched up to approximately 1876, when the first constitution was proclaimed.

The Rescript of 1839 was a charter which proclaimed certain principles concerning the reorganization of the government, the administrative and fiscal sectors of the empire, the judiciary and the military, and the rights of all members of the Ottoman polity. The aim, as stated in the preamble, was to procure through 'new institutions' the benefits of a good administration and 'the regeneration of religion, government, the nation, and the empire'. New laws were to be enacted, based on the principles of the security of life, honour, and property of the subjects; taxation laws were to be revised and regulated so that each

---

[1] M. A. Ubicini, *Letters from Turkey: An Account of the Religious, Political, Social, and Commercial Condition of the Ottoman Empire; The Reformed Institutions, Army, Navy, Etc.*, trans. Lady Easthope (London: John Murray, 1856), Part I, 48–54.

individual would be taxed 'in a ration to his fortune and his ability,' and the tax-farming system was to be abolished; conscription laws and recruitment into the army were to be altered; all accused persons were to be tried publicly and fairly; all the functionaries of the empire were to receive 'suitable salaries' according to their position, and a rigorous law was to be passed 'against the traffic in favours and appointments'; and finally, and perhaps most important, these imperial concessions were to be extended to 'all our subjects, whatever religion or sect they may belong to; and they will enjoy them without any exception'.[2]

The very idea of establishing 'new institutions' or 'new rules' ran contrary to Ottoman Islamic doctrine, but the concept of a multi-national Ottoman brotherhood was by all counts the most novel and revolutionary principle of the rescript. Here for the first time in Ottoman history a *gâvur* (non-believer) and a *râya* (peasant, subject) were—in principle, at least—on a par with the Ottoman Moslem Turk.

The decades after the 1839 Rescript were marked by constant external and internal pressures to bring an empire, which by now even the Ottomans themselves acknowledged as being weak and impoverished, up to the level of a modern, efficient state. New currents of thought emerged, some quite liberal and secular, others a blend of Western liberalism and oriental Islamic values; new institutions of government and new laws for the reorganization of the central and local administration were introduced; new constitutions of the millets were adopted; and a short-lived but historically significant constitution was proclaimed in 1876. Within this ferment for change, which constitutes the prodromal sign of the modernization movement in Turkey, nineteenth-century educational institutions must be examined. For education continued to be regarded as the necessary foundation for the reorganization of the empire and the creation of a cadre of new leaders to maintain it. As one contemporary writer put it, the salvation of the 'sick man' was not through extermination, but through 'education'.[3]

[2] For an English translation of the entire rescript, see Cyrus Hamlin, *Among the Turks* (New York: Robert Carter and Brothers, 1878), pp. 48–54. See also Ubicini, *op. cit.*, 29–30.

[3] Hamlin, *op. cit.*, p. 378.

A NEW EDUCATIONAL FRAMEWORK

The First Phase

The problem of educational reform was originally one of establishing a new framework which would place education more under the supervision of the state than of the ulema group. Considering the traditional hold of the religious bodies over education, opposition to any Western, and hence secular, intrusions was inevitable. Yet, during the nineteenth-century phase of Turkish modernization, there was no intention on the part of the reformers to supplant the traditional system, but rather to complement it or to incorporate innovative elements into it. Also, as will be seen later, not all of the ulema nor all traditionally oriented people opposed Westernizing tendencies.

In 1845, six years after the first Gülhane Rescript, Reshid Pasha, the moving force in this early phase of the Tanzimat, observed that many of the changes proposed by the new regulations had been misunderstood and improperly applied because of a high degree of ignorance among the population. The existing system was painfully unable to meet the demands created by the proposed reforms. Hence, in March of the same year, a commission was appointed with powers 'to seek and examine the most efficacious methods of amending the system of public instruction in Turkey, and to propose to the Government a new and complete course of instruction suited to the growing wants of the Country'.[4] The commission was headed by the sheyhülislâm and included, among others, Ali Efendi, Under-Secretary for Foreign affairs, and Fuad Efendi, Chief Interpreter of the Divan, both of whom were destined to play a major role in the Tanzimat reforms.

The commissioners issued their report in August 1846. It was an ambitious though unrealistic plan for the reorganization of the entire system of public education. It proposed the establishment of a *Mekâtibi Umumiye Nezareti* (Ministry of Public Schools), an Ottoman state university, and the grading of public education into primary or elementary, secondary or intermediate, and higher or superior schools. The report of the commissioners was quickly followed by imperial decrees which gave

---

[4] Ubicini, *op. cit.*, p. 197. Also see Bernard Lewis, *The Emergence of Modern Turkey* (London: Oxford University Press, 1961), pp. 110–11.

statutory sanction to the commission's recommendations: a permanent Council of Public Instruction was set up, entrusted with the responsibility of reforming, 'within the limits set by our religion', the primary schools and the rüshdiyes, the teaching in them of 'those branches of learning and science needed at this time', and of establishing a *darülfünün* (university).[5] The council then proceeded to implement these statutory provisions.

Primary education, as noted earlier, was provided in the religious mektebs or sübyan schools, which were either mosque schools or community schools. In order to set up a uniform organization under state supervision and to bring these schools up to a higher level of efficiency, the council declared that instruction in them should be obligatory and gratuitous, and that teachers should henceforth be paid a fixed salary drawn from the revenues of the schools. Regarding curriculum, the council ordered that better elementary texts, written in the common Turkish dialect, be adopted.

The greatest gap in the educational system was at the secondary or intermediate level. The council, which became the Ministry of Public Schools in 1847, continued the previous policy of establishing rüshdiyes, but without spectacular results. As noted earlier, the first school specifically called rüshdiye was established in 1847. Ubicini records that in 1851 there were only six such schools, attended by 870 students. According to him, the curriculum in the rüshdiyes included Arabic syntax and grammar, orthography, composition and style, sacred history, Ottoman history, universal history, arithmetic, and the elements of geography. Other writers list, in addition to the above, Turkish (reading and writing), the Koran, ritual reciting of the Koran, Persian and drawing.[6] Instruction was free, and the state provided books and instruments, paid the salaries of the teachers, and was responsible for the general maintenance of the schools.

The newly created ministry paid particular attention to the

[5] Ubicini, *op. cit.*, pp. 197–8.

[6] *Ibid.*, p. 201; Richard E. Maynard, 'The Lise and Its Curriculum in the Turkish Educational System' (Ph.D. dissertation, The University of Chicago, 1961), p. 22. See also Edouard Engelhardt, *La Turquie et le Tanzimat ou Histoire des Réformes Dans l'Empire Ottoman Depuis 1826 Jusqu'a nos Jours* (Paris, 1882–84), II, 8.

higher levels of education, but progress in this direction was even slower than that of the rüshdiyes. In 1845 an Italian architect was hired, and the foundations of a university were laid. However, work on the building was soon abandoned, and it was not completed and officially opened until 1863. Even then, the school was poorly attended and staffed, and it was severely criticized by the ulema and the traditional conservative elements in the society. In 1865, only two years after its opening, it was closed.

In addition to these attempts to set up a university, two other higher educational institutions were established during this period: the *Darülmuallim*, which was to train rüshdiye teachers and the *Darülmaarif* or *Valide Mektebi* (College of the Valideh Sultanah), which was intended to prepare young men for the various departments of the government. Of these two institutions, the former continued and became particularly effective later in the century, but the Darülmaarif was abolished in 1872.[7]

Higher education—education beyond the intermediate or secondary level—was supplemented by various types of institutions, many of which were associated with the military establishment. Passing reference has already been made to some of these schools. By the middle of the nineteenth century the network of such institutions included an Army Officers' School, a General Staff College, a Naval School, an Imperial College of Artillery and Engineers, an Imperial School of Medicine, an Agricultural School, and a Veterinary College.[8]

The Second Phase

In spite of the auspicious beginnings of the Gülhane Rescript and the ambitiousness of certain programmes, the tangible results of the reform movement were not spectacular. Although major attention was paid to the military sector, the performance of the new-style army in the Crimean War left much to be desired. In addition to continued internal problems, such as the constant antagonisms of the several millets against each other and against Islam, and continued corruption in the adminis-

---

[7] Ubicini, *op. cit.*, pp. 204–5; Maynard, *op. cit.*, pp. 22–3.
[8] D. A. Rustow, 'The Military: Turkey', in *Political Modernization in Japan and Turkey*, ed. Robert E. Ward and Dankwart A. Rustow (Princeton: Princeton University Press, 1964), p. 357; Ubicini, *op cit.*, pp. 302–8.

tration, the Ottoman Government was pressed by its foreign allies (England and France) to reorganize its administrative system and to put into practice the principle of Christian-Moslem equality which had been promulgated in 1839. The result of this was that in 1856 a new imperial rescript, the *Hatti Hümayun* (Illustrious Rescript), was proclaimed, in an attempt to reform all branches of the administration, 'touching the largest problems of the social order' as Fuad Pasha, a key figure in this second phase of the Tanzimat, said in 1867.[9]

The Illustrious Rescript of 1856, triggered by the approach of the Treaty of Paris, 'confirmed and consolidated' the principles and guarantees of its predecessor, the Gülhane Rescript of 1839: it reaffirmed in even stronger terms religious, social, political and economic equality among all the members of the empire; the six non-Moslem communities known as millets (Greek Orthodox, Gregorian Armenian, Roman Armenian, Jewish, Roman Catholic, Protestant) were to be reorganized under new constitutions; the financial and monetary system was to be overhauled; and public works were to be undertaken in the provinces.[10]

The 1856 Rescript inaugurated a new phase in this era of reorganization. Under the leadership of Ali Pasha and Fuad Pasha, who alternated as grand viziers, a new set of laws, codes and decrees was issued which aimed at the reform of the provincial administration, the legal framework, the training of civil servants, and the system of education.[11] As in the first phase of the Tanzimat, educational change was an integral part of the overall reform movement and was regarded as the *sine qua non* of the creation of a modern state.

In educational administration a *Maarif Umumiye Nezareti* (Ministry of Public Education) replaced the existing Mekâtibi Umumiye Nezareti. The responsibilities of the new Ministry included some control of books used in the medreses and the

---

[9] Quoted by Roderic D. Davison, 'Reform of the Ottoman Empire, 1856–1876' (Ph.D. dissertation, Harvard University, 1942), p. 106. Also published in book form: R. D. Davison, *Reform of the Ottoman Empire, 1856–1876* (Princeton: Princeton University Press, 1963). See also Sir Harry Luke, *The Old Turkey and the New: From Byzantium to Ankara* (London: Geoffrey Bles, 1955), p. 46.

[10] Luke, *op. cit.*, pp. 48–9.

[11] Lewis, *op. cit.*, pp. 113–21.

sübyans, and over the rüshdiyes and other civil and military schools. More important, however, was the issuing of a new set of regulations for a thorough overhauling of the structure of the school system and the setting up of two important and—in many respects epoch-making—institutions; the *mülkiye* (civil service school) and the *Mektebi Sultani* (imperial school) at Galatasaray.

As in many of the educational plans for reform during the Tanzimat, Ottoman leaders looked to France for inspiration and guidance. The French, anxious to strengthen their political and cultural influence in the Near East in the face of a changing balance of power and increasing foreign missionary activity (especially American), accepted this patronage and were only too eager to proffer their advice and services. The eminent Victor Duruy wrote especially for the benefit of Ottoman educational reformers: he recommended that libraries and schools of every type should be opened and that particular attention should be paid to secondary schools and a university, attended by all the nationalities of the empire. The French Minister of Foreign Affairs urged the French Ambassador in Istanbul to see that French educational views should pervade any reorganization scheme. In a note placed before the 'Porte' in 1867, the French government stressed the need for a reorganization of the Ottoman system of education and the creation of more schools, especially mixed secondary schools, as a necessary condition for the fulfilment of the principles of the Hatti Hümayun. And in the same year, Sultan Abdül-Aziz visited Paris, the first time an Ottoman sovereign left the empire as anything other than a conqueror. Apparently he was greatly impressed by the West, especially by the idea that a Western type of education was essential for material progress.[12] In addition to these ideas and activities, Ali Pasha, one of the power figures of the period, wrote a famous memorandum while on a special mission to insurrectionist Crete, stressing the need for Ottoman brotherhood, for a fusion of all the people of the empire, for a Western type of education, and for opening all administrative careers to non-Moslems. 'Learned nations can defeat us,' said Ali

---

[12] Ihsan Sungu, 'Galatasaray Lisesinin Kurulushu,' *Belleten*, VII, No. 28 (1943), 317–18; Davison, *op. cit.*, pp. 301, 309.

Pasha, 'even if we build walls around us like China.'[13]

One of the major outcomes of all this activity and ferment was a rather comprehensive law, passed in 1869, covering all aspects and levels of education. The *Maarifi Umumiye Nizamnamesi* (Regulations for General Education) made the following provisions:[14]

1. Compulsory primary education (in sübyan schools).
2. Reorganization of the central and provincial administration of education, that is, the setting up of administrative units in *vilayets* (provinces).
3. Reorganization and regularization of teaching methods.
4. Provision of clearer criteria concerning the promotion and status of teachers.
5. Increase in 'science' institutions (literature and natural sciences).
6. The school system to be graded and to consist of the following schools:
   a. Primary schools (sübyan or *iptidai*) in all villages and town quarters.
   b. Rüshdiyes in all towns of five hundred or more families.
   c. An *idadi* (preparatory secondary school) in all towns of one thousand families or more.
   d. A *sultani* (lise, or academic secondary school) in each provincial capital.
   e. Men's and women's teachers' training colleges in Istanbul.
   f. A university in Istanbul.
   g. Private rüshdiyes for girls in suitable places.
7. Free education in the sübyan, rüshdiye, and the idadi.

The 1869 Regulations included certain other important provisions concerning the reasons for the reorganization of education and the differentiating characteristics of the various types of schools. Quite clearly, a major motivating force in this reorganization, especially in the emphasis placed upon the second-

---

[13] Sungu, *op. cit.*, p. 322.

[14] For a full analysis of these regulations, see Sadrettin Jelal Antel, 'Tanzimat Maarifi,' in *Tanzimat* (Istanbul: Maarif Matbaasi, 1940), pp. 451–4. See also Hasan Ali Yüjel, *Türkiyede Orta Ogretim* (*Secondary Education in Turkey* [Istanbul: Devlet Basimevi, 1938]), pp. 8–9; and Maynard, *op. cit.*, p. 26.

ary level of education, was the welding of the various nationalities of the empire into a common Ottoman body politic. It was believed that by educating children of diverse religious and ethnic backgrounds together, in integrated schools, a Western-oriented and corporate Ottoman state could be created. Thus the idadis and the sultanis would make it a point to recruit students from both the Moslem and the non-Moslem segments of the empire. Another basic consideration in formulating these regulations was the policy of an Ottoman Western-oriented elite to establish a government-controlled, secularly oriented system of education, independent of the traditional religious system which was in the hands of the religious institution.[15] This modernizing feature was considered necessary for the creation of a corporate Ottoman state and the nourishing of those values associated with Ottomanism about which more will be said later.

This ideological orientation, which constitutes an essential feature of the Tanzimat, was typified in the first lise, the Imperial Lise at Galatasary, established in 1868.

THE GALATASARAY LISE

The influence of French institutional models was nowhere more apparent than in the establishment of the Mektebi Sultani, the first lise in Turkey. This school emerged out of a ferment for educational and social change, and it was the culmination of a series of contacts with French educators and diplomats. When Sultan Abdül-Aziz returned from Paris, he urged that Ottoman education be improved, an idea which was shared by his immediate followers, especially Ali Pasha and Fuad Pasha. Thus, in 1867 an imperial ferman was issued in three languages—Ottoman, Greek, and Armenian—proclaiming the aims, functions, and curriculum of the proposed school and setting down certain provisions concerning tuition fees, scholarships, and entrance examinations. In view of this institution's significance in the movement towards modernity in the Ottoman and Turkish republican period, and the relative paucity of material on it, a more careful look at this original edict would be necessary and helpful.

---

[15] Antel, *op. cit.*, pp. 452, 456. See also Engelhardt, *op. cit.*, p. 11.

The opening paragraph stated explicitly that the purpose of the new school was to prepare young men of various religious groups for all the branches of the public (civil) service by providing a higher type of education consonant with the needs of the empire. Furthermore, this institution was to be regulated in the same manner as similar schools in Western Europe. The course of studies would extend over a five-year period with an additional three-year preparatory course for those who did not possess the necessary background to enter the first class, and a possible sixth-year special course according to the student's special interests. The curriculum would include Turkish, French, Greek etymology, the elements of Latin needed for the study of law, medicine and pharmacy, general and Ottoman history, European and Ottoman geography, mathematics, cosmography, elements of jurisprudence, physics and chemistry, physical history, elements of political economy, rhetoric, geometric drawing, ethics, and practical mechanics. In addition, the Greek and Armenian languages could be elected if the parents so desired, and there would be regular training in gymnastics. Compulsory religious instruction would be provided according to the individual's religious denomination.

The edict further stipulated that the school would accept six hundred students, half of whom would be Ottoman Moslems; students were to be admitted into the preparatory classes between the ages of nine and thirteen; special examinations were to be held for allocation of successful candidates into the other classes of the lise; and, upon successful completion of the entire school course, graduates upon application, were to be admitted into any branch of the civil service. Finally, there would be a liberal provision of scholarships for all Ottoman subjects covering, either fully or partially, tuition fees, food, clothing, lodgings, medical care, books, and stationery.[16]

The founding of Galatasaray was the work of a group of Ottoman modernizers headed by Ali Pasha and Fuad Pasha, a willing sultan, and a coterie of French sympathizers. The French were particularly delighted that their efforts to extend their cultural and political influence into the Middle East finally bore fruit. Bourée, the French Minister of Public Instruction, helped

---

[16] The text of the edict is reproduced in Sungu, *op. cit.*, pp. 336–7. The translation was made by the writer from the Greek text.

in planning the curriculum; French, contrary to the views of the 'Sublime Porte', was adopted as the language of instruction; and a French director (De Salve), with an entourage of French professors, were imported as teachers.[17] At long last there was a French school to rival the recently established American Robert College and other foreign schools, a French lycée, so to speak, within the halls of political power.

The school opened on September 1, 1868, 'amongst the incredulity or rather the indifference which attaches itself to that which did not appear capable of surviving', as the Frenchman, Engelhardt, put it.[18] The immediate reaction was rather mixed. Two leading newspapers in Istanbul—the *Istanbul* and the *Terakki*—heralded the institution as paving the way for the salvation of the empire. 'What we needed most,' wrote the *Terakki*, 'was a school to give us the culture and positive sciences of Europe,' not religious propaganda. 'Now we have a European idea of education,' echoed the *Istanbul*, 'for the time being those who will save us will be those among our children who will graduate from this school.'[19]

The more secular, Western-oriented elite groups surrounding the sultan were among the staunchest supporters of the institution. These were the *Tanzimatci*, the supporters of reform and of Westernization of the institutions and cultural life of the empire. At the other extreme, however, stood the conservative wing, those who upheld the traditional institutions, the champions of Islam and religious schools, the so-called *medreseci*. To the medreseci, the educational changes of the Tanzimat reformers were an infidel infiltration into the religious life of the Ottoman Islamic society. According to Englehardt, however, the ulema in general did not openly oppose this particular institution, perhaps because they were not in a strong position. The astute Frenchman argued that if the head of the ulema had had the same influence and power as before, he would certainly not have been so permissive about it as he was.[20] Other criticisms from Moslem groups were made by people who felt that what the Ottoman state needed was not to import foreign

[17] *Ibid.*, pp. 317–18. See also Engelhardt, *op. cit.*, p. 12.
[18] *Ibid.*, p. 13.
[19] Sungu, *op. cit.*, pp. 328–9.
[20] Engelhardt, *op. cit.*, p. 14.

schools with foreign teachers but to organize and strengthen the indigenous educational institutions. This seemed to be the view of Namik Kemal, a major figure in the Young Ottoman movement of the period.[21]

The non-Moslem groups of the empire were not particularly enthusiastic about the new school. The Greeks complained of restrictions in the study of their language, and they seemed to prefer sending their children to schools in Greece. The Jews for the most part refused to confine their children to a Moslem establishment run by Christians, and the more moderate among them demanded that the Hebraic rites in matters of food be respected. In two successive briefs the Pope forbade his Roman Catholic faithful to attend the school.[22]

Despite these dissenting voices and the many misgivings, 341 students of diverse religious and ethnic groups enrolled at the opening of the school in September, 1868. Among these, there were 147 Moslems, 48 Gregorian Armenians, 36 Greek Orthodox, 34 Jews, 34 Bulgarians, 23 Roman Catholics, and 19 Armenian Catholics. By the end of the second year the number of students had risen to 640.[23]

In the early years of its existence the Galatasaray lise depended greatly on the support of the French, both in terms of moral encouragement and, more significantly, of teacher supply. After the Franco-Prussian War, in 1870, enrolments fell, and many French teachers resigned. In 1871 Ali Pasha, the moving Ottoman power behind the school's founding, died, and in the same year an embittered and disappointed De Salve resigned as the school's director. De Salve was followed by an Armenian director, then two Greeks, and, finally, in 1876, the Sultan Abdül-Hamid entrusted the directorship of the school to the preaching *hoja* (teacher) from the provinces, the strong, Turco-Moslem, unpredictable Ali Suavi. A member of the ulema, he had little use for Europe or for Western reforms, and he had previously been one of the severest critics of such Westernizers as Ali Pasha. Furthermore, French had ceased to occupy its privileged position in the curriculum, and the school moved

[21] Sungu, *op. cit.*, pp. 332–3.
[22] *Ibid.*, pp. 322, 340–1.
[23] Davison, *op. cit.*, p. 310.

67

from the Christian quarter to a completely Moslem section of Istanbul.[24]

But the school continued. Although the 1869 regulations had provided for similar lises to be established in all the provincial capitals, the Galatasaray lise was the only one that materialized. In its subsequent history it acquired more and more significance for certain segments of the Ottoman society and, in turn, played its part in the movement towards modernity. These questions will be examined in the next chapter. The Galatasaray lise, an ambitious experiment in fusing the various nationalities of the Ottoman Empire, became the prototype of the later lises and, in many respects, of the modern Turkish lise.

EDUCATION AND THE MODERNIZATION MOVEMENT

As was previously pointed out, educational reorganization and Westernization were envisaged as a necessary condition in the general movement towards the social and political modernization of the Ottoman State and society. Starting with changes in the institutions for military training, the movement gradually spread into other spheres of educational activity, that is, the schools and the bureaucracy. The Tanzimat period was characterized by attempts to set up a modern administrative framework and a graded system of schools different in many respects from the traditional institutional arrangements. The movement began at the top and was sustained by certain ruling elite elements of the Ottoman State. Moreover, it was a movement which sprang less from unqualified acceptance of Western civilization than from the belief that, by modernizing its institutions, the Ottoman State would be in a stronger position to combat the increasing foreign threat. The tangible results of the innovative elements introduced may not have been spectacular. The reformers may even have been motivated more by considerations of political expediency—namely, pacification of European powers—than by a genuine interest in the creation of a more viable and modern Ottoman State. Yet, as Bernard Lewis has pointed out, the reforms were an important beginning, and they laid the foundation for what ensued.[25] The very

24 *Ibid.*, pp. 250-1, 310.
25 Lewis, *op. cit.*, p. 124.

introduction of Western elements and ideas created conflicts and cleavages within the Ottoman society which were eroding the foundations of the old order. Transplanted into a different social context, and often struggling to survive amidst hostile forces, they gradually acquired different meanings for different people, and they soon vied with traditional beliefs and arrangements for the loyalties of the most powerful groups in the body politic. Nowhere was this process of change more evident than in the field of education.

The Emergence of New Elites

In the early phase of modernization the sultans managed to weaken the powers of traditional groups (Janissaries, ayâns, ulema) and to consolidate their own central position. Through the institutional and educational changes discussed earlier, a new type of bureaucrat emerged who gradually supplanted the traditional groups both at the high levels of administration and in the various government bureaus. In both the elevation and the maintenance of the new bureaucratic elite, education, especially of the Western European type, became an important factor. Education was attained either through attendance at newly established schools or other educational institutions, through foreign travel, or even through self-instruction. At the very highest levels of the bureaucracy, the period of the Tanzimat was dominated by a cosmopolitan group of modernizers, best exemplified in the persons of Reshid Pasha, Ali Pasha, and Fuad Pasha. The formal educational background of these modernizers varied, but all three were well acquainted with European culture, languages and affairs, especially French. Reshid Pasha went to a religious mekteb, but he had a very good command of the French language (which he learned on his own), and he was thoroughly inculcated with Western ideas; Ali Pasha knew French and admired French culture; and Fuad Pasha went to a medical school where the medium of instruction was French, and is said to have been the most elegant and Europeanized of all. Fond of quoting La Fontaine, Fuad Pasha was known as the 'Gâvur Pasha' by his countrymen; and Vambery appropriately characterized him as 'the prototype of upper-class Asiatic society in the early period of Westernization'. Moreover, all three men rose to high positions from within the Ottoman bureaucracy and, in varying capacities, served in European embassies.[26]

In these and other respects these three leaders of the Tanzimat epitomized a new social class which rose to prominence after the administrative innovations of Mahmud II's reign. Called *efendis* (gentlemen), these learned bureaucrats constituted the *kalemiye* (the officials of the pen) branch of the Ottoman Government and occupied positions in the central and provincial administration. The 'Stambuli Efendi Bureaucracy', as Davison labelled them, was a curious combination of the East and the West; it recruited its members largely from the Moslem Turkish population, and, although there was constant replenishment from all social strata, it gradually developed into a separate official aristocracy.[27] Yet it never really became a separate caste. Interestingly enough, although the Ottoman system of government continued to be absolute and despotic, there was still a degree of openness in the recruitment of civil functionaries. Many of the members of the efendi class were 'Westernized', having acquired a knowledge of French language and culture. Indeed, one of the basic preconditions for promotion within the civil bureaucracy was a knowledge of French and an acquaintance with European culture. The most important precondition for entry into the efendi bureaucracy, however, was the ability to read and write. In addition, most of these efendis went through the Translation Bureau, which was as much an educational agency and an avenue for social and occupational mobility as it was a department of government.[28] Thus, basic education opened the doors for government service; but service in the Translation Bureau, coupled with a knowledge of French and an exposure to European modes of life and thought, were important desiderata for advancement and high occupational placement.

The significance of this internal transformation and the rise

[26] For more details on the background and personality of these reformers, see Davison, *op. cit.*, pp. 16–17, 116–18 (unpublished source), and pp. 36–7, 89–90 (published source).

[27] Davison, *op. cit.*, pp. 53–8 (unpublished source) and pp. 32–6 (published source).

[28] *Ibid.*, pp. 28–30. See also Halil Inaljik, 'The Nature of Traditional Society: Turkey,' in *Political Modernization in Japan and Turkey*, ed. Robert E. Ward and Dankwart A. Rustow (Princeton: Princeton University Press, 1964), p. 55.

to power of a bureaucratic elite nourished in Western modernist ideas about education and society can never be exaggerated. As their position solidified, the new political elites arrogated upon themselves the power and authority which had previously been in the sultan's hands, restricted access into their ranks, and vested themselves with the responsibility of regenerating the old Ottoman glory and with the administration of the affairs of the empire. The members of this elite group, especially the higher *kâtibs*, were tied together by bonds of language, culture, religion, personal associations and loyalties, intermarriage, and a style of life. Their overarching ideal was not circumscribed by what was later known as Turkish nationalism; rather, it was an all-embracing, but in many respects amorphous, concept called 'Ottomanism', which meant a multi-racial and multi-religious state in which everybody would enjoy equal rights.

In a society which had previously been characterized by religious orthodoxy and conventional Islamic beliefs and values, the introduction of alien ideas, institutions, and a way of life created conflicts and cleavages, especially within the elite segments of the population (for the most part, the masses of the population remained quite unaffected). The elites of the traditional religious institution—namely, the ulema—still maintained a strong position in the educational, cultural, and even political spheres, not to mention, of course, the ecclesiastical domain. In addition to conflicts between Westernizers and traditionalists, a new intellectual force, known as the Young Ottomans, appeared in the middle decades of the nineteenth century. They too reacted against the reformers of the Tanzimat, but unlike the traditional ulema they introduced into the Ottoman Empire the concept of Turkish nationalism, which was destined to supplant 'Ottomanism' as the motivating ideal.

The Ulema and Westernization

Important as the Stambuli Efendi Bureaucracy was in the modernization movement of the Tanzimat period, its success depended to a large extent on the attitude of the still-powerful corps of the Moslem learned men, namely, the ulema. In their dominance over the religious and educational sectors of the empire, in their control over the judiciary, and in their political participation, the ulema occupied pivotal positions in the dissemination of ideas among the various segments of the society and in the formulation of social policy. The Ottoman State was still a theocratic organization, and the concepts of *din ve devlet* (faith and state) were still the motivating ideals of the society.

The educational background of the ulema in general was radically different from that of the political elites discussed earlier. Invariably, the ulema were educated in the traditional religious schools (the mektebs and the medreses), which, for the most part, remained impervious to Western ideas and influences. Also, the ulema espoused ideals for social organization which were quite different from those held by men who had come under Western influence. Solid antagonism and reaction against any attempts to introduce non-Moslem practices, institutions, and modes of thought would have been expected. However, recent research on this aspect of the modernization movement in the nineteenth century has shown that the role of the ulema was more subtle and multivariant.

In the early phase of modernization (especially during the reigns of Selim III and Mahmud II), many of the highest ulema openly supported and/or sanctioned modernizing reforms. Indeed, some of them, according to Uriel Heyd, 'played a major part in conceiving, suggesting, and planning reforms on European lines'.[29] Even during the later period of the Tanzimat when the more enlightened and liberal members of the institution of the *ilmiye* (learned men) all but disappeared, one finds leading ulema co-operating with the reforming sultans in their efforts to modernize some aspects of the Ottoman society. Certain members of the ulema group were even involved in educational reform. For example, Kemal Efendi (later Kemal Pasha) was active in the original plan for the establishment of the rüshdiyes in 1838, and Sami Pasha, Abdul-Medjid's first Minister of Education, was instrumental in introducing more secular elements into education and was a supporter of the

---

[29] Uriel Heyd, 'The Ottoman "*Ulema*" and Westernization in the Time of Selim III and Mahmud II', *Scripta Hierosolymitana*, I ('Studies in Islamic History and Civilization' [Jerusalem: Magnes Press, Hebrew University, 1961]), p. 64.

Young Ottomans.[30] The co-operation of the ulema and the Young Ottomans in the field of education was specifically expressed in another type of lise established as a counterpart to the lise at Galatasaray. This was the Darüshshafaka Lise, which recruited orphan children and sought to inculcate Islamic ideas, although instruction was carried on along modern Western lines.[31]

There were several reasons why high-ranking ulema were in favour of reforms. From the religious, ideological standpoint, it was argued that by adopting European methods and techniques the Ottoman military power would be strengthened, and thus the Moslem faithful would be in a better position to wage their holy war against the infidels. From the more practical, political standpoint, many mollas were afraid of the growing power of the sultan, especially during Mahmud II's reign. Hence, they were only too eager to submit to their master's wishes, either to gain favour over their rivals, or to maintain their positions. The ulema were also suspicious of the Janissaries and their associates and were eager to see their powers curtailed. In addition, many ulema occupied important positions in the government and were tied to the sultans through bonds of personal friendship. Top members of the ulema hierarchy were often assigned important diplomatic missions which necessitated knowledge of, and familiarity with, 'worldly concerns' and 'external affairs'. As members of the ruling elite they shared with the sultan and the other elite groups the concern for the preservation and stability of the empire which depended to a large extent on maintaining friendly relations with European powers.[32]

Yet those from the upper ranks of the religious institution, who supported or sanctioned innovations based on Western models, were not typical of the ulema corps as a whole or of the other members of the ecclesiastical branch of the body politic. Among the lower ulema and the local imams there was extreme

---

[30] For a fuller discussion of the supportive role of some of the higher ulema during this period, see *ibid.*, pp. 64–9. See also Sherif Mardin, *The Genesis of Young Ottoman Thought: A Study in the Modernization of Turkish Political Ideas* (Princeton: Princeton University Press, 1959), p. 218.

[31] *Ibid.*, p. 219.

[32] Heyd, *op. cit.*, pp. 77 ff.

hostility towards any European innovations. The opposition of these groups stemmed in part from their orthodox Islamic religious ideology, which was alien to any secular and/or rationalistic perturbations; but it was also due to certain important sociological and educational factors. As the Western-oriented elite and the upper ulema consolidated their political and social positions in the social structure, the chances for promotion of those in the lower echelons diminished. By education, social position, and outlook these groups were placed at a disadvantage, and their social opportunities were considerably restricted. Nowhere were such social and educational factors more noticeable as contributing to social conflict than in the *softa* (theological student of the medreses).[33]

The softas were notorious for their intractability, discontent, and troublemaking. Their numbers were large—in the 1830s and 1840s there were about five thousand in Istanbul—and the sources of their turbulence and reaction against the entrenched political and religious elites were multiple. Educated in the traditional religious establishments, these students of orthodox Islam and Moslem learning viewed with suspicion any secularist infiltrations, and reacted violently against any attempts to change the character of Islamic institutions and the essentially Moslem society. But the protest and reactionary fanaticism of the softas, who forced the replacement of the grand vizier and the grand *mufti* (religious leader) in 1876, also stemmed from their underprivileged social position. Having spent many years of study under extremely difficult living conditions, they looked forward to an equally long period of time before they could obtain a remunerative post. At a time when patronage, favouritism, graft, and corruption were rampant in ecclesiastical appointments and promotions, and when the religious aristocracy of mollas, surrounded by luxury, pomp and ceremony, formed a 'closed' hereditary group, the poor and lowly softas saw no possible avenues for their own social and political elevation, or for their economic betterment. Thus the discontent of the softas, as well as the lower ulema, and their opposition to Westernization and authority in general represented both a conflict over education and religious belief and a class struggle

[33] *Ibid.*, pp. 61–74.

within the religious institution itself. The questions of ideology and class interest were also present in the reaction of the Young Ottomans, the group of intellectuals who have been credited with being the originators of the modern concept of Turkish nationalism.

THE YOUNG OTTOMANS AND MODERNIZATION

To understand better the interplay of forces during this period of Ottoman social and political modernization, a more careful look at the Young Ottoman movement[34] is needed. The movement, which gained particular prominence in the last decade of the Tanzimat period, inspired many of the ideological strands that went into the making of Turkish nationalism and political development. The examination of this rather short-lived movement (1865–78) is particularly interesting for several reasons. Unlike the Tanzimat reformers, the Young Ottomans were steeped in traditional Islamic values and beliefs, yet their educational background and political and social ideology were as much nurtured in Western liberal ideas as were those of the other Tanzimat reformers. Moreover, many of the Young Ottoman intellectuals were at one time or another members of the same bureaucracy as the leaders of the Tanzimat and had also served in the famous Translation Bureau. In spite of several obvious affinities, the Young Ottomans reacted strongly against the reform movement initiated by the famous triumvirate (Reshid Pasha, Ali Pasha, and Fuad Pasha) and against the new political elites, although they retained their loyalty to the sultan.

The Young Ottoman movement began in 1865, when the Patriotic Alliance was created by a small group of 'conspirators' who were united by a common dislike of the policies of the ruling elite, by a concern for the rejuvenation of the disintegrating Ottoman Empire, and by a common knowledge of European ideas and institutions. Active both at home and abroad, the Young Ottomans sought to develop a political ideology which incorporated features of the Western liberal

[34] Much of the material for this section is based on Sherif Mardin's book cited earlier, which is the best available study in English. See also Davison, *op. cit.*, pp. 172–233.

tradition, yet was grounded in basic Islamic beliefs about man, society, and government. Their major purpose was to disseminate their ideas among both the leaders of the society and the people, through the use of the media of mass communication. In this sense they may be regarded not only as the political ideologists of the period, but also as important educators in introducing and spreading new ideas concerning constitutionalism and nationalism. Originally members of the bureaucracy they oscillated in their relationships with the sultan and the 'Porte'. Many were exiled, then returned to the bureaucratic fold; one of the most famous of them, Ali Suavi (who had also served as director of the Galatasaray lise), died in an abortive attempt to overthrow Sultan Abdül-Hamid II in 1878, an event which also marked the end of Young Ottomanism as a political movement.

The Young Ottomans were in many respects a diverse group of reformers, and their political philosophy displayed many dissimilar ideals. A sample of the more prominent members of this group included: Mustafa Fazil Pasha, a prince of the imperial family, who advocated a type of constitutional liberty 'which would establish equality and harmony between Musulman and Christian'; Ziya Pasha, a member of the palace group of administrators, the son of a minor customs official, who was educated in the local mekteb and the *Mekteb-i Irfan* (one of the two academies established by Reshid Pasha), and entered the Translation Bureau, where he came under the influence of Fatin Efendi, one of the Ottoman Islamic classicists; Namik Kemal, the eminent poet and perhaps the most famous of the group, who was the son of a court astronomer, went to a rüshdiye and the Translation Bureau, and was deeply immersed in classical Islamic culture; and, of course, Ali Suavi, a member of the ulema group, a colourful activist, who served as director of the Galatasaray lise and who was a ringleader in the abortive attempt to depose Abdül-Hamid. Of all the Young Ottomans, Namik Kemal was the most systematic political ideologist. He sought to weave a political theory of representative government, individual freedom, and human progress, out of intellectual strands which were secular and religious on one hand, and Western and Islamic on the other. He was not always successful in his attempted syntheses, and there are several contradictions and inconsistencies in his thinking. For example, he was not able to reconcile the Islamic belief that government should fulfil the conditions of the sheriat and all that this entailed in terms of origins and legitimacy of political authority and individual freedom, with the Western liberal view of 'justified revolt', *responsible* government, and the view that the state was an 'artificial instrumentality based on the claims of the individual'.

Yet, in spite of a certain failure to reconcile obvious theoretical antitheses in Islamic and Western thought, the Young Ottomans must be assigned an important place in the process of intellectual and educational modernization in Turkey. In spite of their obvious propensities towards the maintenance of the spirit of Islam and of dynastic traditions—both of which were rejected by Atatürk and the revolutionaries of the twentieth century—the Young Ottomans were among the first to introduce and/or popularize such concepts as *hürriyet* (freedom), *vatan* (fatherland), and millet, meaning 'nation' as well as the traditional meaning of 'religious group'. By popularizing these words, the Young Ottomans, especially Namik Kemal, sought to instil the spirit of national allegiance in the individual. The use of such symbols was characterized more by patriotic fervour than by clarity of meaning: in the Young Ottoman political framework vatan signified the territorial boundaries of the polymorphous Ottoman Empire rather than Atatürk's concept of a Turkish national state. Yet the very use and dissemination of such concepts was an important beginning in the ideological development which culminated, in the twentieth century, with the establishment of the Turkish Republic. At this formative stage Turkish nationalism was enmeshed in traditional Islamic beliefs, a substratum which, as Sherif Mardin has observed, was weakened under the Young Turks and was finally eliminated under Atatürk.[35]

This blend of the Islamic and the modern European was also reflected in the educational background of the Young Ottomans themselves and in their views on education. As with the Tanzimat educational reformers, some—Namik Kemal, for example—placed heavy emphasis upon a system of education which would be equally accessible to all members of the Ottoman

[35] Mardin, *op. cit.*, p. 404.

Empire as an important desideratum for the modernization of the polity. But the Young Ottomans also criticized the educational innovations of the Tanzimat reforms, for it seemed to them that the new institutions and practices undermined or did not take into full account the richness and values of traditional Islamic culture. Thus they criticized the nature and character of the Galatasaray lise, and they participated in the establishment of a rival institution, the Darüshshafaka.

The opposition of the Young Ottomans to the educational innovations of the Tanzimat statesmen was part of their general reaction against the Western-educated and Western-oriented ruling elite. The rise to power, the education, and the style of life of these new bureaucrats have already been examined. The Young Ottomans protested against the political entrenchment of the new elites and their formation into what they considered to be a self-perpetuating and closed group, as well as against their methods of government. The religiously puritan Young Ottomans also saw in the new bureaucratic elite the embodiment of what they rejected in Western education. Further, the Young Ottomans, many of whom had emerged from the bureaucracy itself, may be viewed as a group of angry intellectuals who reacted against the closing of opportunities for social advancement into the upper ranks of the government. Although their education and literary skills would previously have been sufficient qualifications for occupational advancement and high social status, they now found that they could not go beyond the middle levels of the bureaucracy. Thus, as in the case of the middle and lower ulema, the Young Ottoman reaction to the Tanzimat reforms was the result of an interplay of forces: educational, social, and ideological.

CHAPTER IV

REACTION AND REVOLUTION: EDUCATION AND THE FOUNDATIONS OF MODERN TURKISH NATIONALISM

THE period from the accession of Sultan Abdül-Hamid II in 1876 to the Revolution of 1923 witnessed some of the most turbulent episodes in Ottoman history. Pressed by the zealous reformer Midhat Pasha and the Young Ottomans, the new sultan proclaimed the first *meshrutiyet* (constitutional government) ever promulgated in the empire. But the new constitution was short-lived. Within three years, Midhat Pasha, who had in the meantime been appointed grand vizier, was ignominiously dismissed; another war broke out with Russia; and Abdül-Hamid dissolved the newly-convened chamber of deputies and reverted to a tighter form of despotism than any of his predecessors had exercised. In 1908, the Hamidian regime was overthrown by the Young Turks, who forced the restoration of constitutional government upon the new sultan. The second meshrutiyet likewise ended in failure and disappointment. The Ottoman Empire was soon embroiled in wars with the Balkan states and with the European allied powers, events which also sealed its fate. World War I ended with Allied forces stationed in Istanbul and, in 1919, with Greek forces landing at Izmir. In that same year Mustafa Kemal also landed at Samsun, thus starting a chain of events which ultimately culminated in the demise of Ottoman Islamic rule and the birth of the Turkish Republic.

THE SYSTEM OF EDUCATION AND THE SCHOOLS

The despotic, autocratic, and reactionary character of Abdül-

Hamid has been legendary among observers, historians, and people who had come to know him, either directly or indirectly. Surrounded by the malleable creatures of the palace secretariat, Abdül-Hamid wielded personal authority throughout the Ottoman realm through a network of spies and informers. More than any other ruler of recent years he utilized his office of caliph to exert power over the Moslem members of his empire. As the legitimate ruler of the Ottoman State, he ruthlessly stamped out seeds of rebellion, by Armenians or by his own co-religionists and friends. A more dispassionate and objective historical appraisal, however, reveals that, insofar as Ottoman rulers were concerned, Abdül-Hamid was also a man of unusual entrepreneurial scope. More pertinent to this study, he had considerable faith in the value of education and enlightenment. Moreover, far from being a period of political reaction and stagnation, the Hamidian years, especially the early years, saw the consolidation of many of the ideas and reforms of the Tanzimat. In short, as Bernard Lewis points out, Abdül-Hamid was 'a willing and active modernizer, the true heir of Sultan Abdülaziz and the statesmen of the Tanzimat'.[1]

The Constitution of 1876 provided that all schools should be under government supervision and that the first stage of education should be compulsory. Although these principles were discarded along with the constitution, the idea of educational reform survived. Indeed, as in the period of the Tanzimat, education was considered the cornerstone of any and all improvements in the judicial, legal, administrative, and military advancement of the state. This view was entertained by Said Pasha, an Anglophile, a descendant of a family of ulema and a key figure in the educational reforms associated with the Hamidian era.

We have previously noted that the 1869 Regulations provided for the establishment of a network of schools throughout the empire, ranging from primary schools to a university in Istanbul. The progress in setting up schools at the lowest rungs of the educational ladder was perhaps the slowest. In 1876 responsibility for the sübyans was placed in the hands of local school boards, which were to consist of the imam and the

[1] Bernard Lewis, *The Emergence of Modern Turkey* (London: Oxford University Press, 1961), p. 174.

muhtar (local official civil leader). The teaching staff was to be appointed by the Minister of Education, the course of study was to extend over three years, and the school was to be supported by combined funds from the pious foundations, from fees charged to wealthy parents, and from fines imposed on delinquent parents who did not send their children to school. However, no attempt was made to enforce this regulation, and the growth of these schools was rather slow. Nor did their previous character change; the sübyan continued to be a school supported by the Evkaf and by fees, and its curriculum was predominantly religious in orientation.

An English lady writing in 1878 compared the religious character of these schools with that of the old British national schools which were operated by the Church of England. She recorded that in a typical school in Istanbul the pupils, normally amounting to one or two hundred, were closely assembled in a room. Under the superintendence of monitors and the direction of an old hoja, they learned and recited verses written in Arabic from the Koran. In her own words:

'Kneeling in rows, divided into tens by monitors who superintend their lessons, they learn partly from the book and partly by rote, all reading out the lesson at the same time, and swaying their bodies backwards and forwards. An old Hodja, with his assistant, sits cross-legged on a mat at one end of the room, before the chest which serves the double purpose of desk and bookcase. With the cane of discipline in one hand, a pipe in the other, and the Koran before him, the old pedagogue listens to and directs the proceedings of the pupils.'[2]

There was great ceremony surrounding a child's first day at school. Well dressed and carrying a copy of the Koran, the child was led to school by his father. After reciting the Moslem creed, the novice kissed the teacher's hand and then joined his future schoolmates. After the day's session the other children took the newcomer home, the teacher leading the procession and chanting prayers and the children joining in the response. When they reached the pupil's home, they would all be offered

[2] Stanley L. Poole (ed.), *The People of Turkey: Twenty Years' Residence among Bulgarians, Greeks, Albanians, Turks and Armenians, by a Consul's Daughter and Wife* (London: John Murray, 1878), pp. 165–7.

refreshments and ten *para* (about a half penny) each by the parents of the new scholar.

The character of these schools remained essentially the same until the period of the republic. An American observer from New England, writing in 1908, noted the same initiation ceremonies, methods, and content of teaching. In a slightly over-romanticized tone this observer described the ritualistic procession after the first day at school as follows:

'Dressed in his holiday suit, and bedecked with all the jewels and personal ornaments . . . his little fez almost concealed with strings of gold coins, pendants, pearl tassels, and various little objects worn as charms against "the evil eye", and his finger-tips tinged with henna, he is mounted on a superbly caparisoned horse, and led in pompous procession through the streets of the neighbourhood. In front of him his future instructors walk backwards, slowly and gravely, as if to prolong the ceremony. . . . Behind these come all his future school fellows, walking two and two, chanting verses said to have been composed by the Prophet extolling the pleasures of knowledge, exhorting to love of one's neighbour, inciting to industry, and concluding with good wishes for their new companion, eulogies of his parents and teachers, and finally glorification of the Sultan, all the bystanders loyally joining in the refrain. *Amin! Amin!*'[3]

In his moving autobiographical novel, *Portrait of a Turkish Family*, Irfan Orga, who had been sent to such a school early in the twentieth century, presents a graphic but uncomplimentary picture of his first day at school: the perennial hoja and his ten-foot-long stick, the single room with children seated cross-legged on cushions on the floor, chanting verses from the Koran and '*Padishahim chok yasha*' (Long live my Sultan); and, to sweeten everybody's taste, if not his mind, the tray of *lokma* (a heavy, syrupy sweet). Young Irfan was disappointed with his first entry into the Moslem halls of learning, and so were his parents. After the boy recounted what transpired at school, his father declared firmly: 'Ahmet was right. He must be sent to the French school at Gedik Pasha.'[4]

[3] W. S. Monroe, *Turkey and the Turks: An Account of the Lands, the Peoples, and the Institutions of the Ottoman Empire* (London: G. Bell & Sons, 1908), pp. 165–6.
[4] Irfan Orga, *Portrait of a Turkish Family* (New York: The Macmillan Company, 1950), pp. 52–3.

Under the Young Turk regime another attempt was made to reform the system of primary education. In 1913 a new law was passed, aimed at public support of primary schools and better organization of the programme of study. The *Tedrisati Iptidai Kanunu* (Provisory Primary Education Law) of 1913 included: (a) compulsory and free six-year education in public schools, and (b) limitation of class size to not more than fifty pupils. The purpose of these schools was stated as preparation for secondary education, and Article 23 laid down in specific terms the content of the curriculum as follows:

'Primary schools shall teach the following: The Ku'ran (to Muslim students only); elements of religion (to non-Muslims, the elements of their own religion); reading and writing; Ottoman language; geography, especially Ottoman geography; arithmetic and geometry; history, especially Ottoman history; civics, science and hygiene; handiwork and drawing; religious and patriotic poetry; physical education and school games; for boys military training; for girls, housekeeping and sewing.'[5]

Regarding teacher-training, the law provided that regular teachers must be graduates of normal schools and that assistant teachers must have temporary licenses stating that they are qualified to teach.

The type of institution envisaged by this law was in reality a combination of the old iptidai and the rüshdiye. After the 1869 Regulations, there was a sudden increase in the number of rüshdiyes. In 1876, there were already 253 throughout the empire, 21 of which were located in Istanbul. Foreign observers noted that there were rüshdiyes in all the large towns of the empire.

Above the rüshdiye were the idadis, and at the apex of the system were the two famous schools of Galatasaray and Darüshshafaka. The idadi, which recruited students from the rüshdiyes, provided what might be called middle and lower secondary education. Although the 1869 Regulations stipulated the establishment of such schools, the lack of government funds stunted their growth at first, so the first such school was not established until 1879. After 1884, however, when a special

[5] For the text of the Provisory Law, see *Milli Egitim le Ilgili Kanunlar* (Ankara: Milli Egitim Basimevi, 1953), pp. 931–52.

tax was levied through the efforts of Said Pasha, the idadi grew rapidly. By 1895, there were fifty-five idadis with an enrolment of about 7,200. Of these, two were in Istanbul, and the rest, in the provinces. Idadis were either four-year boarding schools or two-year day schools. Foreign observers commented that some of them were quite similar to the leading secondary school of Galatasaray. In 1914, Stanley Cobb, an American, visited the idadi at Kabatash (a section of Istanbul) and was quite impressed by the cultural atmosphere of the school and its scientific equipment.[6]

By that time, however, the idadis had already become the centre of criticism for their functions overlapped those of the lises. Accordingly, it was suggested that the idadi be transformed into a quasi-vocational or practical institution to cater to the agricultural and industrial needs of the country. As a result, practical divisions (commercial, agricultural, and industrial) were added to the day idadis, and the boarding schools were converted into lises. By 1923, twelve out of sixty-nine day idadis had practical divisions. With the reorganization of the schools under the republic, all existing idadis were converted to *orta* (middle) schools.

Important as the idadis were, the pride of the Ottomans in the period lay in the upper secondary schools, and other higher institutions. Outstanding examples among these were the already mentioned schools of Galatasaray and Darüshshafaka, the mülkiye established during the period of the Tanzimat, and the Darülfünün Shahane, later known as Istanbul University, established in 1900. Although the 1869 Regulations provided for the establishment of sultanis in each of the provincial capitals, their growth was rather slow. However, by 1914, twenty-six such schools, with a student enrolment of 8,380, had been created. Schools of this nature were modelled upon the original institution at Galatasaray, which had remained the secondary school par excellence.

In spite of its being a borrowed institution, the Galatasaray was gradually becoming Ottoman Turkish in character and an integral part of the educational and socio-political development of the country. By 1876 De Salve, the French Director of

---

[6] Stanley Cobb, *The Real Turk* (Boston: The Pilgrim Press, 1914), pp. 134-5.

Studies, had left for his homeland, reminiscing about the progress and disappointments of this Franco-Ottoman enterprise; and the school had already moved into an entirely Turkish quarter of the capital. During Abdül-Hamid's reign, Latin was abolished and the amount of Turkish instruction increased, although French continued to occupy a prominent place in the curriculum. As time passed it recruited most of its students from the Turkish population and developed into an exclusive institution for the upper, affluent, social strata.[7]

Contemporary descriptions by foreign observers were, in the main, laudatory. Stanley Cobb wrote: 'The courses of instruction here are thoroughly modern, with five lecture rooms, laboratories, and dormitories for the resident students, and the young men who graduate are at the point in education reached by our juniors at college.'[8]

By the opening decades of the twentieth century, the desire to spread the sultani type of education had increased. This, however, raised questions about the relationship of such an institution to the other secondary schools, the idadis, and to the educational system of the country in general. The essential function of schools like the sultani was the provision of a general, humanistic, type of education and preparation of a small number of students, the elite, for higher education and high careers in the society. It would recruit its students mostly from the *güzide sinif* (elite group), although it could also draw exceptionally bright children from the poorer classes through scholarship awards. When Emrullah Efendi, the Minister of Education, proposed to change the character of the idadis in 1910 and to open ten new sultanis, the plan was criticized, for fear that it would alter the character and function of the idadis. Emrullah Efendi had proposed that French should be emphasized in the lower classes of the new sultanis, and that science and mathematics in the upper classes should be taught in French. When ten boarding idadis were renamed sultanis, following the minister's proposals, only one of Emrullah's curriculum suggestions was put into effect; science and mathematics continued to be taught in Turkish. The idea of expanding

[7] Osman Ergin, *Türkiye Maarif Tarihi* (*History of Turkish Education* [Istanbul: Osmanbey Matbaasi, 1939–43]), III, 743.

[8] Cobb, *op. cit.*, p. 134.

a sultani type of education continued to evoke criticism. Some feared that expansion would mean the blurring of the schools' distinctive social and intellectual features, and the creation of disenchanted outcasts. Thus, for example, Ismail Hakki Baltajioglu felt in 1918 that the sultani should maintain its elitist and humanistic nature; the education of prospective *ish adamlar* (business and similar people) belonged to other types of schools.[9]

No one expressed better the distinct educational and social characteristics of the sultani-lise than the eminent Ziya Gökalp. Obviously influenced by French ideas, Gökalp drew a distinction between education and training: the former aimed at culture; and the latter, instruction in particular techniques. The lises, according to him, were purely educational institutions, whereas the primary, trade, and professional schools, were institutions of training. Moreover, the function of the lise was to educate the elite, namely, the future lawyers, doctors, writers, government officials and teachers. Gökalp summed up as follows:

'During their undergraduate years the youth, who are later expected to specialize as doctors, engineers, chemists, etc., badly need teaching in literature, philosophy and social sciences, in other words in cultural sciences. Later they are going to study in great detail the sciences in their respective fields of specialization. As they will not get a cultural education as graduates, they need a thorough cultural education as undergraduates. Therefore, these schools should be entirely devoted to education in the humanities.'[10]

In contrast to the Galatasaray lise, the Darüshshafaka started out as a charitable institution. During the Hamidian period, its course was rather stormy; it also affords an example of Abdül-Hamid's suspicions of the possible results of the concentration of too many intellectuals in the capital. Largely through the efforts of Said Pasha, the government took a more active interest in the schools of Istanbul, especially the Darüshshafaka. In 1884, Said Pasha visited the school and was quite impressed with the work done in it. In the same year he wrote a report to the government, which responded by increasing its

[9] Ergin, *op. cit.*, III, 1194–1203.
[10] Niyazi Berkes (ed.), *Turkish Nationalism and Western Civilization: Selected Essays of Ziya Gökalp* (London: Allen & Unwin; New York: Columbia University Press, 1959), pp. 240–1.

subsidies to the school. In 1888, the Darüshshafaka passed under the direct control of the sultan—in Ergin's words it became 'a private institution run by the palace'. Entrance examinations were abolished, and students were accepted solely on the basis of recommendations. Enrolments soared from four hundred to seven hundred, thereby creating problems of accommodation and support. In 1903 the students responded by riots and protestations in front of the grand vizier's chancery, asking for more food and clothes. Their purpose was merely to attract the sultan's attention, for they shouted 'Long live the sultan' when they arrived at the chancery, and they returned to their schools. By this time, however, Abdül-Hamid had grown too suspicious to brook any kind of protest or student impertinence. He reacted by peremptorily ordering that all students be deported to Tripoli and that the school be closed. A high governmental official, who happened to be a graduate of the school and near the sultan when the order was given, saved the day. The students were spared, but the director of the school was exiled to Anatolia. A number of students were sent to other schools outside Istanbul, strict discipline over the affairs of the school and the students was imposed, and the institution was incorporated into the government system of education. Abdül-Hamid kept a constant vigilance over any potential student trouble-makers. Ergin reports that the new principal spied on students 'to find out whether there were political influences from outside'.

In 1908, after the Young Turk revolt, the graduates of the Darüshshafaka asked for changes in the governing of the school. A new committee was appointed which asked that the school revert to its original status. The government agreed and donated 6,000 liras to its support. Since 1909 the Darüshshafaka has remained a private lise.[11]

The third educational institution which grew into considerable importance during this period was the Mülkiye. Literally translated 'civilian', the word mülkiye came to mean 'civil service' in general, and the Mülkiye, a civil service training school. The Mülkiye was founded in 1859 for the explicit purpose of selecting and training persons to occupy positions in the

[11] For the full account of the trials and tribulations of the Darüshshafaka during Abdül-Hamid's autocracy, see Ergin, *op. cit.*, III, 744 ff.

expanding bureaucracy. Like the school at Galatasary, it was essentially a secular establishment and was part of the general movement to modernize the institutions and the functioning of the government. Originally, the Mülkiye course lasted only one year and its students were recruited from qualified kâtibs who were already government employees serving in the various bureaus. Soon, however, such training became inadequate. In 1872 Djevdet Pasha, a leading intellectual, submitted a memorandum to the grand vizier urging him to reorganize the programme of studies at the mülkiye so that the civil service would be staffed with better-trained individuals. In 1877 the course of study was lengthened to two, three, or four years, depending on the educational background of the student, and the curriculum was modernized. The students who entered the school were no longer limited to the kâtib class, but had varied prior educational experiences. A breakdown of the Mülkiye graduates from 1860 to 1900 has shown that, of 287 such persons for which information on educational background was available, 92, or 32 per cent, had gone to an idadi; about the same number (90) had attended a rüshdiye; 21, or 7 per cent, the Galatasaray lise; 15, a medrese or other religious school; and the rest had received their education elsewhere (abroad, privately, etc.). After 1900 the idadis and Galatasaray became major preparatory schools for the Mülkiye.[12] As it became better organized and resembled an institution of higher learning, admission into it presupposed a modern, primarily secular, secondary school training which at the time was provided in the two previously mentioned types of institutions. Students from the medreses were admitted, provided they passed certain examinations or had gone through an idadi as well.

The Mülkiye continued to flourish, even under the repressive Hamidian regime. Indeed, Abdül-Hamid himself supported the institution, as he did the military schools, from funds directly allocated by him, in spite of the fact that many students and professors were critical of his policies. After a brief eclipse during World War I, the Mülkiye reopened in 1918; in 1934 its name was changed to School of Political Sciences; two years later it

[12] The data on the characteristics of the graduates of the Mulkiye were tabulated from the biographical information given by Mujellitoglu Ali Chankaya, *Mülkiye Tarihi ve Mülkiyeliler* (Ankara: Ornek Matbaasi, 1954), Vol. II.

was moved to Ankara; and in 1950 it was attached to the University of Ankara as the Faculty of Political Sciences (*Siyasal Bilqiler Fakültesi*).

The Mülkiye, like the Galatasaray Lise, was socially a selective institution in the sense that a relatively large number of its students came from specific occupational and social groups. For example, of 289 students who graduated during the period 1860–1909 and for which information was gathered, about 40 per cent had fathers who had a position as high or low *memur* (member of the civil bureaucracy). Considering the fact that the school itself prepared for careers in the civil bureaucracy —almost all the graduates became a memur, a *kaymakam* (governor of a sub-province), a *vali* (governor of a province), etc.—it could be said that there was a tendency for the official class to perpetuate itself. Nevertheless, the Mülkiye was not exclusively a bureaucrats' school; nor is there evidence to show that the majority of the students were recruited from the bureaucracy.[13] Investigation into paternal occupation of all graduates up to the period of the Young Turk Revolution revealed that the pattern of recruitment seems to have been quite diverse. For example, of the sample of 289 graduates, 40 per cent indicated that their fathers belonged to the civil bureaucracy, but 12 per cent had fathers who were religious leaders, and about the same percentage had a business family background. In addition, about 7 per cent indicated 'educator' as paternal occupation, and 9 per cent 'judge'; the rest included 'free professions', military officer, farmer, and 'tribal chief'.

Clearly, the overwhelming majority came from the 'white-collar' group, which constituted a very small segment of the Ottoman society and was largely located in Istanbul and the European provinces of the empire: of a sample of 765 graduates, 40 per cent were born in Istanbul; 21 per cent, in the European provinces; and about 25 per cent, in small towns in Anatolia. Apparently, therefore, the Mülkiye reflected the growing importance of the efendi bureaucracy, which was largely concentrated in the Istanbul and the Rumelian regions of the Ottoman Empire.

---

[13] This seems to be the view taken by Chambers. See Robert E. Ward and Dankwart A. Rustow (eds.), *Political Modernization in Japan and Turkey* (Princeton: Princeton University Press, 1964), p. 306.

The variations in the recruitment pattern of the Mülkiye were not reflected in the occupational destinations of its students. The school continued to be a training ground for officials in the government service. A breakdown of the highest positions attained by the students who graduated from 1860 to 1909 has shown the following occupational distribution:

Position	Percentage of Graduates (N = 792)
Vali	5·3
Mutasarrif (deputy governor)	9·4
Kaymakam	28·3
Memur	45·6
Vekil (minister)	4·4
Diplomat (ambassador, etc.)	1·8
Nahiye Müdürü (local government official)	·7
Hâkim (judge)	2·1
No information	2·4

Since all of the above positions were appointive civil service posts, the official career orientation of the institution is quite obvious.

At the very apex of the emerging system of education there was the Darülfünun. Although attempts had been made earlier, only in 1900 was an institution of higher learning approximating a university created. The original University of Istanbul included faculties of theology, literature and science, and mathematics; faculties of law and medicine were later incorporated. Students were recruited only from graduates of the sultanis. A foreign observer, writing in 1914, described the Darülfünun as follows:

'Its work is much limited by scholasticism, and it cannot be said to turn out real scholars. It forms a basis, however, upon which a real university may some day be erected. It is well equipped with seats and desks, but there are no libraries to study from and no laboratories for the direct study of the physical sciences. The chief means of instruction is by lectures, as in the medieval universities of Europe. Even the textbooks are ancient. Until a few years ago physics was taught from an Arabic textbook over a thousand years old—dating from the Cordova period.'[14]

[14] Cobb, op. cit., pp. 136–7.

During this period there were several other educational establishments at the secondary and primary level. Some of these, such as the normal schools, which prepared primary school teachers, were under the Ministry of Education; others, like the trade, technical, and agricultural schools, the Veterinary School, the School for Customs Officials, and the Police School, were under other ministries—Agriculture, Health and so on. The School of Engineering and the Higher Commercial School also provided a higher type of education. Finally, the different military schools of varying grades for the training of officers and technicians should be included. These were outside the general educational system, since they belonged to the Ministry of Defence.

The Medreses

Although the skeleton of a modern state system of schools was being formed by the outbreak of World War I, the traditional religious higher schools continued to occupy a central position in education in the Ottoman Empire. The medreses, supported by funds from the mosques, provided free tuition, lodging, and a small sum of money for food. Partly because of such free education and the fact that graduation from them meant exemption from military service, these establishments were able to attract and sustain large numbers of students of all ages. One writer estimated that in 1908 there were one hundred medreses with six thousand students in Istanbul alone;[15] another, put the figure as high as twenty thousand at about the same time.[16]

The medreses differed from the other higher schools in almost all respects. They recruited their students from the lower and middle classes; they provided an Islamic, religious type of education with emphasis upon Arabic and the Koran; they were free; they trained mostly for ecclesiastical careers; they had a very loose system of examinations; they were relatively conservative in their beliefs; and, in general, they were in a stage of decline as intellectual centres of the empire. The Young Turks sought to improve the status of these schools, but their general condition continued to decline. To those who

[15] Monroe, *op. cit.*, p. 167.
[16] Cobb, *op. cit.*, p. 137.

wanted to modernize the society the medrese symbolized reaction, conservatism, and a static state of affairs. In her pene-
trating lectures on the conflict between East and West, the
eminent Halide Edib associated the medreses and their products with a stagnant scholasticism and the propagation of a
state of mind which was averse to Western modes of thought
and progress. The type of education they offered and their outlook on life were not substantially different from what they had
been in the thirteenth century.[17]

Technical and Commercial Education

During the early period of their history, the Ottoman Turks
were well known for their domestic arts and crafts and their
manufacture of military weapons. But by the nineteenth century, when European countries were being swept by new inven-
tions and new techniques, the Ottoman Empire still relied
heavily on primitive methods of manufacturing. Financial difficulties paved the way for commercial agreements with foreign
countries, which were granted certain privileges in business
transactions. This was the notorious system of capitulations,
which allowed foreigners to engage in business with the Ottomans under minimal trade restrictions. Importation of foreign
goods increased out of proportion with exports in the nineteenth
century. Ottoman goods could not compete in the foreign
markets, and manufactures were limited to simple articles for
the limited village markets. The Ottoman elites preferred
European dress and the European type of military uniform to
the rustic fabrics made on hand looms.

During the period of the Tanzimat, some attempts were
made to set up factories and to organize local petty industries
into larger corporations. In the Istanbul Exposition of 1862,
Turkish articles made by local craftsmen were displayed in the
hope that this would check the inflow of foreign goods which
plunged the nation into economic difficulties. At the same time,
attempts were made to establish trade schools, the beginnings of
which have been attributed to Midhat Pasha. While he was
governor of the Danube Provinces, Midhat Pasha founded re-
formatories to provide shelter for orphans, waifs, and strays,

[17] Halide Edib, *Conflict of East and West in Turkey* (Lahore: Shaikh Muham-
mad Ashraf, 1935), p. 52.

and to teach a basic trade. When he returned to Istanbul as head of the Council of State, he established a trade school, an idea which was emulated in the provinces. The growth of these institutions was rather haphazard, however, and they remained essentially reform or orphan schools. The 1869 Regulations omitted any mention of vocational or technical education. Although Said Pasha recognized the need for such a type of education, no state action was taken until 1913. By the Provisory Law of that year these so-called industrial schools were included in the provincial educational budgets. Although this arrangement helped to stabilize such schools, the system of technical education lacked co-ordination. It was not until the republican period that concerted efforts were made to strengthen this type of education and to bring it into closer relation with the needs of the country.[18]

Like technical schools, commercial education was also neglected by the Ottomans. Although a commercial school—the Hamidiye Commercial College—was established in Istanbul in 1883, any commercial education provided at the time was in the hands of the minority groups of the empire. This, of course, paralleled the commercial activities of the society at large. Moslem merchants, as one official document put it, 'retired from business life and left commerce in the hands of foreigners and the minorities as they sent their children to the new military and civilian schools opened during that epoch'.[19] Even at the Hamidiye Commercial College, the majority of the students were non-Moslem. After the Young Turk Revolution some commercial training was provided in the idadis, but progress in the provision of commercial training prior to the period of the republic was quite negligible.

Minority and Missionary Schools

Although many of the new schools established by the state, particularly at the post-primary level, were also intended for the non-Moslem members of the Ottoman Empire, the millets provided and operated their own schools. Contemporary ac-

---

[18] *Technical Education for Men in Turkey* (Ankara: Milli Egitim Basimevi, 1951), pp. 1–4.

[19] *Schools of Commercial Education in Turkey* (Ministry of Education, Statistics and Publications Department [Ankara: Bengi Printing House, 1962]), p. 6.

counts pay particular attention to the educational activities of the Greek Orthodox, one of the largest millets.

Greek education was for the most part supported and regulated by the several communities from private contributions and from church donations. The central agency was centred in the patriarchate located in the Fener section of the old city of Constantinople. Each local community managed its own Greek school, where children were taught Greek letters and history, and the Greek Orthodox religion. In Istanbul, there were old educational establishments dating to the period after the conquest of Constantinople. These were centred in the National Training School at Fener and the more recently established (1844) Theological Seminary at Halki, one of the islands in the Sea of Marmara. During and after the Hamidian regime, the network of Greek schools spread rapidly. According to Ergin, in 1904 there were 64 elementary and secondary schools and 360 teachers in Istanbul alone, without counting special schools directly under the patriarchate. Graduates of the better-known secondary schools like Heybeliada, Fener, Zografyon, Haji Hiristo, Zapyon and Yoakimyon, could enter any university in Europe and Greece without entrance examinations. The Greek Patriarch was also instrumental in setting up a multiracial school, largely for Europeans, which would teach Turkish, English, German, French, and Greek. In requesting permission from the sultan, he argued that such a school would train officials who would take up posts in business enterprises especially those connected with European transactions. The school was opened at Beyoglu, the fashionable section of larger Istanbul, and was used as both a language school and a commercial lise. It continued to function until the republican period, when it was replaced by a Turkish elementary school.[20]

As in the larger Ottoman society, the wealthier sections of the Greek millet received more and better education than the average individual. Istanbul and other cities like Prusa (*Bursa*), Smyrna (*Izmir*), and Salonika (*Selanik*), had some of the best-staffed and equipped schools in the empire. Many of the Ottoman Greek elites sent their children to them and to the other famous Ottoman schools like the Galatasaray lise, but others

[20] Ergin, *op. cit.*, III, 841–51.

preferred to send them to schools in Athens. In most of the
Greek schools, the motivating ideal was the Helleno-Christian
tradition. In the curriculum and in the values sought, the
Greeks aimed at transmitting their Hellenic heritage and in-
stilling what they felt were inseparable twin values, namely,
Greek nationalism and the Orthodox faith. A girls' school in
Salonica taught such subjects as ancient Greek, history of
Greece, catechism, sacred history, political and physical geography, mathematics, pedagogy, plain and fancy needlework,
vocal music, physics, and psychology. Boys' schools were called
gymnasia and, except for subjects solely intended for girls,
focused on the same curriculum as the schools for girls, plus
more advanced mathematics, philosophy and logic, and Latin.[21]
No Turkish was taught in the Greek schools until 1895, when
the Ottoman government made Turkish a required subject.
Although the Greeks constituted a part of the Ottoman nation,
there was little in their education and their aspirations which
was in any way connected with such a nation. Indeed, following
the Greek Revolution, and increasingly during the period under
study, their eyes were turned to Greece rather than to their
Ottoman rulers, which rendered any concept of Pan-Ottoman-
ism quite unrealistic. Those who studied in Greece returned
home eager to spread the ideas of Greek nationalism and
Hellenic culture rather than to settle down for the multiracial,
cohesive body politic envisaged by the Ottoman modernizers.

In addition to the educational activities of the ethnic minorities, there were missionary activities by the Protestant and
Catholic denominations. An American observer writing in 1908
estimated that throughout the Ottoman Empire Protestant
missions operated 527 schools with 23,572 pupils, and 45 colleges with 3,004 pupils. Roman Catholic missions, particularly
the Jesuits, had fewer institutions.[22] An outstanding example
of the Protestant missionary zeal was Robert College, the
cornerstone of which was ceremoniously laid on July 4, 1869,
in Bebek, near the fortification of Rumeli Hisar built by Mehmet
II, the conqueror of Constantinople. In one of the many ora-
tions delivered in English, French, Turkish, Greek, Armenian,
and Bulgarian, the following analogy was drawn between the

[21] See Poole, *op. cit.*, pp. 193–9.
[22] Monroe, *op. cit.*, p. 173.

school and Mehmet II's castle: 'It [the school] stands on higher ground than those towers. It dominates them. Its forces are spiritual and eternal. It shall see them pass away.'[23]

The purpose of Robert College was to give 'a non-sectarian Christian education', similar to contemporary New England colleges, to young men of all creeds and nationalities. At the same time, this and other missionary schools hoped to provide a better spiritual hearth, especially for the Turkish non-believer. The accomplishments of such missionary enterprises in proselytizing the youth of the empire were not great; nor did they seem to be effective at this time in recruiting Ottoman Moslem children. Indeed, Abdül-Hamid forbade attendance of Turks in such institutions. Ramsay reports that by 1909, only two Mohammedan girls had graduated from the American College for Women, opened in 1871 at Scutari (Üsküdar) on the Anatolian side of the Bosphorus.[24] The missionary schools drew their students almost exclusively from the non-Moslem religious groups: Americans, Greeks, Armenians, Bulgarians, Jews, and so forth. When the Young Turks came to power, a special fund was set aside to educate five young Turkish men each year at Robert College and five young women at the American College for Women; but it was not until the period of the republic that schools like Robert College became favoured places for the non-Christian inhabitants of Turkey.

EDUCATION AND POLITICS: ABDÜL-HAMID AND THE YOUNG TURKS

The short-lived Midhat Constitution of 1876 was a momentous event in Ottoman history. Midhat Pasha and his liberal followers had become increasingly aware of the weaknesses of the Oriental dynastic and administrative features of the Ottoman system and, influenced by Western models, they wanted to establish a constitutional form of government which could curb the authority of the sultan and create a viable Ottoman cosmopolitan state. The first parliament ever assembled in the

---

[23] Cyrus Hamlin, *Among the Turks* (New York: Robert Carter and Brothers, 1878), p. 297.
[24] W. M. Ramsay, *The Revolution in Constantinople and Turkey* (London, 1909), p. 147.

Gate of Felicity represented a prima facie triumph of this idea: Jews, Christians, and Moslems from all parts of the empire and from all walks of life gathered in the august halls of the palace and there, before the divine ruler, proclaimed the rights of the Ottoman subjects to enjoy certain basic liberties and to participate in the affairs of the government.

There is little doubt that the proclamation of the first constitutional government in Turkey bore the imprint of Western influences, since the very idea of a constitutional monarch was alien to the Ottoman Islamic tradition. Many of the leaders and deputies were members of the civil bureaucracy who, in some form or another, were exposed to Western ideas and a Western type of education. Sava Pasha, the Director of the Imperial Lise at Galatasaray, Ziya Bey, the Undersecretary of Education, and Namik Kemal were among the members of the Constitution Drafting Commission. More important, perhaps, than the role which the Western-educated or Western-oriented efendi bureaucracy played, was the fact that such people were joined by many members of the ulema group and by others from several segments of the Ottoman Empire. For example, among the members of the Drafting Commission, there were ten who belonged to the religious hierarchy, and not less than six were Christians. Among the deputies there were merchants, Christians, and mosque teachers.[25]

Despite these auspicious beginnings, the first attempts at constitutional government in the Ottoman Empire were quite ephemeral. Paradoxically, some of the factors which brought it about contributed also to its failure. The liberal modernist tendencies which forced Abdül-Hamid to promulgate the constitution also created a strong anti-modernist reaction by the palace clique and by members of the 'Sublime Porte'. However, the collapse of the constitution was also due to the absence of a foundation solid enough to sustain such an experiment. In the first place, there was a lack of political consensus, not only among the various segments of the population, but also among the deputies themselves. In the second place, there was no public opinion which would act as a restraining force to Abdül-

[25] Robert Devereux, *The First Ottoman Constitutional Period: A Study of the Midhat Constitution and Parliament* (Baltimore: The Johns Hopkins Press, 1963), pp. 259–82.

Hamid's reactionary proclivities. Even in Istanbul, the main centre of political activity, there was no articulate group which could arouse public opinion. In the third place, Ottoman society continued to be rent by sharp cleavages between urban and rural, elite and masses, rulers and ruled. The overwhelmingly large peasant groups were politically, economically, and intellectually separated from Istanbul and the other urban centres; they were mostly, if not completely, illiterate; they engaged in subsistence-level economic activities; they were a non-participating mass; and they viewed themselves as subjects of the sultan rather than as citizens of a state.[26] Added to these was the fact that Abdül-Hamid was able to impose tight censorship and to organize a system of surveillance over the activities of all the people, which prevented the rapid dissemination of ideas and helped to hold insurrectionist plots at bay.

Abdül-Hamid succeeded in suspending the constitution, in dissolving the chamber, and in eliminating liberal or revolutionary leaders like Midhat Pasha and Ali Suavi. For the next thirty years he ruled like a despot from his favourite residence, surrounded by a coterie of sheikhs, mollas, dervishes, astrologers, Albanian militiamen, and a small group of trusted friends like Zarifi, the Greek banker, and Dr. Mavroyeni, his personal physician. Although he was able to maintain his hold on the House of Osman longer than many of his predecessors, he did not succeed in either checking the fast disintegration of the empire or in stamping out the nascent liberal modernist movements. The Midhat Constitution itself, though dead, remained a source of inspiration for those who aimed at the creation of a multiracial and multireligious polity based on constitutional principles; and educational institutions like the rüshdiyes, the lise at Galatasaray, and the Mülkiye, were beginning to produce a more liberal and Western-oriented group of modernizers. In addition, the military schools, which Abdül-Hamid himself encouraged more than any of the other educational establishments, turned out to be hotbeds of rebellion against their own patron. In the end, they provided the activist branch of the Young Turk Revolution of 1908, which deposed the sultan and restored the 1876 Constitution.

[26] *Ibid.*, pp. 251–6.

Of the many forces which contributed to the Revolution of 1908 and the beginning of the second meshrutiyet, a Western type of education and Western liberal ideas among the Ottoman intelligentsia have been assigned major roles by historians. Just how education actually performed such a function remains rather unclear. According to Edwin Pears, a contemporary, the revolution was a 'popular movement', in the sense that a revolutionary spirit had pervaded diverse elements in the society, ranging from the military to the mollas and the truculent softas.[27] The policies of Abdül-Hamid apparently aroused the antagonism not only of the intellectuals who inherited the liberal doctrines of the Tanzimat, or of those educated in the newly established secular and military schools, but also of people who continued to be educated in the traditional Islamic medreses, and of others who, for various reasons, wanted the authority of the sultan curtailed.

Since the beginnings of modernization, in the latter part of the eighteenth century, reform of the military wing of the government had been a major preoccupation of all ruling sultans. New military schools were established and new methods of instruction were introduced. Abdül-Hamid, despite his other reactionary policies, continued the policies of his predecessors; indeed, he accelerated the pace of reform by building and subsidizing new military academies[28] and other schools associated with the military forces. It was during his reign that German influence began to infiltrate into the Ottoman Empire. At the sultan's invitation, the famous German scholar-soldier General von der Goltz came to Constantinople to modernize the Ottoman army along European lines. In 1889, the German Emperor William II of Hohenzollern paid a visit to the Imperial City, soon to be followed by an array of generals, technicians, and commercial travellers.[29] Ironically, although Abdül-Hamid man-

[27] See Edwin Pears, *Forty Years in Constantinople* (New York: D. Appleton and Company, 1916), pp. 236 ff.

[28] In addition to military schools, several 'technical' schools were established, e.g., School for Vaccinators (1894), Civil Veterinary School (1889), School for Civil Engineering (1884), etc. See Ward and Rustow, *op. cit.*, p. 215.

[29] See Joan Haslip, *The Sultan: The Life of Abdülhamid* (London: Cassell and Co., Ltd., 1958), pp. 189 ff. See also Ernest Jackh, *The Rising Crescent: Turkey Yesterday, Today and Tomorrow* (New York: Farrar and Rinehart, 1944), pp. 91 ff.

aged to keep the empire relatively intact during his reign, his army also provided the Achilles' heel of his regime and ultimately played a major part in his deposition.

It was among the cadets of the Imperial Medical School, within the Old Seraglio, that the first revolutionary group, the Committee of Union and Progress, was formed in 1889. Patterned after the famed Italian Carbonari, this committee, which marked the beginning of the Young Turk movement, adopted as its expressed purpose the overthrow of Abdül-Hamid and his despotic government. The revolutionary spirit soon spread throughout the medical school and overflowed into other government military and naval schools and into the Mülkiye. The ranks of the original conspirators were quickly swollen by students from these groups and by dissatisfied liberals both at home and abroad.[30]

Many of the revolutionaries were exposed to Western ideas and to an education which drew a great deal from Western models; and interestingly they included members of several ethnic groups of the empire. For example, of the original nucleus of four at the medical school, Ibrahim Temo, the driving spirit behind the establishment of the society, was an Albanian who had travelled to Europe and Italy; Abdullah Jevdet was a Kurd and an erudite physician who translated French, Italian, German, Persian, and English works, including Shakespeare's works, into Turkish; Ishak Sükuti was another Kurd who was well acquainted with the works of Namik Kemal; and Mehmet Reshid was a Circassian.

The influence of the West was most apparent among the cadets of the various military schools. Among these original cadets, who soon became the officer class of the empire, revolutionary cells were formed for the purpose of overthrowing the government and restoring the Midhat Constitution. And in the end, the army units of Macedonia forced the sultan to restore the constitution by threatening to march into Istanbul.

The influence of Western ideas was not confined to the military schools; nor can the revolutionary reaction to Abdül-Hamid's autocracy be interpreted solely in terms of a military coup d'état. The Young Turk movement was a complex

[30] See E. E. Ramsaur, *The Young Turks: Prelude to the Revolution of 1908* (Princeton: Princeton University Press, 1957), pp. 14 ff.

phenomenon drawing from people of many beliefs, backgrounds, and walks of life.

Many of the other revolutionaries were people who had also come under the influence of Western liberal ideas and Western culture, either through their education at home, or through travel and education abroad. An outstanding example was Ahmet Riza Bey, the son of Ali Riza Bey, known as 'Ingiliz Ali' (the Englishman Ali) because of his strong affinities with the English. Ahmet Riza had gone to the lise at Galatasaray and had studied agriculture in France. He served as director of education at Bursa; but he abandoned his post and returned to Paris in 1889, after joining the revolutionaries. There he participated in the activities of the revolutionary exiles and fell under the influence of the positivist philosophy of Auguste Comte. Through the columns of his journal the *Meshveret* (Consultation), which was secretly smuggled into Constantinople, he conducted a campaign against the reigning Ottoman dynasty. (Much of the activity of the Young Turks was conducted by Ottoman exiles from Paris, Geneva, and Egypt, especially after the seeming collapse of the movement in 1897.)

Another outstanding example of the impact of Western ideas on the Young Turks was Prince Sabahettin, a member of the Imperial family, who, with his father, Damat Mahmut Jelaleddin Pasha and his brother Lütfullah, made a dramatic flight to France and joined the revolutionary exiles. Sabahettin received the type of private education befitting a royal prince, but in France he fell under the spell of Edmond Desmolins' *A quoi tient la Supériorité des Anglo-Saxons?* with its emphasis upon individualism and decentralization as the cornerstones of patriotism and constitutional government. According to Sabahettin, the development of such traits, which Desmolins felt were the hallmarks of Anglo-Saxon superiority over the French, rested on the system of national education. Hence, in his campaign for reform of the Ottoman outlook on life and the system of government, Sabahettin placed great emphasis upon reforming education, which he considered to be the greatest weakness of his country. He felt that through education, especially the social studies, it was possible to stir up private initiative and lead towards administrative decentralization. Accordingly, he urged the Ottoman youth who had been ex-

posed to Occidental civilization to steer away from the traditional paths in the civil service and the military and, instead,
to turn with ardour towards 'independent and productive
careers'.[31] In Sabahettin the role which Western education performed—or was perceived to perform—in the modernization
movement in the Ottoman Empire during this period is discerned: on one hand, it opened the doors for new political ideologies which challenged the traditional Ottoman ones; and on
the other, it was considered a condition necessary for the
emergence and consolidation of a modern polity.

The liberal modernist spirit seems also to have been felt in
the two famous Western-oriented schools for the training of
civil servants, namely, the Galatasaray lise and the Mülkiye.
Contemporary accounts by graduates of these and other schools
depict a ferment of discontent against the regime: how the
teachers and students read the proscribed writings of Young
Ottoman intellectuals like Namik Kemal, Shinasi, and Ziya
Pasha, and how they talked about freedom, patriotism, and so
on. Murad Bey, another key figure among the Young Turk intellectuals, was probably educated in St Petersburg and became a member of the revolutionary society while he was a
teacher of history at the Mülkiye.[32]

The amount of influence, however, which such schools had
upon the general movement towards modernity can only be
indirectly established. It is difficult to trace a causal connection
between a Western type of formal education and either the
modernization of political ideas or the actual revolutionary
spirit. Of course, institutions like the imperial lise and the
Mülkiye provided a modern type of education largely based on
Western European, especially French, models. Furthermore,
many of the Galatasaray graduates, and almost all those of the
Mülkiye, entered careers in the civil bureaucracy. It might be
reasonable, therefore, to infer that, having been exposed to a
type of education different from the traditional Islamic one and
to more liberal ideas, as civil servants they would react against
the autocratic and reactionary policies of Abdül-Hamid and
would desire changes along modern lines. However, to assess

[31] *Ibid.*, pp. 81–5.
[32] *Ibid.*, pp. 27–8. See also Bernard Lewis, *The Emergence of Modern Turkey*
(London: Oxford University Press, 1961), pp. 191–2.

more accurately the role, which these schools played, the exact careers of their graduates and the part which they played in the total process would have to be examined. A breakdown of a random sample of the graduates of the Galatasaray lise shows that until the opening decades of the twentieth century the majority of them (60–70 per cent) entered careers in the military, diplomatic, and civil bureaucracies. Of the whole sample, however, only a small number (about five) attained very high posts. The first Turkish graduate (1873) was Abdurrahman Sheref, who served as director of the school and then as Minister of Education. Four other graduates of Turkish origin were a Bulgarian Comisar, an ambassador to Madrid, a general, and an ambassador to Tehran; one Bulgarian graduate became *bash vekili* (prime minister) and another, Minister of War. After 1900, however, most of the graduates entered the free professions (lawyers, doctors, engineers, etc.), or took up appointments in banks and in business. A relatively small number entered the diplomatic, civil, or military bureaucracies.[33]

Some writers have ascribed a major role in the emergence of modern Turkey to the Galatasaray lise. For example, Bernard Lewis has asserted:

'The influence of the Galatasaray school on the rise of modern Turkey has been enormous. As the need for administrators, diplomats and others with a Western education and a capacity to handle Western administrative apparatus became more and more pressing, the graduates of Galatasaray came to play a preponderant role in the politics and administration of the Ottoman Empire, and after it, of the Turkish Republic. The Imperial Ottoman Lycée had no playing-fields, but not a few of the victories of modern Turkey were won in its classrooms.'[34]

However, in view of the absence of evidence as to the precise nature of this school's influence, Lewis' statement must be regarded as a hypothesis rather than as a conclusion. In addition to the type of information presented above, the extent to which

[33] These data were gathered from the records available in the school at Istanbul, *50a Yil Kitabi* (Istanbul: Matbeayi Amire, 1918); *Ders Yil, Mezunlari, 1918–1945*; and through a personal interview with the director and vice-director of the school.

[34] Lewis, *op. cit.*, p. 120.

Ottoman and Turkish leaders who played a part in the modernization movement attended the school at Galatasaray and whether their experiences there influenced their subsequent thoughts and actions, must be known. Since full information of this kind is lacking, any statements on this are perforce speculative and hypothetical.

Opposition to Abdül-Hamid and his repressive policies was not confined to the military officers and cadets or to Western-oriented intellectuals.[35] Eyewitnesses on that memorable day of July 28, 1908, when the famous *irade* (decree) proclaiming the constitution was published, observed that among the jubilant crowds assembled at Ayia Sophia and Galata Bridge, softas and mollas were seen wearing symbols of liberty.[36] Yet the actual role that such religious groups and the religious medreses which educated them played in the general Young Turk movement and the Revolution of 1908 must not be exaggerated. Whatever the reasons for their discontent, their political ideology and their general outlook on life were firmly entrenched in the conservatism and traditionalism of Ottoman Islam. Indeed, as Ramsaur has pointed out, it was the softas who formed the backbone of the abortive counter-revolution of 1909.[37]

In examining the role of education in the process of modernization during the Hamidian period and the ascendance of the Young Turks, the following observations could be made. The military schools provided a cadre of activist leaders and officers who, for various reasons, adopted the revolutionary policy of overthrowing the existing system of government. These military groups represented one section of the Ottoman elite who, because of their education and outlook and the policies of the government, became alienated from the sultan and his court. The sultan, in turn, restricted access into his own councils of state, adopted an extremely reactionary policy towards any liberalizing tendencies on the part of the military, and allowed for graft, corruption, bribery, and incompetence in the recruitment of members of the military and ruling elites and in the general affairs of the government. Thus the Ottoman Empire at this time represented a classic case of a state which prevented

[35] Pears, *op. cit.*, pp. 236–7.
[36] See Haslip, *op. cit.*, p. 263.
[37] Ramsaur, *op. cit.*, p. 21.

the assimilation of a new type of elite into the ruling branch of the government. The 'circulation of elites', to use Pareto's classic phrase, had ceased to vitalize the functioning of government, and the powerful military leaders who commanded the support of the rank and file among the soldiers had lost complete faith in the ability of the sultan to maintain a strong government and a unified state. The only possible alternative under the circumstances was a revolution rather than a peaceful modification of the existing system. By background, training, and political outlook, the military leaders of the movement typified a type of emergent force which was the logical outcome of the modernizing tendencies of the nineteenth century. The military leaders had traditionally been an important part of the ruling classes. Although there had been frictions with the other branches of the government in the past, a rapprochement or, in the hands of powerful sultans, a solution had always been found which preserved the existing institutional arrangement. But by the end of the nineteenth century this working relationship had ceased to operate, and a violent outburst ensued. The emergence of this powerful force inevitably created conflicts among the elites themselves, although the Young Turks were not bent on overthrowing the entire system of Ottoman government nor of its Islamic foundations. Yet a crack in the edifice had already been made—and under Mustafa Kemal it widened, causing irreparable damage to the entire structure of the Ottoman State.

These observations on the military elites also apply to the other liberal elements in the society and to the Ottoman intelligentsia. Schools like the Galatasaray lise and the Mülkiye represented different patterns of education from the traditional medreses. Although in the past this twofold institutional arrangement existed between the Palace School and the medrese, by the end of the nineteenth century the lines of separation between the two types of education were more sharply drawn. In the past, both the 'secular' and the 'religious' elements supported the existing governmental structure and indeed furnished the leadership for its sustenance. But the secularist or quasi-secularist character of the new schools and the types of leaders they trained contributed more to disenchantment with the 'purity' of traditional patterns and modes of thought. The reactionary regime of Abdül-Hamid did not provide avenues for the accommodation of these ideas or of the individuals espousing them. Some of the products of the Galatasaray took an active and leading part in the modernization movement. But it is suggested here that the role this institution played lay more in providing a fertile ground and a substratum of bureaucrats, administrators, professionals, and so on, who were ready to accept innovation and the modernization of the institutions of government. And this, it is speculated, was also the role of the Mülkiye during the pre-republican period of the modernization movement, especially during Abdül-Hamid's reign. This is based on the fact that the great body of the bureaucrats was not actively engaged in the reaction against Abdül-Hamid's policies; indeed, the valis, the kaymakams, and the memurs, that is, the group most heavily represented among the Mülkiye graduates, were used as agents to support such policies.

THE QUEST FOR AN IDEOLOGICAL IDENTITY:
ZIYA GOKALP AND TURKISH NATIONALISM

The Young Turk Revolution and the deposition of Abdül-Hamid in 1909 was a clear signal that the days of the old Ottoman political order were numbered. Henceforth, the destinies of the empire were placed in the hands of a new type of leadership, mostly men who were schooled in the military colleges, and equally important, men fired by a Moslem Turkish patriotism. Soon after the Young Turks assumed power, it was apparent that the hopes of previous Ottoman reformers, namely, the creation of a corporate body politic where people of diverse ethnic and religious backgrounds would enjoy equal rights and be assimilated into a great Ottoman state, was a dream entertained only by a few visionary utopians. The emergence of modern Turkey, according to one writer, had its genesis in the Young Turk pre-Kemalist period.[38] Yet, in spite of the obvious bad omens, the aim of the Young Turks was not to dissolve, but rather to reform the empire and its major institutions. In

[38] See Richard D. Robinson, *The First Turkish Republic: A Case Study in National Development* (Cambridge, Mass.: Harvard University Press, 1963), p. 5.

the words of Bernard Lewis, 'both their actions and their discussions revolved around this central problem—*Bu devlet nasil
kurtarilabilir?*—How can this state be saved?'[39] Thus the period
following the collapse of Hamidian absolutism can best be
viewed as a transitional stage in the reform movement which
culminated in the Kemalist Revolution and the proclamation
of the republic in 1923. As in most transitional phases of a
country's development, the Young Turk period was marked by
confusion, turbulence and groping. This was most saliently
manifested in the cultural and intellectual spheres in which,
according to one authority, the Young Turk years are 'most
interesting and most significant'.[40]

During the stage of fermentation in the two decades preceding
the overthrow of Abdül-Hamid's despotism, several currents of
thought characterized the Young Turk movement. Broadly
speaking, they were either modernist-positivistic or Islamic
conservative, the former represented by Ahmet Riza Bey and
the latter by Murad Mizanci.[41] It was not until after 1908–9,
when the lid was lifted, that an intellectual outburst took place;
various types of 'isms', some with roots in the past, others new,
acquired renewed vitality or new forms. In addition to Ottomanism, there were Pan-Islamism, Pan-Turanianism, Pan-Turkism,
and Turkish nationalism. Pan-Islamism or Islamism was the
ideological weapon of the more conservative groups who attributed the weaknesses of the Ottoman Empire to the abandon-
ment of orthodox Islamic principles and institutions. The
Islamists included fundamentalists who felt there was no room
for compromise in matters of faith and the Holy Law, and
moderates who aimed at some reform of Islam and an accommodation of modern civilization within an essentially Islamic
framework. The moderate Islamists envisaged a Pan-Islamic
unity and a regeneration from within rather than from ideas
introduced from the West. Pan-Turanianism and Pan-Turkism,
both expressions of an emerging nationalist ideology, envisaged
a cultural unity of all peoples (Moslem Turks as well as Christians) claiming descent from the land of Turan, or a cultural

[39] Lewis, *op. cit.*, p. 208.
[40] *Ibid.*, p. 225.
[41] Kemal H. Karpat, *Turkey's Politics: The Transition to a Multi-Party
System* (Princeton: Princeton University Press, 1959), pp. 18–19.

unification of all Moslem Turks inside and outside the empire. Ottomanism, as already described, meant the vitalization and 'democratization' of a multiracial and multireligious polity which could be coextensive with much of the existing empire. But Turkish nationalism would be confined to a more religiously, culturally, and ethnically homogeneous, and a more geographically limited, empire-state. These several ideological strands could also be distinguished by their conservative or modernist features, the latter in particular reflecting the influence of Western ideas and education. In spite of variations in emphasis, the Westernizers or modernizers did not formulate a nationalist ideology which would completely eliminate either the Islamic or the imperial features of the existing order. This was manifested even in the thought of Ziya Gökalp, perhaps the greatest nationalist intellectual spokesman of the period.

Gökalp occupies a pivotal position in the intellectual and educational modernization of Turkey, especially during this formative period of Turkey's national development. Atatürk claimed him as his intellectual 'father', and Turcologists refer to him as the first Turk who formulated a systematic theory of Turkish nationalism.[42] He was also the first Turk to articulate a systematic theory of education.

Ziya Gökalp's educational background included both traditional Islamic and Western, secular characteristics. After finishing a local mekteb in Diyarbakir, he attended a military rüshdiye and then an idadi where, in addition to the traditional type of Oriental education, he began to study French. He later followed up his modern education in the Veterinary College of Istanbul. At the same time, he avidly read the Islamic classics, the writings of the Young Ottomans, and those of Western thinkers, particularly the French sociologist Émile Durkheim. Gökalp was as much the product of an Islamic culture as he was an ardent student of French sociology. He seems to have

[42] The best study in English on Gökalp's work and his contribution to the emergence of Turkish nationalism is Uriel Heyd, *Foundations of Turkish Nationalism: The Life and Teachings of Ziya Gökalp* (London: Luzac & Company, Ltd., and the Harvill Press, Ltd., 1950). For a collection of selected writings and a good introduction by the editor, see Berkes. For other views on Gökalp, see Charles Warren Hostler, *Turkism and the Soviets: The Turks of the World and Their Political Objectives* (London: George Allen & Unwin, Ltd., 1957), pp. 101–8; and Karpat, *op. cit.*, pp. 25–7.

followed the advice of his father, Tevfik Efendi, concerning his own educational training and outlook. Gökalp's father criticized exclusive study of the 'European sciences' at the neglect of 'our own national feeling' on the one hand, and a pure medrese education on the other. The best education for the Turkish youth was 'a mastery of both Western (essentially French) and Eastern (especially Arabic, Persian, Islamic) learning'; and then, according to him, the youth 'must discover the great truths which our nation needs by comparing and combining Western and Eastern learning'.[43]

Gökalp's intellectual preoccupations spanned several fields: politics, poetry, sociology, history, and education. But, as with the Young Ottomans before him, his whole work could be viewed as essentially educational in scope and intent. Gökalp sought to clarify the various conflicting currents of thought which befuddled contemporary Turks and to reconcile what he felt were several dichotomies and contradictions in the society of the time. His mission was to educate his compatriots in a type of nationalism which was grounded in an indigenous culture but which also drew from Western civilization. Gökalp attributed the existing intellectual confusion and the conflicting values to education, to which he also assigned a major role in the creation of a national cultural synthesis. In the following excerpt from one of his writings, Gökalp not only made an astute sociological observation about the contemporary Ottoman society, but he also raised a fundamental educational question:

'In this country there are three layers of people differing from each other by civilization and education: the common people, the men educated in *medreses*, the men educated in (modern) secular schools. The first still are not freed from the effects of Far Eastern civilization; the second are still living in Eastern civilization; it is only the third group which has had some benefits from Western civilization. That means that one portion of our nation is living in an ancient, another in a medieval, and a third in a modern age. How can the life of a nation be normal with such a threefold life? How can we be a real nation without unifying this threefold education?'

[43] Berkes, *op. cit.*, p. 36.

On the basis of his historical and sociological conclusions and observations he felt that the salvation of the 'sick man' lay in the pursuit of the following social policy: 'to be of the Turkish nation, of the Islamic religion, and of European civilization.'[44] Within such an ideological framework Gökalp sought political and educational modernization of the Ottoman State.

At first Gökalp espoused Ottomanism, but later he abandoned it as a political ideal, developing his political theory instead around *Türchülük* (the concept of Turkism). The new life of the nation, according to him, must be drawn from a rediscovery of the indigenous Turkish culture: its traditions, values, and spirit. A true nation will be built if it becomes conscious of its own culture, which he defined as 'the integrated system of religious, moral, legal, intellectual, aesthetic, linguistic, economic, and technological spheres of life'.[45] Thus defined, culture differs from civilization, which is international rather than national, a rational product created consciously by man and shared by several nations. The distinction between civilization and culture provided Gökalp with a valuable rationale to judge what should be borrowed from the West and what the education of the modern Turks should include. Thus he would have introduced Western civilization into Turkey, that is, science and technology as well as scientific methods and the scientific spirit; but spiritual and moral values should be derived from the national and religious heritage. The complete education of the Turks, according to Gökalp, should be based on three principles: Turkism, Islamism, and Modernism. Hence, it should include (a) Turkish language, literature, and history, (b) *tejvid* (reading the Koran with the proper rhythm and pronunciation), catechism, the history of Islam and Islamic languages (Arabic and Persian), and (c) mathematics, natural sciences and European languages, as well as handicrafts and gymnastics. His approach to religion, however, was novel. Although 'Islamization' was an integral part of his theoretical and educational orientation, he advocated a more rational approach to the Islamic religion and called for its reform. His aim was the separation of church and state, and of religion and Oriental civilization, thus making it possible to maintain 'the fundamental values of Islam side by

[44] *Ibid.*, pp. 278–9.
[45] *Ibid.*, p. 245.

side with European civilization and Turkish national culture'.[46]

In establishing a nationalist self-consciousness, Gökalp placed major emphasis upon education and assigned a pre-eminent role to an educated elite. He was critical of both the traditional Islamic education and the Ottoman elites; the latter, according to him, constituted a separate class by themselves, totally different in culture, training, and outlook from the Turkish mass. The lines of cleavage were very sharply drawn and the two classes—the Ottoman cosmopolitan and the Turkish peasant 'red-heads'—actually hated each other. Clearly this state of affairs was detrimental to the development of a social and political solidarity and the emergence of a nation, for the Ottoman elites ignored a most fundamental principle: that the source of a national identity is the ideals and values of the 'common people'. Yet popular culture is only the raw material and the source of a bond between the rulers and the ruled. A nation must possess an enlightened class which will guide the destinies of all the people, articulate their ideas, values, and aspirations, and introduce the fruits of modern civilization to them. Thus, although Gökalp envisaged a type of national democracy, he would place the responsibility of government not in the masses, but in a national educated elite. A 'leader' in Gökalp's theory was a pre-eminent figure in whom, as Heyd put it, 'the consciousness of society crystallizes', and who, in times of crises, might even be justified in assuming absolute power.[47]

From these sociological concepts and observations, Gökalp drew several conclusions concerning education. In the first place, 'since education inculcates culture and culture is national, education must be national'; in the second place, the basic education of the Turkish child must be 'according to Turkish culture'; in the third place, a major aim of Turkish education must be to develop 'idealists' who will also be 'national types'; and lastly, special attention must be paid to the education of 'unselfish, patriotic, self-sacrificing men', the guiding elite of the nation. The education of the elite was of particular signi-

---

[46] For a fuller analysis of Gökalp's approach to Islam, see Heyd, *op. cit.*, pp. 82 ff. For his views on the aims and content of education, see Berkes, *op. cit.*, pp. 233–5.

[47] Heyd, *op. cit.*, pp. 69–70; Hostler, *op. cit.*, p. 107; Berkes, *op. cit.*, pp. 107–8.

cance to Gökalp, as indeed it was to other modernizers of the period, especially Emrullah Efendi, a Minister of Education. This view was often justified on what was known as the *tuba agaji nazariyesi* (the theory of the tree of Heaven). In Turkish folklore the tuba agaji was a tree which had its roots in heaven and cast its delightful shade and fruit on the earth. It was therefore felt that if in educational reform top priority were given to the schools which trained the elites (lises and higher institutions), society would be established on a firmer footing.[48]

Gökalp's activities were not limited to writing and teaching. In Diyarbakir, Constantinople, and Salonica he took an active part in revolutionary activities: he was a key member and the intellectual spokesman of the famous Committee of Union and Progress; and he was actively engaged in the *Ojagi* (Turkish Hearth) movement whose task was to work 'for the national education of the Turkish people' and to contribute to 'the uplift of the Turkish race'.[49] After the defeat of the Ottoman Empire and the Allied occupation of Istanbul, Gölkap was arrested and exiled, together with other revolutionaries, to Malta. But he resumed his involvement in the nationalist movement when Kemal Atatürk assumed power, and in 1923 he represented Diyarbakir in the new assembly. In addition, he was elected to the new Parliamentary Education Committee which formulated proposals for the reform of the school curriculum.

Gökalp died in 1924, but his ideas provided the bedrock upon which Atatürk and the new Turks constructed the revolutionary ideology.[50] His theories continued to underlie educational developments during the republican period.

---

[48] On Gökalp's statements on education, see Berkes, pp. 236–43. On the tuba agaji nazariyesi, see Ergin, *op. cit.*, III, 1056–7.

[49] On the educational and political significance of this movement, see Ahmed Emin, *Turkey in the World War* (New Haven: Yale University Press, 1930), pp. 192–3.

[50] Heyd, *op. cit.*, p. 170.

PART TWO

FROM MEKTEB TO OKUL: TOWARDS A NATIONAL SYSTEM OF EDUCATION

CHAPTER V

THE STRUCTURE
OF THE EDUCATIONAL SYSTEM
UNDER THE REPUBLIC

IN embarking upon the task of building a new nation, Atatürk
and his associates conceived of education as the most important
foundation. In the emerging ideology of Atatürkism, education
was inextricably bound up with political, economic, and cultural independence and with breaking the shackles of traditional
beliefs and outlooks; it was the means of nourishing national,
aspirations, creating the consensus necessary to sustain a free,
national state, training new Turkish leaders, and paving the
way towards a dynamic and modern society. Knowledge and
science were regarded as power and as the leverage in transforming and uplifting the entire society. Atatürk made several
statements on the important role assigned to education. In
1921, he said that 'our national system of education should be
something different from the old and something that grows out
of our own nation . . . and national genius can only be developed
through our national culture'; on another occasion, that 'education makes a nation either free, famous and enlightened, or
poor and under the domination of others';[1] and, of course, there
is his famous 'Message to the Youth' with which he ended his
marathon six-day speech delivered before the national assembly
in 1927. In this message, which has become a veritable creed
and is today framed in almost every school in Turkey, Atatürk
placed the future of the republic squarely in the hands of the

---

[1] Enver Ziya Karal, *Atatürk'ten Düshünjeler* (Ankara: Dogus, Ltd., shti.
Matbaasi, n.d.), p. 77.

schools and the younger generation, whom he exhorted 'ever to preserve and defend the National Independence of the Turkish Republic'.[2]

The nation builders were confronted with an immense under-undertaking. The comprehensive Education Act of 1913 was little more than a dead letter; educational provision was negligible; the medreses were in a pitiful state; and the illiteracy rate exceeded 90 per cent. In order to pave the way for a new state and a new society, it was necessary to transform the entire system and the entire value orientation of the people, to provide a more effective administrative machinery, to organize a graded system of schools and teacher training institutions, to change the curriculum, to vest educational authority, supervision and control in the hands of the state, and generally to provide more and better educational opportunities for the people. The whole problem of creating a unified national system of education, one of the three main points emphasized by Atatürk in his speech at the opening session of the Grand National Assembly in 1924, was also bound up with questions affecting the place of the religious schools and the role of the 'church' vis-à-vis the state in the education of the people. The rest of this study will be devoted to the educational reforms and policies under the republic and to the progress made to date. In line with this approach, education will also be examined within the context of the broader Turkish society and culture.

ADMINISTRATION AND CONTROL OF EDUCATION

When the republic was proclaimed, the legal and administrative structure of the educational system was as follows: excluding the medreses, the organization, the types of schools, and the programme of instruction were governed by the Provisory Primary Education Law of 1913, which was discussed in Chapter IV. Authority in 'public' education was vested in the Minister of Public Education, who performed his functions through three educational divisions or departments (Divisions of Primary, Secondary, and Higher Education). In addition, there was a Higher Educational Council consisting of two sub-

[2] *A Speech Delivered by Ghazi Mustafa Kemal, President of the Turkish Republic* (Leipzig: K. F. Koehler, 1929), p. 724.

divisions: the Permanent and the Annual. The council, which included high officials in the ministry, directors of certain schools in the capital, and selected teachers and administrators, advised the minister on such questions of educational policy as the selection of the textbooks, the curriculum, and so on. The minister prescribed courses of study, school regulations, certification, salaries, and promotions of teachers; he appointed inspectors and local 'school superintendents'; and he was responsible for secondary and higher education. Financing and administration of primary schools were largely in the hands of local school boards (provincial and divisional). A Secondary School Commission in each province, comprising local school officials, advised the minister on measures and regulations affecting the administration of the local schools.[3]

Thus by the time of the revolution, a 'modern' administrative framework indeed existed. But the 1913 Law was not strictly enforced; and, because of the war years—especially the period of the revolution (1919–23)—the educational picture was rather chaotic. Schools overlapped in their functions, there was no administrative co-ordination, and generally there were two systems of administration and of schools (state and religious), not to mention the commercial, military, and technical schools run by the several other ministries.

No sooner had the republic been proclaimed than steps were taken to centralize the system further, to reassert and implement certain of the provisions of previous enactments, to abolish the dual control and organization of schools, and to pave the way for a uniform graded system of public education. The first Constitution of the Turkish Republic placed all education under the supervision and control of the state, and it reaffirmed the previous principle that 'primary education is obligatory for all Turks and shall be gratuitous in the government schools'.[4] On March 3, 1924, the *Official Gazette* published the *Tevhidi Tedrisat*

---

[3] See Hasan Ali Yujel, *Türkiyede Orta Ogretim* (*Secondary Education in Turkey* [Istanbul: Devlet Basimevi, 1938]), pp. 34–7. See also Richard E. Maynard, 'The Lise and Its Curriculum in the Turkish Educational System' (Ph.D. dissertation, The University of Chicago, 1961), pp. 86–8.

[4] Articles 80 and 87. For the full text of this constitution, see Donald E. Webster, *The Turkey of Atatürk: Social Process in the Turkish Reformation* (Philadelphia: The American Academy of Political and Social Science, 1939), Appendix D, pp. 298–306.

Kanunu (Law of Unification of Instruction), which provided that 'all educational institutions are to be placed under the control of the Ministry of Education'. This included control of all religious schools as well as funds used by the Evkaf for educational purposes. Another law (Law No. 637), published on the twenty-second of April of the same year, again placed military schools under the Ministry of Defence. Subsequent laws allowed for the opening of special schools by other ministries (technical schools by the Ministry of Public Works, etc.), but in such cases the respective ministries were responsible jointly with the Ministry of Education for preparing the courses of study. Even private schools came under the purview of the central educational ministry; the central authority had to grant permission for their opening, approve their courses of study and regulations governing their operation, and inspect them.[5] Other enactments, beginning in April, 1926 (Law No. 789), defined the structure and functions of the central and local authorities and laid out certain provisions concerning the relations between the several units of the administrative arrangements.

As it developed under the republic, administration and control of Turkish education has been centred in the National Ministry of Education. The minister makes all final decisions affecting the administration of all the schools in the country; he must sign all orders, even those pertaining to relatively minor matters (e.g., use of textbooks in the schools). In the performance of his functions, the minister is advised by three bodies: the Educational Council, the Committee on Instruction and Education, and the Commission of General Directors. The Educational Council (in shortened form, called *Shura*) is made up of high officials in the ministry, rectors of the universities, deans of the faculties, a number of school principals, inspectors, teachers, and other specialists nominated by the minister. It discusses and advises on all matters of educational policy, especially on curriculum questions and school regulations. The total number of Shura members varies, but in general it exceeds three hundred; it is supposed to meet at least once every three years. The Committee on Instruction and Education, consisting of six members, prepares courses of study for all schools for submission to the Shura, examines textbooks, and passes judg-

[5] For the text of these laws, sec Yüjel, *op. cit.*, pp. 277–8.

ment on proposed legislation. In general, its duties are to examine and report to the minister any measure for the improvement of the educational system. The Commission of the General Directors, which comprises the various department heads in the ministry, considers matters relating to the administration of schools, and is especially responsible for the appointment and transfer of teachers and administrators in the post-elementary schools.

The general directors and the office of the *müsteshar* (undersecretary) conduct most of the administrative affairs of the ministry. The two permanent müsteshars theoretically are not political appointees but career educators. One of the müsteshars is responsible for all types of technical and vocational schools, including technical or commercial teacher training institutions; the other, called the regular müsteshar, for all other types of education and affairs of the ministry. Under the regular müsteshar there are at least nine other directorates: the General Directorates of Primary Education, Secondary Education, Higher Education, Teacher Education, Private Education, Fine Arts, and Physical Education, and the Directorates of Libraries, Museums and Antiquities. The General Director of Primary Education generally controls primary schools through provincial inspectors, and he is responsible for the curriculum, the assignment of teachers to provinces, and to some extent, the supervision of provincial budgets. Likewise, the General Director of Secondary Education is in charge of the *ortaokullar* (middle schools), lises, six recently established *kolej* (colleges), and the schools for the training of religious leaders. In contrast to the primary education department, the secondary department exercises direct control over the administration and the educational activities of each individual school. The Director of Private Schools supervises the programme of studies and the physical provisions of all private schools including the minority and the foreign-operated institutions. In the secondary private schools, this department exercises its functions through the local superintendent of education rather than directly, as is the case with the department of secondary education. Although the undersecretaries and the general directors carry out almost all the administrative functions of the ministry, the minister's approval in all cases is mandatory.

Since 1926, there have been several changes in administration at the provincial and local levels. The country was originally divided into twelve districts with one or more provinces in each. In each of the districts there was a *maarif emini* ('superintendent' of education) who was authorized to appoint, remove, and discipline the personnel of the primary schools, and who was responsible for the financing of these institutions. He also exercised the same authority over the personnel of the secondary schools directed by the ministry, and, in conjunction with the local boards, had some control over secondary schools. In 1931, the provinces became the unit of educational government below the ministry, and secondary schools came directly under the central authority, which also assumed responsibility for the appointment and dismissal of primary school teachers.

The present system of local administration dates from 1949. At this local level, the vali of each of the sixty-seven provinces, who is appointed by the central government, acts as the representative of the Minister of Education. Theoretically, therefore, each governor is responsible for all education in his povince. The governor is assisted and advised by a council consisting of a *maarif müdürü* (director of education), who is appointed by the minister and is responsible to the governor, and by the heads of various local political units. This provincial administrative body is in charge of primary education, but it operates within a framework of regulations set up by the central ministry. It appoints, assigns, disciplines, and removes teachers; it appropriates monies for the construction and operation of schools; and, through a corps of school inspectors, it sees that the directives and regulations of the ministry are carried out.

Each province is further divided into *kazas* (sub-provinces) governed by a kaymakam, who is also a civil servant. In each sub-province there is a *maarif memuru* (education officer), appointed by the ministry and responsible to the kaymakam of each subprovince, as well as to the provincial director of education for the administration of primary education.

Although the administrative arrangements outlined above bear the semblance of a balance between central and local control of education, the Turkish system of education is a clear example of a highly centralized pattern where policy making and school administration are conducted and regulated at the ministerial level. This is even more apparent in secondary education. The ministry at Ankara appoints teachers and principals; it appropriates money, which is earmarked in the national budget, for buildings, repairs, and equipment; and it has its own inspectors, although the provincial governor also has the right to inspect secondary schools and to report any observed irregularities. The tight bureaucratic control over schools is typified further in the duties and powers of the local *müdür* (school director or principal). The responsibilities of the müdür encompass administration of the affairs of the school and supervision of classroom instruction, but these duties are minutely prescribed by regulations issued by the central office. The director is authorized to inspect classes and the work of the teachers; he is expected to see that each teacher provides monthly course outlines; he has the power to report to the ministry if the outline is not followed; he checks on homework assignments; he administers the finances of the school; he must hold meetings with teachers to discuss matters of school policy; and at the end of the year he must evaluate teacher performance for purposes of promotion or transfer.

Principals of foreign schools who have worked in Turkey for a number of years find government control and regulation of schools rather stifling. One such person wrote: 'It is difficult to imagine a system in which less opportunity is given for individual schools and teachers to exercise initiative, and in which all changes and adjustments must come from a place as remote from the real school situation.'[6]

ORGANIZATION AND TYPES OF SCHOOLS

As stated earlier, a graded system of schools had emerged prior to the Kemalist Revolution; but it was not until the period of the republic that a concerted effort was made to establish a public national system of schools with clearly defined functions. The framework of a uniform state system of education was charted in 1924.[7] The primary school course (which according to the Law of 1913 extended over six years) was re-

[6] Maynard, *op. cit.*, p. 103.
[7] For the text of the laws reorganizing the system of general education, see Yüjel, *op. cit.*, pp. 278 ff, and pp. 25 ff.

duced to five, and the secondary course, from seven to six years. At this latter level, the previous sultanis were all named lises and they were divided into two separate three-year cycles. Subsequently, the first or middle cycle was called *ortaokul* (middle school) and the second, lise. In 1949, after a bitter debate, the lise course was lengthened by one year, but in 1954 it again reverted to four. This pattern (5–3–3) characterizes the Turkish state system of general education today, and it is the main gateway to the universities.

Technical and Vocational Schools

In addition to the schools of general education, attempts have been made since 1923 to establish a network of vocational and technical schools, teacher-training institutions, and other special or professional schools. Although there were several vocational schools in Istanbul at the time of the proclamation of the republic, they soon became insufficient for the policy of development and modernization. Foreign advisers (including John Dewey) were invited to Turkey to investigate existing educational deficiencies and to recommend a programme of reorganization. In 1927, the General Directorate of Higher Education was reorganized and its name changed to the General Directorate of Higher and Vocational Education. All but few of the commercial and vocational schools were placed under the control of this department, a branch of the central Ministry of Education. They continued, however, to be supported by local agencies. In 1933, a new department, the Department of Vocational and Technical Education was created, and in 1935, the central ministry assumed financial responsibility for all vocational and technical schools.[8]

Today there are several types of technical and/or vocational schools which constitute different systems of post-primary education. There are trade schools for boys, trade schools for girls, commercial schools, agricultural and nursing schools, boys' institutes, girls' institutes, and so forth. Perhaps the technical-vocational aspect of Turkish education is better described as several interlocking educational paths or tracks. Vocational or professional education begins after the five-year primary stage,

[8] *Technical Education for Men in Turkey* (Ankara: Milli Egitim Basimevi, 1951), pp. 4–5.

and it consists of three cycles, each of which is also terminal. The middle cycle, which is parallel to the orta school cycle, consists mainly of various kinds of three-year trade schools (building, tailors, chemical, trade, and the like). The middle-level trade schools provide a terminal education and prepare for the second cycle, comprising higher schools of the same type (lise-level schools) which are of one-, two-, or three-year duration. At the apex of the technical-vocational ladder are the institutions of higher learning, such as technical colleges, technicians' schools, secretariat schools, and the School for Applied Arts. A boy finishing the Building Trades Middle School, a three-year school, may enter a two-year Building Trades Institute and then a two-year higher technical school. Likewise, a girl finishing a three-year Middle Trade School may enter a two-year Girls' Trade Institute and then a two-year Secretariat School. Boys or girls may enter the various lise-level institutes after graduation from the orta schools, and the higher technical schools after graduation from the lises.

Other educational tracks include the *imam-hatib* (religious schools), teacher training institutions, and commercial schools. The schools for imams comprise middle-level (three years) and lise-level (three years) schools, and a four-year Higher Islamic Institute. Likewise, the commercial track consists of three-year middle schools, three-year commercial lises, and four-year colleges of commerce and economics.

Teacher-Training Institutions

Finally, there are various levels of teacher education corresponding to the various levels and types of schools: elementary teacher-training schools, or normal schools, which offer a six-year course after the primary stage; pedagogical institutes, two-year teacher-training institutions for orta school teachers, which accept graduates of normal schools or lises after an entrance examination; the four-year higher technical teacher-training colleges; a three-year Commercial Teacher Training College which accepts graduates of the commercial or the general lises; and two four-year higher teachers schools which are connected with the universities and prepare lise teachers. However, the greatest source of supply of lise teachers are the universities themselves. Theoretically, all lise teachers must be university graduates who have also taken a number of courses in education and psychology. But, in practice, there are teachers who are certified to teach in the lises without any professional work in education and who are graduates of such pedagogical institutes as the *Gazi Egitim Enstitüsü* (Gazi Pedagogical Institute of Ankara).

Owing to the tremendous shortage of teachers, especially at the village primary school level, several other programmes outside the general system have been designed. The first experiment started in 1937. Village men in particular, who were literate (i.e., who could read and write) and knew something about farming, were assigned, after a one-year course in a special institute operated by the Ministries of Education and Agriculture, as *egitmen* (trainers) to one-room village schools with a maximum of three grades. After successful completion of the course these 'trainers' were appointed 'to teach in a village and to act as advisers to the villagers in the use of scientific methods in agriculture'. The work of these individuals was supervised by a travelling master teacher who was responsible for a group of villages. The peak of egitmen teachers was reached in 1950–51, when 6,654 primary school teachers came from this group. Subsequently, the experiment declined, and, although there were still about two thousand such teachers in service in 1960, no more are being trained.[9]

A more colourful project, acclaimed by several writers as a most significant experiment in modern Turkish education and in Turkey's programme for planned change, was the controversial *köy enstitüsü* (village institute), established in 1940. The motivating consideration in embarking upon this innovation was to meet the village teacher shortage by recruiting village youth and then assigning them to village schools. The prospective teachers, technical leaders, or 'advisers', were to be trained in village institutes set up in selected villages for a period of five years following graduation from village primary schools. In turn, they were obligated to work for twenty years in places to which they would be appointed by the Ministry of Education. If they did not meet this obligation, they would pay twice the amount spent on their education to the government.

Actually, the purpose of the village institutes was more than

[9] Maynard, *op. cit.*, pp. 110–11.

the training of village teachers; it was also raising the general level of village communities and fostering economic development in the country. The teachers were expected:

'To do all kinds of teaching in their villages. In order to insure that farming in their villages is done in a scientific manner, they are to bring into existence in their villages model fields, vineyards, gardens, and workshops to serve as models and guides for the villagers. They are also to see that the villagers make use of (or derive benefit from) these facilities.'[10]

The social role of these institutions will be discussed later in this study. Suffice it to add here that for several reasons, mostly political, they were closed in the early fifties and were converted into regular teacher-training colleges—but not until they had trained several thousand (by 1950 their enrolments reached fourteen thousand) village youth who would not have had the chance for a more advanced type of education.

Another, more recent, experiment in meeting the acute village teacher shortage is the *yedek subay* (reserve officer) teacher project initiated in 1960 by the Revolutionary Committee of National Union. Prior to this year, graduates of the lises entered the officer corps during their years of military service. After the 1960 Revolution, only graduates of the universities and other institutions of higher learning were given this privilege. According to the yedek subay project, graduates of lises, lise-level institutions, normal schools, and university students who had failed in their courses and could not continue their education, could opt to become village teachers in lieu of their military service, except for the summer months when they would still be subjected to military training. Those who were graduates of normal schools could start teaching in places assigned by the Ministry of Education, but the others were so assigned after attending a short teacher-training course in designated places in the provinces. Upon completion of their teaching duties, which lasted for the same period as normal military service, such individuals were to be honourably discharged with the rank of officer (lieutenant). According to the figures available for 1962, there were 22,452 yedek subay teachers, of whom 12,575 were graduates of the normal schools,

---

[10] Quoted in *ibid.*, p. 112.

and 9,877 of lises or equivalent institutions. The effectiveness of this project is at present being investigated by the Research and Measurement Bureau of the Ministry of Education. A survey of the opinions of directors of education and elementary school inspectors revealed some dissatisfaction, especially with respect to the nature of the pre-service course.[11]

In the state system of post-elementary schools, no institutions occupy a more crucial position than the orta schools and the lises: they enrol the largest number of students; they are the main gateways to institutions of higher learning and leadership positions in the society; they are the schools most preferred by parents and children; and, in large part, they epitomize the Turkish view of what the nature and content of education should be. Therefore, a more detailed examination of some of their main characteristics is necessary for a better understanding of Turkish education and for the analysis of its relation to society in subsequent chapters.

The Ortaokul

Prior to 1930, the orta school was a mere adjunct to the lise, which was mainly a college-preparatory institution, although after 1924, it was also considered a complete unit in itself. In 1930, the ortaokul established itself both as a terminal institution with specific functions of its own, and as a feeder school for academic and higher technical schools. Its educational functions were: (a) to give a general education beyond the primary school with a modicum of practical knowledge; (b) to prepare for academic and other types of lise; and (c) to prepare for higher trade and professional schools. Up to 1934–36, the overwhelming majority (over 90 per cent) of the graduates of this school continued their education, and about 70 per cent of them did so in lises. Since then, attempts have been made to make the orta school less of a lise-preparatory institution and more of a terminal school organically related to elementary education—one which would channel more students into non-academic secondary schools. Thus it was recommended that more practical courses, such as typing, be introduced so that

[11] For an analysis of this survey and of the nature of the project, see Semahat Sozalan ve Ibrahim Ozgentash, *Yedek Subay Adayi Ogretmenler Hakkinda* (Ankara: M. Eg. B. Arashtirmalari ve Degerlendirme Merkezi, 1962).

students would be better equipped to enter lower positions in government and in other offices, and in 1941 many vocational schools opened special classes for orta graduates who could be admitted without examinations. Attempts to introduce practical elements into the orta curriculum were not very successful, nor was the policy of the government to divert the majority of the orta graduates from entering lises. In 1945, the Minister of Education stated that it was the government's intention that 90 per cent of the elementary and orta school graduates should go to technical and vocational schools; and in 1948, he asserted that the orta school should really be a terminal, quasi-practical institution to meet the needs of the local communities. 'The orta school,' according to him, 'used to be a city school and the threshold of the lise—now it is a small town school . . . The son of the cloth-seller, who had a primary education, will be a cloth-seller, but with an orta education.'[12]

After a relative decline between 1939 and 1950, however, the number of orta graduates entering the lises steadily increased. In 1951–52, about 45 per cent of orta graduates continued their education in the lises, but this percentage rose to 75 in 1957–58. Recently, the number of orta students entering the lises has levelled off. On the basis of the latest figures available, an estimated 40 per cent of such students enter the lises. Chapter VII contains more about the growth in the number of orta schools and in enrolments. Students and parents, however, continue to prefer a lise type to any other type of education after the middle school. In a recent survey conducted by the present writer in 1962–63, over 85 per cent of the students in the four major types of the present lise (the public, the private Turkish, the minority, and the foreign) indicated that they would rather go to a lise than to a technical or vocational school, for three major reasons: (a) they wanted to continue their education in a university; (b) they felt they could get a broader general education; and (c) they wanted to get a better job (see Table XVI in Appendix B). On another question, which read: 'Suppose a friend of yours finished an ortaokul with just a passing mark. Do you think he should go to a lise like your own, to a commercial lise or to a vocational school?' Fifty-two per cent answered that he should go to a vocational school,

[12] Quoted in Maynard, *op. cit.*, p. 120.

9 per cent, to a commercial lise, and 31 per cent, to 'a lise like my own'. To most students a vocational or a commercial type of educational training apparently is more appropriate for the less competent orta graduate, and by implication, that if he could make it, an orta graduate would prefer a lise to any other type of secondary school.

The educational functions of the orta school have been a constant theme discussed by the Shura, by the government, and by many Turkish educators. The most recent activity in this connection was manifest at the meeting of the Seventh National Educational Council in February 1962. The Shura accepted the recommendations of the Second Committee (General and Technical Education) that the main educational functions of the orta school should be: (a) general education for graduates of the elementary schools according to their 'age-level and readiness'; (b) 'assessment and improvement of interests, aptitudes, and abilities of the students with due recognition to the economic characteristics of the environment'; and (c) preparation for further education. The Shura also endorsed the suggestion that the subjects of the orta curriculum should be divided into required general subjects and electives— the latter in accordance with the needs and interests of the students—and that the same principles be applied to all middle-level institutions.[13] These statements were in part based upon the findings and suggestions of a survey conducted by the Research and Measurement Bureau of the National Ministry of Education.[14] Interestingly, those who conducted the survey were Turkish educators trained in American universities. Some other members of the Shura itself have had training in American colleges and universities. It may not be a coincidence, therefore, that the ideas and principles in the Shura statements echo American pedagogical language.

The influence of American ideas and practices is further apparent in the movement for the establishment of 'compre-

[13] *Yedinji Milli Egitim Shurasi, 5–15 Shubat, 1962: Chalishma Esaslari Konunlar ve Kararlar* (T. C. Milli Egitim Bakanligi [1962]), pp. 123, 179.

[14] *Responses to the Questionnaire of the National Education Shura, 1962: Questionnaire on Proposals Submitted to the 7th Educational Shura* (Ministry of Education, Board of Education, Educational Research and Evaluation Center [Ankara: Research and Measurement Bureau, 1962]).

hensive' orta schools.[15] This movement started in 1953-4, when three *muhtelif gayeli orta okul* (multipurpose orta schools) were established on an experimental basis in the cities of Mustafa Kemal Pasha (Bursa), Nevshehir, and Mush. Originators of these schools clearly had in mind American high schools, as well as some experiments with the 'multilateral' idea in England, Belgium, and Sweden. In the first year of the 'multipurpose' orta school, all students followed the same curriculum, which included general subjects (Turkish, history, geography, civics, mathematics, hygiene, foreign languages, etc.) plus commerce, agriculture, home economics for girls, and manual trades for boys. In the second and third years there were three streams: the general, the boys' technical or trade, and the girls' home economics. Students in all the three branches took the same number of weekly hours in Turkish, mathematics, and foreign languages. There were variations in weekly hours spent on the other subjects, depending on the stream, but in general, the preparation was such that a student who went through any stream could enter either a lise or a higher vocational school. The rationale for the establishment of these schools was that such a 'comprehensive' arrangement would allow students to follow an educational path more in line with their interests and abilities, and that it would also break the monolithic orta-lise sequence. It was also felt that the vocational-academic dichotomy of education would be bridged.[16] Actually, in the opinion of some observers these experimental schools were 'comprehensive' only in name. What they did was merely juxtapose the existing types of schools under one roof.[17]

The 'comprehensive' school idea lingered on, in spite of the fact that the number of schools established has remained con-

---

[15] For a good analysis of the comprehensive school idea in Turkey, which also illustrates the American influence, see Selâhattin Ertürk, *Chok-Gayeli Okullar Meselesi* (*The Question of Multi-Purpose Schools* [Ankara: Egitim Arashtirmalari ve Degerlendirme Merkezi, 1962]). Dr Ertürk informed the writer that this pamphlet was distributed to all the members of the 7th Educational Shura prior to its convening.

[16] For more details on these early experiments, see Reshat Ozalp, *Türkiye'de Mesleki ve Teknik Ogretim* (Orta Derejeli Okullar [Ankara: Maarif Basimevi, 1956]), I, 119-21.

[17] This statement is based on conversations with some of the recent advocates of the comprehensive schools.

siderably small (today there are only five such schools in the country), and that a clear idea of what 'comprehensiveness' means has not crystallized. The common middle-level school arrangement was considered unsatisfactory by some leading educators and by many members of the Shura. Before the meeting of the Seventh Shura the previously mentioned questionnaire was sent to all the Shura members, and one of the items pertained to this arrangement. Briefly, the item stated that, according to the present system, elementary school graduates who enter the various types of middle-level schools are not selected on the basis of aptitude or ability, and once they do enter such schools, they have no choice but to follow the prescribed course; again they do not receive an education according to their interests and abilities. One of the main points was that the age of eleven or twelve was too early for educational selection to take place. This prevented subsequent transfers and did not provide a diagnostic stage during which the student's aptitudes and abilities might be better expressed and assessed. Over 50 per cent of the Shura members agreed that the present system was not satisfactory, and 35 per cent, that the orta and the various kinds of vocational schools should be replaced by 'comprehensive middle schools' with programmes which should include both compulsory and elective subjects.[18] The Seventh Shura discussed the comprehensive school idea and accepted the recommendation that the present arrangements should be replaced by comprehensive schools. The ministry also accepted the Shura recommendations in principle. However, no plans have yet been made to embark upon this undertaking on a nationwide scale, and the comprehensive school is still at the experimental stage. Also, the concept is unclear to administrators, teachers, and the general public.

More recent discussion on this topic indicates a shift in the concept of the comprehensive school from that of the earlier 'multipurpose' or 'multilateral' schools. According to some advocates of the comprehensive school idea, all students, regardless of their destinations or interests, would follow a general programme; but there would also be elective courses

[18] Selâhattin Ertürk, Shefik Uysal, and Ibrahim Yurt, 7. *Milli Egitim Shurasi Ile Ilgili Anket Sonuchlari* (Ankara: Talim ve Terbiye Dairesi, Egitim Arashtirmalari ve Degerlendirme Merkezi, 1962), p. 20.

(academic, vocational, etc.) according to individual aptitudes and inclinations.[19] This first cycle of studies would then lead into the second, a three-year comprehensive lise with essentially the same kind of arrangement. In other words, the comprehensive pattern would extend beyond the middle stage of education and encompass the lise stage as well, so that a student who elected to follow a vocational path in the middle school would continue along a similar path in the lise. The Seventh Shura rejected the inclusion of the lise stage and accepted only a comprehensive middle stage. This clearly would make the comprehensive experiment dubious or at best limited. Knowing that orta students prefer the lise to other types of institutions of the same level and certainly to the higher vocational schools, it would seem natural that, barring continuation into a lise, the students who elect to follow a vocational or practical path in the comprehensive middle school would consider such a path as being of lesser prestige and not so good as the academic path. So long as the lise occupies the position it does and remains unchanged, any comprehensive arrangements at the lower level would not take strong roots. Considering the forces of tradition and the people's perceptions of the value and role of the lise, it seems unlikely that this institution will be modified in the foreseeable future.

The Lise

The modern Turkish lise is an outgrowth, or perhaps a continuation, of the Ottoman sultanis which were themselves modelled on the Galatasaray lise discussed in Part I of this book. The coping stone of the state system of general education, it follows the three-year orta school, and it is the main gateway to the universities. Like the orta school, it has frequently been the focus of controversy where 'traditionalists' have vied with 'modernists'—and, more recently, Americanophiles with Francophiles and others—over what its aims, nature and function should be in relation to the other units of the educational structure and to the society. Some assumptions and characteristics of this institution have remained quite stable; others have changed. The sultani, as noted earlier, was envisaged to be an institution belonging to the European family of secondary

[19] Personal interview with Dr Selâhattin Ertürk.

131

academic schools—the English Grammar School, the French lycée, and the German Gymnasium. Oriented perhaps more to the French prototype, it sought to provide *genel kültür* (general culture), interpreted in similar terms as the French *culture générale*. Ziya Gökalp, interpreted 'cultural education' to be the acquisition of knowledge rather than technical skills, knowledge aimed at the cultivation 'of non-utilitarian and altruistic sentiments which do not seek ulterior sentiments'. According to Gökalp, since the university and the technical and professional schools were specialized institutions, genel kültür must be provided by the lises. And since the sciences were more related to specialized education, which the students would acquire in the universities, the lises 'should be entirely devoted to the humanities'.[20]

In addition to these educational aspects, the Ottoman lise had social and political connotations: in the first place, it was envisaged to be an elite institution; and second, it was considered an important recruiting place for political leaders, the civil bureaucracy, and the professions. Moreover, in the minds of people like Ziya Gökalp, a lise education, like all 'good education', should aim at the creation of a 'national culture' and a 'national type'. Prior to the Kemalist Revolution, the nationalistic aspect of the lise was not clearly defined, but it was expressed by some of the ideological forefathers of modern Turkish nationalism. Referring specifically to the sultani [lise], Gökalp stated that its purpose is 'to furnish those who will make up the ruling class with the spirit of unselfishness and dedication [to their country]'.[21] Similarly, in 1918, Ismail Hakki Baltajioglu described the nature and function of the lise as follows: '*Sultanis* (*lises*) are the institutions responsible for giving that general, philosophical, nationalistic and humanistic (training) which is needed by those who are going to get a specialized education in the university ... To the *sultani* and the university we must only send students who are suited to be members of the elite.'[22]

[20] Niyazi Berkes (ed.), *Turkish Nationalism and Western Civilization: Selected Essays of Ziya Gökalp* (New York: Columbia University Press, 1959), pp. 240–3.
[21] *Ibid.*, pp. 243–4
[22] Quoted in Maynard, *op. cit.*, p. 171.

Like its European counterparts of the nineteenth century, the sultani was based on certain similar educational and social assumptions: (a) that 'culture' and 'cultural education' are defined primarily in terms of the humanities; (b) that secondary education should essentially be general and non-utilitarian in the sense that its benefits lay more in disciplining the mind, or in developing intellectual, moral, social, and aesthetic traits and habits which were often associated with a 'cultivated personality'; (c) that schools offering this type of education should be selective and distinct (educationally and socially) from other kinds of schools; and (d) that the best governed society is that which places its intellectual elite at the helm of the statecraft. To these, Gökalp's further assumption implicit in his statement could be added: 'The real representatives of a nation are men of genius and heroes. The genius is the hero of the intellect, and the hero is the genius of the will.'[23] In other words, the man of intellect, assumed to be created through a lise type of education, is also the man most capable of representing or leading the nation.

Some of these general characteristics and assumptions would apply to the modern Turkish lise as well. The Atatürk Revolution did not radically alter this aspect of Turkish society; rather, it solidified what was already nascent during the pre-republican decades. However, the lise under the republic *did* undergo important transformations. An attempt will be made in this study to show the elements of continuity and change, and to qualify the contention made by some writers that the functions of the lise have remained the same because its curriculum and organization have not changed substantially.[24]

Throughout the republican period, there have been changes in the curriculum of the lise, which will be discussed in a subsequent section. Basically, however, the *educational* function of the lise has remained the same, namely, (a) to provide a general course in the essential 'disciplines' as the best training for the development of cultured and moral men and women, and (b) to prepare for the universities. There have been variations concerning the university preparatory aim of the lise,

[23] Berkes, *op cit.*, p. 244.
[24] This is the conclusion reached by Maynard, the only writer who has made an extensive study of the Turkish lise. See Maynard, *op. cit.*, p. 352.

but to a great extent the lise course continues to be regarded as a selective mechanism for admission into the universities and institutions of higher learning. At first, successful completion of the lise entitled one to enter the university. In 1935–36 the *olgunluk* (a maturity examination) was instituted. This meant that, in addition to the completion of a lise course, a student had to pass another examination before he gained the right to enter a university. The olgunluk was abolished in 1955 and the State Lise Completion Examination was instituted. Those who passed this examination were entitled to enter a university. Of course, not *all* lise graduates enter a university or institutions of higher learning. But a substantial percentage of them do, as Chapter VII will show. What is equally important is that the majority of students prefer the lise to any other type of secondary school because they aspire to continue their education in an institution of higher learning.[25] Successful completion of the lise course and continuation in higher institutions have come to be so closely related that when the government recently instituted university entrance examinations as an additional screening device for entrance into the University of Ankara, unsuccessful candidates carried placards and marched through the main street of Ankara, protesting such additional selective procedures, and asserting that it was their *right* to be admitted to a university.[26] Unfortunately, no information is available as to the number of lise graduates who entered institutions of higher learning during the Ottoman period. But from the analysis of the sultani it is reasonable to infer that the percentage of graduates who entered institutions of higher learning was not so great as during the republican period.

The lise has been regarded as a selective institution for the few rather than as a universal secondary school for all, as it

[25] In the survey of lise students, 65 per cent stated that the main reason for choosing a lise was because they wanted to go to a university. Over 90 per cent wanted, under ideal circumstances, to continue their education in an institution of higher learning.

[26] Personal observation by the writer. On October 23, 1962, the newspaper *Jumhuriyet* reported that about 5,000 lise students marched to the Ministry of Education carrying placards which read: 'Either knowledge or death', 'Close the lises', "Let the press support our claims', 'Without knowledge life is a grave', etc. Subsequently, places were found for all students. Since then the tests have been used for admission to other universities.

was during the Ottoman period. During his lise years, and upon completion of the course, the student is frequently subjected to oral and written examinations and to teachers' evaluations. One of the main purposes of these selective devices is to eliminate those who are not able to meet the standards and to allow the others to proceed. Since 1923, many changes have been made in the rules and regulations governing the system of examinations,[27] but their selective function has constantly been maintained. It has been an avowed policy of the authorities that the lise must seek to educate only the students who are intellectually superior, and one way of finding out who such persons are is through examinations. Whether those who attend the lise or who are able to graduate are in fact intellectually superior students is another matter. Some writers have expressed strong doubts as to whether the examinations accomplish their aim of screening the most able students, or of being used as pedagogical devices to provide an education according to the needs of the students. According to Maynard:

'Despite the apparent faith of the Turkish authorities in regulations as a tool for improving education, the examination and promotion regulations and the perpetual manipulation of them did not promote the attainment of the objectives of the school nor did they serve to adapt the schools to the needs of the students, especially in the face of rapidly increasing enrollments. They have resulted in waste of manpower and resources of the nation and must have resulted in untold anguish to and tensions in the students. Perhaps the right to take another and yet another examination has deadened the pain of failure, but it is doubtful.'[28]

One should remember, however, that these sorts of problems are encountered in all systems of education which put heavy emphasis upon examinations. In Turkey, as in other countries, other factors influence the selection process. It is equally doubtful whether a 'better' system of examinations would obviate the social, cultural, and economic elements which go into the examination system and into the selection of the students for further education. More will be said about this

---

[27] For the most detailed account of these changes, see Maynard, *op. cit.*, pp. 266–308.
[28] *Ibid.*, pp. 207–308.

later in this study. Suffice it to mention here that during the republican period, attempts were made to base selection more on achievement than on ascriptive criteria. As a subsequent chapter will show, the present lise, although still catering to a small segment of the population, recruits its students from wider social strata than its predecessor, the sultani. In other words, although certain of the lise's structural characteristics and assumptions are similar to the sultani's and the academic schools of Europe, many of its social functions have changed. It is no longer a European school or a 'borrowed' institution. It is as Turkish as any other institution, in the sense that it has acquired a meaning for the Turks themselves. This is also manifest in the emphasis which the Turks have placed upon the lise for the training of Turkish leaders, imbued with nationalistic sentiments and the tenets of the revolutionary ideology, and of individuals who will enter the ranks of the new occupations. Several statements to this effect have been made by official bodies and by leading educators. In 1937, Hasan Ali Yüjel, at the time general director of secondary education, stated that 'the lise, both in itself and in the elements of education it gives, represents a nation's concept of civilization'. In the 1959 'Official Rules and Regulations for the *Lises*', the following appears: 'Lises are schools preparing for higher education. [Their function] is to prepare useful hard-working citizens for the Turkish Republic, who have adopted as their own the national character [ethic] and to bring students to that level of learning and culture needed for higher education.' And, according to the Committee on Ethical Education of the First Shura, the first objective of the lise is 'to train a Turk who is committed to the Turkish language, the principles and policies of the Turkish revolution and in general to Turkish ideals'.[29] This represents a marked ideological shift in the conception of the lise, even though whether the lise actually accomplishes these aims is not quite clear. It will be suggested later that the political education of Turkish youth takes place in lower types of schools (elementary and middle), so that by the time a person enters the lise his political values to a large extent have been formed.

[29] These quotations were taken from Maynard's translations. *Ibid.*, pp. 171–4, 208.

The question of whether the lise should be college preparatory and selective or not has frequently been debated among official circles and Turkish educators. More recent controversy over these problems occurred at the meeting of the Seventh Shura. In the questionnaire sent to the Shura members prior to its convening, the following question was asked: 'The lises should be considered as institutions which prepare students not only for higher education, but also for life (a living).' Of 263 individuals who responded, 62 per cent expressed agreement, while 33 per cent felt that the lises should be 'academic schools' preparing only for institutions of higher learning.[30] The Shura accepted the latter aim of the lise, but the Ministry of Education accepted the former dual purpose.

During the Shura debates, one group adhered rigidly to the view that the lise should be a highly selective institution for the intellectually competent who will most probably continue their education after graduation. They maintained that the lise must be selective if it is to merit that nomenclature, otherwise 'all levels of higher education will suffer because students who are not well prepared will then be admitted'. According to another group, however, the lise should also consider those students who do not intend to continue their education; for such students 'we must have institutions which will offer a general education and a general culture above the *orta* school ... in order to cover the needs of the society and the government'. It is true, they argued, that the lise is the main source of 'scientists, artists and intellectuals (thinkers)'; but besides specialization in that direction, 'we must accept the other principle which is to make good citizens out of students ... who through scientific methods will acquire knowledge and be able to grasp the world and tackle local problems'. Finally, this group maintained that selection would not be advantageous in the case of provincial lises because of lack of teachers and economic factors. In any case, they concluded, selection does take place in the orta schools.[31]

Interestingly, neither group envisaged the lise as performing

---

[30] Ertürk, Uysal, and Yurt, *op. cit.*, p. 21.

[31] *Orta Ogretim Komitesi Raporu* (T. C. Milli Egitim Bakanligi, VII Milli Egitim Shurasi Dokumanlari [Ankara: Milli Egitim Basimevi, 1961]), pp. 25–8.

any 'vocational' functions. The main point in both positions was that a lise education should essentially be a a general education and that the lise should train the future leaders of the society. Currently, however, there *is* a concern for these questions in Turkey. As enrolments in the lises increase, it is realized that a monolithic type of education will not serve the needs of all the students. There is even talk of expanding the idea of comprehensive schools to encompass the lises, and the government, as in the case of the *orta* schools, has accepted this idea in principle. Here again the movement seems to be spearheaded by people who have had training in the United States or have been exposed to American educational ideas and practices. At the lise level, some experiments have been made in the direction of 'comprehensiveness', but they have not yet taken root. Experimental schools of this kind are comprehensive only in name. The author visited *Bahchelievler Deneme Lisesi* (an experimental lise in Ankara), which was established seven years ago and was, for a time, indirectly supported by the Ford Foundation. A substantial proportion of its teachers (40 to 50 per cent) had received some training in the United States. The only experimental feature of the school, which differentiated it from the other lises, was that curriculum diversification began with the first lise class, instead of with the second and third classes, as in the normal lises. In addition, daily twenty-minute 'homerooms' were provided. The curriculum diversification took the form of three streams (literature and social studies, natural sciences, and mathematics) rather than of two (literature and science) as is common with other lises. The programme of studies was essentially academic, and the students aspired to higher education.

In addition to the commercial schools, there are currently two main types of lises in Turkey: public and private. The public lises, enrolling the great majority of students (about 88,000), are entirely controlled and supported by the Ministry of Education. The private lises are of three kinds: (a) *özel Türk* (private Turkish), which are partly supported by private contributions, but are still under the control of the ministry; (b) the *azinlik* (for the Greek, Armenian, and Jewish minorities), all of which are located in Istanbul and are entirely private schools, except that the curriculum must include Turkish and

Turkish history taught by Turkish teachers; and (c) *yabanji* (foreign-operated) schools (English, American, German, Italian, French, Austrian), also entirely private on matters of support and control, and similar to the minority schools in the special curriculum provision. To repeat, even though they are privately supported and controlled, minority and foreign lises come under the supervision of the Ministry of Education: the minister approves their opening and their curriculum and has the right to inspect them. Foreign and private Turkish schools in general include some of the most prestigious lises in Turkey, and, considering the number of students enrolled in them, they have comparatively high success in the university entrance examinations.[32]

Within the public school category, there are six schools of lise level called 'colleges', four of which were opened in 1955. They are located in Izmir, Istanbul (Kadiköy), Eskishehir, Konya, Samsun and Diyarbakir, and they enrol about 550 students in all. The difference between these 'colleges' and the regular public lises lies in the curriculum; in the former, which are also boarding schools, all subjects except Turkish language and literature are taught in English.

---

[32] Abdurrahman Sh. Sanay, *Ankara Universitesi 1962 Girish Imtihanlarinda Liselerin Basharilari* (Ankara: M. Eg. Bak., Talim, ve Terbiye Dairesi, Egitim Arashtirmalari ve Degerlendirme Merkesi, 1962), pp. 7–8.

CHAPTER VI

THE CURRICULUM

PRIMARY SCHOOLS

DURING the Ottoman period, the main function of primary schools was to socialize the children, to make them 'good Moslems', and in some cases to train them in reading and writing. Reflecting on village education in the early part of the nineteenth century, the elders of Hasanoglu, a village situated thirty-four kilometres north-east of Ankara, remembered Shükrü Hoja, the teacher-priest, who 'taught the village children to recite the verses in the Koran and the prayers and to copy calligraphy samples, and he taught especially able children outside school hours and helped them to go to the medrese in Ankara and Konya'.[1] After the revolution, the teaching of religion was proscribed, and a secular elementary school programme was substituted.[2] As in other countries, the purpose of the elementary school since then has been to teach the rudiments of knowledge and to induct the young into the values of the society. Education at all levels became an important agency for the development of political consensus and a feeling of nationalism. In addition, and largely because of Turkish local conditions (e.g., the urban-rural differences), an attempt has been made to adjust the curriculum to the pupils' environment. Finally, statements about the programme of the elementary schools have reflected efforts to base pedagogical practice on modern psychological principles, a point which is also reflected

[1] Ibrahim Yasa, *Hasanoglan: Socio-Economic Structure of a Turkish Village* (Ankara: Yeni Matbaa, 1957), pp. 128–9.

[2] The secularization of education and the reintroduction of religion are discussed more fully in Chapter VIII.

in the programmes of the elementary school teacher-training institutions.

The reform of the curriculum began in 1926, two years after John Dewey was invited to advise the Turkish government on ways to build up a modern educational system. In 1948, new regulations governing the curriculum of the elementary schools were issued. More recently, there has been considerable activity to revamp the curriculum, but in the main, the 1948 Regulations are still in force.

A study of John Dewey's influence on Turkish pedagogical theory and practice and of the more recent impact of American educational ideas has yet to be written. But, as noted earlier, there is a marked congruence of what is expressed in Turkey concerning the principles and aims of education and what one reads in American educational literature. This is most apparent in the statements on elementary education and the curriculum of elementary schools. In his 'Report and Recommendation upon Turkish Education', Dewey urged that the content of studies 'should be modified in different sections of the country to be adapted to local conditions and needs'. In true Deweyan fashion, he continued that 'without this change, the school studies will not be connected with the life of the pupils, and hence will neither serve them practically nor enlist their full interest and attention'. Dewey stressed that the elementary system should be flexible 'to accommodate itself to special local conditions, especially economic', and that the schools should be made 'centers of community life especially in the rural districts'.[3]

The question of adapting the schools to local conditions and of making them cultural community centres has constantly been reiterated in republican Turkey. As indicated earlier, experiments with the egitmen teachers and the village institutes were attempts in that direction. Moreover, there are some variations in the curriculum of urban and rural schools, the most important being that in the latter, six hours per week are devoted to agriculture during the entire five-year elementary school course, but no agriculture is taught in urban schools. Apparently, in order to compensate for this provision,

[3] *The John Dewey Report* (Ankara: Ministry of Education, Research and Measurement Bureau, 1960), pp. 1–2, 17–18.

more hours are devoted to drawing and manual work in the urban schools.[4] Emphasis on agricultural subjects in agricultural areas was more recently underscored by the Directorate General of Primary education,[5] and the idea of adapting the programme to local conditions, by the Turkish National Commission on Education. The latter is rather interesting for several reasons. One of many indications of the growing post-World War II involvement of American advisers in Turkey's attempts at educational change, its report was suppressed by the Menderes government. Only after the Revolution of 1960 was it made public. Regarding the primary school programme, the commission felt that 'a complete overhaul' was necessary and recommended that 'the syllabus must be adjustable to the characteristics of the area and the peculiarities of the village; therefore the programme to be drawn up by the central authority should be in the form of a general outline'.[6] Nowhere, however, is there more similarity between American and Turkish educational terminology than in the report by the Directorate General of Primary Education, a document which, in the opinion of this writer, is as comprehensive concerning the aims of primary education and the principles upon which it should be based as it is unrealistic in the demands made upon primary schools, their teachers, and their pupils.

The first part of this report classifies the objectives of primary education, which are derived from four major sources or 'standpoints': the individual, 'human relations', 'economic life', and 'social life'. In connection with these sources, primary schools are called upon to perform a gargantuan task, namely, to accomplish no less than nine-five objectives. For example, children are expected to do the following, in addition to developing basic skills of literacy and computation: (a) to learn habits

[4] *Facilities for Education in Rural Areas* (International Burea of Education, XXXIst International Conference on Public Education, Geneva, 1958), p. 201. See also *World Survey of Education*, Vol. II, Primary Education (UNESCO, 1958), p. 999.

[5] *Report on Proposed Revisions in the Primary School Program* (Ministry of Education, Directorate General of Primary Education [Ankara: Ministry of Education Printing Plant, 1962]), p. 20. Hereafter cited as *Report on Proposed Revisions.*

[6] *The Report of the Turkish National Commission on Education* (Istanbul: American Board Publication Department, 1961), p. 48. Hereafter cited as *National Commission Report.*

conducive to a hygienic way of living; (b) to 'attach a special value on all mortals and lifeless objects' around them; (c) to utilize the senses more efficiently; (d) to make good judgments and to learn 'scientific thinking methods'; (e) to acquire the feeling and outlook for making good use of their spare time; (f) 'not to despair in case of failure'; (g) to grasp basic principles of a good family life, and to attach a value to the family; (h) to learn simple housework and skills needed in daily family life; (i) to grasp 'the role of manpower and natural resources in the development of the community and the whole country'; (j) to grasp 'the importance of good consumers in the economy of the country'; (k) to learn the importance of scientific knowledge and technique in the advancement and development of societies; and (l) to develop the feelings of patriotism, of democratic living and behaving, and 'to feel proud for being the son of a great nation with an honourable history'.[7]

A list follows of 'principles of education' upon which the primary school programme should be based if it is to accomplish these objectives. Such principles are classified in three major categories: (1) principles concerning the child, (2) principles concerning the school and the community, and (3) principles concerning the problems of teaching and teaching methods. Here emphasis is placed upon 'knowing the child', recognizing individual interests and 'the basic needs of a human being', adjusting the school activities to the child's environment, developing 'national' as well as aesthetic feelings, training good citizens, making the school 'a cultural centre of the community', 'learning by doing', and so on. Finally, recommendations are made on content, namely, that the social sciences should include Turkish geography and history and 'historical events of the nations which are related to Turkish history, from the citizenship point of view'; that within the natural sciences, agricultural subjects should be emphasized in the rural areas; that a revision must be made of the geometry curriculum by taking out 'surface calculations of pyramid, cone, globe and the volumetric measures', since they are difficult to learn and of no interest to the children; that 'audio-training and singing classes' should be included in music education; that teachers should avoid being dogmatic in teaching religion, but instead

[7] *Report on Proposed Revisions, op cit.*, pp. 3–11.

should 'give a tender, sweet and warm inspiration'; and so on.[8]

These recommendations clearly attest to the movement towards establishing a modern rationale upon which the primary school curriculum should be based. Regardless of the reservations made, they are a departure from traditional beliefs and practices. This is also reflected in the latest 'teacher's guide', which presents the principles upon which elementary education should be based and detailed instructions concerning daily lessons, examinations, holidays, and the like. The guide also tells about the social, personal, economic, and human sources of objectives, about discipline based not on fear or severity, but on democratic principles, and about instruction according to the natural growth of the child.[9] Unfortunately, no evidence on the extent to which these pedagogical principles are being applied is available. Observers have commented on the excessive uniformity that prevails at all levels of education, the persistence of formal methods of instruction, and the control exerted by the central authorities. To generalize, there is probably more application of such pedagogical ideas in primary schools than in other levels of education.

At present, the curriculum of the elementary schools includes the following subjects: Turkish language, history, geography, civics, natural sciences, mathematics, writing, music (only in urban schools), study of the environment, drawing and manual work, agriculture (only in rural schools), physical education (only in urban schools) and domestic science. The largest single block of time is devoted to Turkish language (28 per cent of the total weekly class periods in the urban, and 30 per cent in the rural, schools). The second largest block is occupied by mathematics in urban schools (15 per cent) and by agriculture in rural schools (24 per cent); in the latter schools 18 per cent of the total class periods is devoted to mathematics. In urban schools sixteen weekly periods (12 per cent of the total periods) are spent on drawing and manual work, but in rural schools only five periods are spent on these subjects. There are some other urban-rural variations: no music or physical education is taught in the rural schools, and the time spent on the study

[8] *Ibid.*, pp. 11–23.
[9] See Jevdet Ekemen, *et al.*, *Ogretmen Rehberi* (Ankara: Ayyildiz Matbaasi, 1961), pp. 123 ff.

of the environment and on such subjects as history, geography, civics, natural science, domestic science, and writing is somewhat less in these schools than in the urban ones.[10]

THE ORTA SCHOOLS AND THE LISES

The nature and educational functions of the orta schools and the lises and the controversies surrounding them have been discussed in a previous chapter. In connection with those aspects, reference was made to several developments concerning the curriculum, namely, the attempts to introduce practical studies in the orta schools and to set up comprehensive or experimental schools in which there would be greater curriculum flexibility. In the orta schools, except for what has already been said, the courses of study have generally remained the same since the early years of the republic. Some of the most important changes were the introduction of commercial and agricultural subjects, 'free study' periods, and, in some cases, combination of zoology, physiology, botany, and geology into one course in 'natural science'.[11] Today the curriculum of the orta school includes Turkish, modern foreign languages, civics, history, geography, natural science, physics, chemistry, mathematics, religion (Islam), drawing, music, physical education, housekeeping and child care, commerce and agriculture. Of these subjects, the humanities (Turkish, modern foreign languages, history, religion, music) occupy by far the largest single portion in terms of weekly periods taught (35 per cent of the total weekly instructional period). Science and mathematics come second, with 21 per cent of the weekly hours, and commerce and agriculture third, with 6 per cent. Three periods (one in each grade) are devoted to civics, drawing, and physical education. Within the humanities group (a total of thirty-four instructional periods), fourteen periods are devoted to Turkish language and reading.[12] There are no electives in the orta

[10] *World Survey of Education, loc. cit.*

[11] For a comparison of the courses of study in 1925 and 1959, see Richard E. Maynard, 'The Lise and Its Curriculum in the Turkish Educational System' (Ph.D. dissertation, The University of Chicago, 1961), p. 122.

[12] *World Survey of Education*, Vol. III, Secondary Education (UNESCO, 1961), p. 1097.

curriculum except in the experimental schools; if a student fails in two or three of the fourteen courses, he must remain in the same grade and repeat the whole year.

To conclude that because there has been little change in the courses of study, the conception of the curriculum has also remained unchanged is only partially true. As in the primary schools, there has been a shift in Turkish pedagogical thinking about the objectives of the orta curriculum and the principles upon which it should be based. The parallel between primary and middle school general education in this respect is striking. In the first place, the objectives and curriculum of the orta school are derived from the same sources as those of the primary school. Hence, they are listed in such categories as 'social objectives', 'individual objectives', objectives relating to human relationships, to economic life, and so forth. In addition, courses of study include specific instructions to teachers as to how the objectives are to be accomplished and supplements on the basic psychological principles upon which teaching and learning are based. In summary, the curriculum of the orta school is envisaged as performing the following tasks: (a) to develop national consciousness and the feeling of patriotism; (b) to 'protect' the values of Turkish culture and history and to follow the principles of Turkish reforms; (c) to respect the Constitution of the Turkish Republic and its laws; (d) to protect Turkey's natural resources and to understand the importance of science and the scientific method in the development and improvement of life; (e) to improve the ability to read, write, and speak the Turkish language correctly; (f) to 'enjoy nature and the fine arts'; (g) 'to love and respect all the members of one's family'; (h) 'to enjoy working', to choose a suitable job, to be 'able to earn a living', and to 'spend wisely'; and (i) to develop moral character, responsibility, and the like.[13]

Whether these objectives are being accomplished, or whether the psychological principles upon which curriculum statements are made are being adhered to, is not quite clear. Turkish educators and foreign observers have some doubts

[13] *Orta Okul Programi* (Türkiye Jumhuriyeti, Milli Egitim Bakanligi [Ankara: Milli Egitim Basimevi, 1949]), pp. 5–6. See also Maynard, *op. cit.*, p. 124. More recently there has been a movement to revamp the orta curriculum, but no information is available on any proposed plans.

about this. Commenting specifically on the principles embodied in the revised 'Orta School Program' of 1949, John Rufi, an American consultant, wrote:

'I found almost no evidence that the statements of the major objectives and the principles of secondary education so well set forth in this publication are being translated into practice in the schools ... I am in accord with the philosophy set forth in the opening sections of the 1949 Program for the Junior High Schools, but ... the practices in the middle schools and lycees I have visited almost completely disregard and violate the positive theories which are so well enunciated in this official publication.'[14]

In a study on the evaluation of student progress in the secondary schools, a Turkish educator concluded that objectives seem to be established through 'armchair discussions', and that there is a gap between their theoretical formulation and their practical application.[15] Significantly, though, a concerted effort is being made to formulate more clearly a rationale upon which the curriculum should be based and to break away from the traditional rigidity and views on the ideological bases of education.

Moving up the educational ladder, the development and present status of the lise curriculum reflect more clearly the Turkish conception of what the nature and function of the lise proper is or should be, a topic which was discussed in the previous chapter. Not unexpectedly, therefore, the curriculum has mainly been built around certain academic disciplines— literature and language, history, the sciences, mathematics, philosophy, sociology, and so on. Since the period of the sultani, there have been several reforms of the amount of time spent on each subject, the emphasis given to certain subjects (notably those connected with the Turkish language and culture), the arrangement into streams (scientific and literary), and the number of subjects to be included in the entire lise course.

---

[14] John J. Rufi, *Secondary Education in Turkey: Observations, Problems, and Recommendations* (mimeographed, Ankara, 1952), pp. 10–11. See also Maynard, *op. cit.*, p. 125.

[15] Shefik Uysal, 'Evaluation of Pupil Progress in Secondary Schools of Turkey' (Ed.D. thesis, The University of Illinois, 1961), p. 128. This was essentially the impression derived by the present writer in his talks with Turkish teachers and educators.

Some changes are particularly important in that they reflected significant developments in the society at large. The revolutionary plan to 'Turkicize' the people, their language, and their culture was most saliently echoed in changes in the curriculum of the lise, as well as in the other schools. Thus, Turkish language and literature replaced the previous Ottoman language in 1924, and religion was eliminated; after the 1927 language reform,[16] Arabic and Persian were dropped; the history of Turkey and the Turkish race became the 'pivot' of history courses at all levels of education; pre-Islamic Turkish literature was given more emphasis; and, after 1929, the new Turkish Latin alphabet became compulsory as the only medium of writing and instruction. Plans to Turkicize the language were inextricably intertwined with the nationalistic policies of the republic; and one of the main purposes of the lise curriculum has been 'to train a Turk who is committed to the Turkish language, the principles and policies of the Turkish revolution and in general to Turkish ideals'. Indeed, during the period of the thirties, when dubious theories, theses, and diatribes were produced 'proving' that all civilizations and languages originated with the Turks, one aim of the lise history courses was 'to teach the student the thesis that our race has been a leader in civilization. It [the course] will show how Central Asia was the cradle of civilization and the importance of this fact and its development throughout history from prehistoric times up to today.'[17] It was also during this ultranationalistic period that military training, even for girls, was added to the programme of studies. Changes in other areas of the curriculum were made at the same time. For example, attempts were made to emphasize laboratory work in the teaching of science and to simplify science and mathematics, bringing them more within the conceptual reach of the students.

The next major step in revamping the curriculum was made in 1949, when the lise course was extended from three to four years. During the preceding decade, the lise course of study was

---

[16] The language reform by which the Arabic script was replaced by Latin letters is discussed more fully in a later chapter.

[17] Hasan Ali Yüjel, *Türkiyede Orta Ogretim* (*Secondary Education in Turkey* [Istanbul: Devlet Basimevi, 1938]), p. 198. The translation of this passage is by Maynard, *op. cit.*, p. 227.

criticized as too demanding in its many details; too theoretical and not geared to the interests of the students; too restrictive, in that it omitted subjects like art and music and paid relatively little attention to sports, physical education, and foreign languages; and too difficult in terms of the language in which textbooks were written, and not integrated in its constituent parts. Critics attributed the large number of failures to these factors. At the Fourth Shura meeting there was a debate over the merits and demerits of the ministry's proposal to lengthen the school course, and in the end the Shura voted to accept this change. The most significant curriculum changes made at that time were: (a) the introduction of tutorial classes or seminars; (b) the provision of electives to be chosen from art, history of art, or music; (c) a somewhat lesser emphasis upon Turkish ideals and Turkish history and a greater one on social and economic history; and (d) a revision of Turkish language and literature (more hours were added, with more emphasis upon language composition and folk literature, and less importance was given to literary history, etc.). In his extensive treatment of the development of the curriculum up to this time, Maynard has concluded that 'all in all . . . the 1949 course of study was a considerable step forward. In all respects it appears to be better thought out, better organized, and especially more concerned with the student and the nature of the society of today and less concerned with arbitrary concepts about what should be studied.'[18]

In 1954, the lise course was again reduced to three years. In 1957, diversification into science and literature streams began with the second class, rather than with the third, as was the case prior to the 1949 revisions. In the pre-revolutionary period it began with the first lise class. According to these revisions, tutorial classes and seminars were dropped, and although the topics in most courses were rearranged, the content remained essentially the same. The 1957 provisions are in force today, and the relative distribution of the weekly periods in the various subjects is indicated in Table XVII.[19]

[18] Richard E. Maynard, *op. cit.*, p. 236.
[19] For a detailed description of the content of the various courses, see M. Sitki Bilmen, *The Turkish Lycée: Its Stable Characteristics and Curriculum* (Ankara: Maarif Basimevi, 1960); and *Lise Müfredat Programi* (T. C. Maarif Vekaleti [Ankara: Maarif Basimevi, 1956]).

The lise curriculum continues to be a major focus of controversy and criticism. In 1952, Rufi complained that the programme was too heavy for both pupils and teachers, and that teaching was 'extremely formal and bookish'. He also observed that the pupil was given little opportunity 'to learn by doing, or by first hand experience'.[20] Clearly, in this second comment Rufi was influenced by American ideas about how teaching and learning should take place, perhaps without taking into consideration that some of the functions of the Turkish lise are different from the American high school. But the lise curriculum has also been criticized by the Turks themselves. The Turkish National Commission on Education attributed failures in secondary schools to 'the lack of proper co-ordination between the programmes and teaching methods of primary and secondary schools, and the fact that children passing from primary to secondary school find great difficulty in adapting themselves to the latter grade'. According to the commission, the lises 'were incapable of producing young people who possess all the qualities demanded for the Turkish universities'. It stressed that teachers and facilities 'should be speedily brought up to the required standard', and that the programmes and teaching methods should be completely revised. In addition, the commission recommended that the student be given the opportunity for 'free activity and the development of talent in either the fine arts or in mechanics and handicrafts, according to his ability and inclination'. Finally, it suggested that diversification into streams should begin in the first class, and that in small cities and towns some sort of comprehensive school arrangement should be introduced.[21] More recently, as was shown in the previous chapter, questions bearing on the lise curriculum were discussed at the meeting of the Seventh Sura.

Curriculum questions are not always *sui generis*; they are also related to external factors beyond the control of the school. It is not always self-evident, for example, that changes in the content of instruction or in the teaching methods will bring about desired results if no other concomitant changes take place. One of the crucial educational functions of the lise is to

[20] Rufi, *op. cit.*, p. 12.
[21] *National Commission Report*, *op. cit.*, pp. 52–55.

prepare students for the universities. In order to do this, there is a rigorous system of examinations in certain academic subjects. Furthermore, students attach a great deal of importance to such examinations (in the survey, for instance, more than 60 per cent of the students agreed that 'the most important thing in my life at school is to pass my examination'), and to entrance into the universities. Under these circumstances, it is rather unrealistic to expect that modifications in the methods of teaching, or even in the content of the curriculum, will take root in and of themselves. Some critics attribute the high dropout rate and the failures among lise students to the excessive load and to the demands made upon the student. This may indeed be true. But the lise is perceived to be a selective institution; there are not sufficient university places for all lise students; and many of them come from cultural backgrounds not conducive to optimum school performance. Further, in criticizing the schools for being formal and rigid in discipline or expectations, patterns of authority in the society must be considered. It is unrealistic to expect a school to be a microcosmic nirvana. And finally, bland comments about the need for 'free activity', 'learning by doing', 'democratic classroom interaction', and the like, often made by foreign advisers or experts, are based on certain assumptions about what education should do or should be, which are derived from different, especially Western, models. There is no concrete and unquestioned evidence that the products of the lises are 'less democratic', or that they lack initiative *because* of the type of instruction or experiences in such schools.

TECHNICAL AND VOCATIONAL SCHOOLS

Reference has already been made to the various types of technical and vocational institutions and to the steps taken by the government to bring technical education under its control and direction. Since 1936, the government has sought to strengthen non-academic education and to make it more attractive to students and parents, partly through efforts to introduce practical subjects in the orta schools and general subjects in the technical and vocational schools. Although considerable progress has been made in terms of growth of enrolments, as the next chapter will show, technical and vocational education in Turkey, as indeed in many other developing societies, has not grown to the lusty proportions expected or relative to other types of education. Such an education seemingly continues to be regarded as second best and to attract the less competent (intellectually), less affluent type of individual, for reasons which will be discussed in a subsequent chapter.

Owing to the great variation in types of technical and vocational schools, statements about curriculum that would hold true for all are difficult to make. In general, whether such schools are of middle or lise level, courses are distributed into general, professional (technical), and practical (workshop) subjects. For example, in the boys' middle trade schools, the percentage distribution of subjects in the first year programme is: 58 per cent 'general knowledge', 8 per cent professional, and 34 per cent practical. In the second and third years, the percentages change to about 32, 23, and 45 per cent respectively. The general subjects include Turkish, history, geography, citizenship, biology, foreign language, music, and religious studies. As the student moves into the lise level trade institutes, the hours in practical work increase to about 55 per cent of the total, and those in general subjects decrease to between 18 and 29 per cent.[22]

The curriculum of the vocational schools for girls is organized on similar principles. At the middle school level, the programme includes the same general subjects as those of the equivalent boys' schools, as well as drawing, home economics and 'workshop classes' (dressmaking, millinery and artificial flower making, underwear and embroidery, home management and cooking, and child care and education). Unlike the trade schools for boys, in the girls' schools the amount of time spent on practical subjects remains relatively constant in all three years (approximately 28 per cent of the total weekly hours). At the lise level (girls' institutes), there is a decrease in the hours devoted to general subjects and an increase in the subjects in the category of 'home economics and workshop classes'. History, geography, and physics are replaced by psychology, and theo-

---

[22] Reshat Ozalp, *Türkiye'de Mesleki ve Teknik Ogretim* (Orta Derejeli Okullar [Ankara: Maarif Basimevi, 1956]), p. 60.

retical chemistry and physics, and by applied chemistry and physics.[23]

Lastly, mention should be made of commercial schools, which have registered a steady growth since 1941. These are likewise organized in terms of two stages: middle and lise. In the past, the programme was almost equally divided between general and commercial courses. More recently, there was a decrease in the vocational-practical component of the curriculum. Out of a total of thirty-three weekly hours in the first year of the middle commercial schools, only five are devoted to 'office practice', all the rest being general courses (history, Turkish, geography, civics, natural sciences, music, foreign languages, religious education, etc.). In the second and third years, there is comparatively little change in the distribution of courses (some increase in the vocational courses and a corresponding decrease in the general). In the third year, 76 per cent of the weekly hours are spent on general subjects, and 24 per cent on vocational subjects (office practice, commercial correspondence, commodities and typing). Greater vocational specialization takes place in the commercial lises: by the time a student reaches the third and last class, he spends 37 per cent of his time on general subjects and 63 per cent on vocational subjects, the number of which is increased and includes economics, finance, statistics, shorthand, financial algebra, and so on.[24]

Turkish efforts to expand technical education and to modernize the curriculum of vocational schools were part of the general movement to modernize the society, and to develop the skills necessary for the various industrial, commercial, and business enterprises. Schools (and more recently correspondence courses) and technical training through adult education programmes have aimed at developing new approaches to the means of producing and distributing goods and to a modern, scientific way of thinking. Yet the actual results have not met the expectations of those engaged in such educational planning,

[23] *Vocational and Technical Education: Girls' Institutes* (Ministry of Education, Statistics and Publications Department [Ankara: Bengi Printing House, 1961]), pp. 12–16.

[24] *Schools of Commercial Education in Turkey* (Ministry of Education, Statistics and Publications Department [Ankara: Bengi Printing House, 1962]), pp. 39–41.

and it is unlikely that efforts to change the curriculum alone will bring about the desired outcomes. In a conversation with a Turkish expert on technical education, the present writer was informed that the demand for technical or vocational education is not so high as expected, not because of the types of training which go by that name, but rather because the rewards after graduation from vocational schools are not so enticing or great as those accruing from attendance at other schools. Recently, in fact, many trained Turkish technicians have been emigrating to countries like West Germany, primarily for higher pay.[25] To reiterate a point made previously, mere curriculum changes, without concomitant social and cultural changes, are at best palliatives, not educational cures.

TEACHING AND TEACHERS

The organized content of instruction, the principles upon which it is based, and the objectives it seeks to accomplish do not, in and of themselves, sufficiently define the nature of education or of the curriculum. The efficiency of an education system depends in no small part on the quality of instruction, which is itself influenced by the 'technology' of education and the calibre of the teaching staff. A full and adequate assessment of these qualitative aspects of Turkish education is at present quite impossible, due to the lack of reliable material on the subject. The following comments, therefore, are based on statements, mostly impressionistic, made by other writers and on the author's casual observations of classroom procedures in some secondary and technical schools. Several factors (teacher preparation, classroom size, methods of administering examinations or evaluating student performance, etc.) will be considered as possible clues to an assessment of quality of instruction.

Foreign observers, especially Americans, have frequently commented on and criticized what seemed to be a highly formal and rigid classroom atmosphere, where no free discussion takes place, where teachers control and direct most classroom activities, and where pupils memorize and merely recite what

[25] Personal interview with Mr Reshat Ozalp, Director of the Department of Statistics of Technical Education.

they have learned from their textbooks. At the lise level, in particular, instruction is in the form of lectures by the teacher and recitation by the students. Student participation often consists of repetition of memorized parts from textbooks in answer to rather general questions by the teacher. Although teachers have recently been urged or pressed to adopt what is called an 'active method' of teaching and hence to allow for a greater interchange of ideas in the classroom, this does not seem to have occurred because of overcrowded classrooms and lack of appropriate training on the part of the teachers.[26] Unfortunately, there is no evidence on the actual results of such types of teaching on pupil learnings and on the attitudes which such classroom procedures develop in the students. They could affect not only the mental development, but also the general socialization of the individual.

In examining the quality of instruction in Turkish classrooms, it is safer to look at the quality of the teachers and the conditions under which they work. Here again factors *assumed* to be related to quality in teaching must be relied upon for lack of data concerning the teaching act itself.

As noted earlier in this study, there are certain basic qualifications that a teacher must possess before teaching in the various levels of schools. However, because of the tremendous teacher shortage which has resulted from the expansion of the system, several stopgap measures have been adopted from time to time, and people with less than adequate qualifications were licensed to teach. In some instances, especially in distant provinces, teachers who were only qualified to teach in elementary schools have been allowed to teach in orta schools, and even in lises, where by law they are supposed to be graduates of a university or an equivalent institution. At the lise level, many teachers assume teaching responsibilities for which they have no preparation or experience. A study by Jemal Mihchioglu records that in the 'outer provinces' retired artillery majors taught physics, officers in the gendarmery taught literature, chemists in sugar factories taught chemistry, and in one lise (at Kars) at least nine elementary school teachers taught sections in orta and lise schools. This author attributed the poor record of these schools in the university entrance examinations

[26] See, for example, Maynard, *op. cit.*, pp. 255-7, 311 ff.

to such practices and to overcrowded classrooms.[27] Of course, success or failure in school or university examinations may also be related to other factors (socio-economic background, conditions under which a student studies, etc.), but in view of the standard of the university entrance examinations, satisfactory performance could hardly be expected from candidates taught by teachers who have had what for all practical purposes is a lise-level school training. Likewise, the quality of instruction in the middle schools must suffer when at least 38 per cent of the teachers have an educational background of a normal school or less.

It could also be hypothesized that the quality of teaching suffers because of certain rules and regulations governing recruitment, appointments, promotions, tenure, salaries, and transfers of teachers. In Turkey, all teachers are members of the civil service, and as such their professional status is minutely regulated by the central authority. As civil servants, teachers are on the same salary scale as all other members of the civil service. The step in the salary scale at which a teacher starts depends on his education: for example, a primary school teacher who has graduated from a 'normal school' starts at step thirteen (the next to the lowest), which in 1959 meant a monthly salary of 350 Turkish liras (about $40); the beginning monthly salary of a secondary school teacher who has graduated from a two-year teacher institute is 400 Turkish liras (about $45, representing just one step above the primary school teacher); and a teacher who has graduated from a four-year university course starts at step eleven which means a monthly salary of 450 Turkish liras (about $50). This beginning salary pattern applies uniformly to all teachers throughout Turkey, except that if a person has demonstrated, by passing an examination, that he is proficient in one foreign language, he is entitled to a step higher than the one for which he is originally qualified.

A teacher is considered for promotion after a specified number of years in the service. This is done at the end of every three years, and his eligibility for promotion is based on the reports of his superiors in the school system, that is, principals

---

[27] Jemal Mihchioglu, *Universiteye Girish Sinavlarinin Yeniden Düzenlenmesi* (Ankara: Sevinch Matbaasi, 1962), pp. 81–5.

and inspectors. Recommendations for promotion seem to be automatic, but actual promotions depend on the availability of positions within the various ascending steps. Promotion means moving one step higher in the salary scale; sometimes teachers may receive the salary associated with a certain step, but not the rank.[28]

Uniformity in salary emoluments and the step-by-step system of promotions, which is based more on years of service than on meritorious performance, may in one sense be construed as equalitarian; but the effects of these policies on ambitious and highly capable teachers, or on the types of individuals who would consider entering teaching might be questioned. Moreover, centralized control of appointments and transfers (a teacher may be arbitrarily placed or transferred to any region of Turkey) often adds to the lack of enthusiasm on the part of interested and capable individuals, especially women, to become teachers. In conversation with several girls in urban lises, this writer was informed that, although the girls liked teaching, they did not plan to enter the profession for several reasons, chief of which seemed to be that they felt they could not 'be safe' outside the big metropolitan centres; and even if they were prepared to take up an assignment away from these centres or from home, their parents would not allow them to do so. The possibility of being appointed or transferred to a remote town in Eastern Anatolia also seems to be a factor which discourages young men from choosing teaching as a career. In addition to these considerations, the low salaries and the bleak possibilities of advancement render the problem of recruiting competent teachers more difficult; it also results in many resignations from the service.

The teacher's task becomes quite onerous and the quality of his teaching is likely to suffer from the heavy demands made upon his time, the size of classes, and the physical environment within which he is forced to perform his services. Teachers are overburdened by extracurricular activities and grading of examinations; and they often find themselves in poorly equipped and overcrowded classrooms. In several schools visited by the writer, it was not uncommon to find sixty, eighty, or more students squeezed together in threes or fours on benches fit

[28] Maynard, *op. cit.*, pp. 73–8.

only for two. A constant complaint of teachers and administrators was that classes were too big for any good teaching or learning to take place; and sometimes schools operate in double shifts.

Although data on the subject are insufficient, all available information suggests that, taking the whole educational system into consideration, the quality of instruction in the Turkish schools leaves much to be desired. This was also one of the major points stressed quite often by the Turkish National Commission on Education under the chairmanship of Fahir Iz, a distinguished professor of Istanbul University. The general criticism made by this commission was that the schools of Turkey 'are unable to prepare children adequately for life', and that, 'socially, culturally and economically', education was 'not functional'. More specifically, the report noted that the quality of teaching, the teachers, and the physical facilities would have to be greatly improved if Turkey was to attain the level of development and Westernization to which it aspired.[29]

[29] *National Commission Report, op. cit.*, pp. 24, 47 ff.

CHAPTER VII

EDUCATIONAL EXPANSION AND
OPPORTUNITIES

THE new Turkish leaders adopted as their policy not only the modernization of the structure of the educational system and the curriculum, but also the expansion of educational opportunities. They believed that the spread of knowledge and the development of new skills and habits of thought held the key to economic and political development as well as to the solution of many social evils. According to Atatürk, 'the most important real guide to life, success and civilization is science and knowledge'.[1] In view of the republic's commitment to the spread of education and to the expansion of educational opportunities for all segments of the population, it is necessary to examine the progress made in this direction and to assess the record to date. Such an inquiry acquires added significance when it is remembered that students of modernization have observed that the expansion of education, in terms of amount and level of schooling available for the relevant school age cohorts, is related to the stage of development of a country. Accordingly, a look will be taken at the growth of the educational enterprise and the extent to which certain traditional geographical and socio-economic factors continue to play an important part in educational attainment and in the opportunities available for the population.

---

[1] Enver Ziya Karal, *Atatürk'ten Düshünjeler* (Ankara: Dogus, Ltd., Shti. Matbaasi, n.d.), p. 80.

GROWTH AND PRESENT SIZE OF THE EDUCATIONAL ENTERPRISE

During the last decades of the Ottoman period, the number of children attending schools was extremely small, and there were glaring disparities in the general diffusion of education. In sheer numbers, the growth of education under the republic has been quite spectacular (see Table I). In 1923, there were only 336,000 persons enrolled in primary schools; about forty years later, enrolments soared to over three million. The growth of the middle, the lise, the vocational, and the higher levels of education was even more dramatic. Enrolments in the lise in particular have grown proportionately more than in any other type of school (the increase was approximately 88 times more). Interestingly, increases at the post-primary level were considerably higher than those at the primary level. It would appear that the Ottoman tuba agaji theory of education continued to be a motivating factor even after the demise of the Ottoman Empire.

Over-all enrolments in the primary schools increased steadily throughout the forty-year period, but relatively more so since 1955. The growth of the orta schools and the lises displayed more dramatic and uneven changes. In 1923, there were seventy-two middle schools and twenty-three lises; by 1935 the number of orta schools doubled, but that of the lises increased only to thirty-six. In that year, the Republican People's Party, the party in power, adopted the principle that an orta school be established in every kaza. This would have meant the creation of about 317 more orta schools. This goal, however, was not reached until the fifties. In 1950, when the Democratic Party came to power, the number of orta schools stood at 285, but in 1961–62, it soared to 694. Likewise, between 1949–50 and 1961–62 the number of public lises rose from 59 to about 139. Dramatic increases were registered after the year 1957–58, when, within a four-year period, 39 new lises were added.[2] There were similar uneven sharp increases

<hr />

[2] These figures were taken from statistics released by the Research and Measurement Bureau of the Ministry of Education and from the following: *1959 Istatistik Yilligi* (T. C. Bashbakanlik Istatistik Genel Müdürlügü) No. 380, pp. 157–9; and Richard E. Maynard, 'The Lise and Its Curriculum in the Turkish Educational Eystem' (Ph.D. dissertation, The University of Chicago, 1961), pp. 115, 184.

in the enrolments of these post-primary institutions: in the middle schools there was actually a decline between 1945 and 1950, but sharp increases followed, especially after 1955; and in the lises there was a most spectacular increase, between 1960–61 and 1962–63, of about 20,000 students.

We might look at the over-all expansion of education from different points of view. Between 1927–28 and 1960–61, the number of full-time students in all educational establishments below the universities rose from 497,300 to 3,396,857 (see Table II). In the former year about 4 per cent of the total population attended school, but in the latter, 12·0 per cent did so; and although the percentage of the total population in primary schools increased about two and one-half times, that in secondary schools rose by about three and one-half times. In 1935, an estimated 18 per cent of children between the ages of six and eighteen attended schools, but twenty years later the percentage rose to 44 (see Table III). Taking an age range from six to fourteen years, about 44 per cent of the children were at school in 1955, this figure being double that of twenty years earlier. On the basis of gross population figures available for the year 1960, these percentages are estimated to have remained relatively the same as those of 1955.[3]

In order to assess more fully the progress in the expansion of education, certain other dimensions of the problem must also be considered, namely, the comparative growth of girls' and boys' education, the geographical distribution of education, the urban-rural developments, and so on. When attention is turned to these aspects of education, several noteworthy features may be discerned. School attendance on the part of girls has consistently lagged behind that of boys, although in terms of percentages the increases have been greater. For example, in 1923–24, there were only 63,000 girls attending public and private elementary schools; but in 1961–62, the number rose to slightly over 1,200,000, while the corresponding figures for boys were 273,000 and slightly over 2,000,000. Disparities in boy–girl enrolments have been greater at the post-elementary levels of education: in 1924–25, enrolments according to sex in the orta schools were: 8,000 boys, and 2,000 girls; in 1961–62,

---

[3] See also Jefferson Eastmond, *Availability and Efficiency of Schools in Turkey* (Ankara: Research and Measurement Bureau, 1964), No. 3, p. 23.

the figures in the public schools were 244,500 and 72,000 respectively. Stated in different terms: of the total number of children attending middle schools or lises, only about 23 per cent are girls.

However, the greatest disparities in the growth and present status of the educational enterprise are evident in the geographical distribution of education. The progress and the present diffusion of education varies markedly from province to province. For example, in the province of Van, in the eastern part of Turkey, enrolments in the public elementary schools from 1953–54 to 1959–60 increased from 6,000 to 8,000, but in the province of Ushak, in the western part of the country, the increase was from 16,000 to 23,500; and yet, according to the 1960 census, Van had a population of 211,034, and Ushak, 184,733. The same two provinces registered sharp differences in orta school enrolments during the same period: in Van, in 1953–54, there were 74 students attending public orta schools which were not attached to lises; in 1959–60, the numbers rose to 267. But in Ushak, the figures for the two years were 97 and 1,000 respectively.[4] Provincial variations in the provision of primary and secondary education are illustrated in Table IV.

Table IV also shows what percentages of the total population of each province enrolments in the elementary schools represent. The disparities are obvious. If these percentages are compared with those for Turkey as a whole (about 10 per cent as shown in Table II), at least twenty-five provinces fall short of the national average, and only fourteen register percentages of eleven and above. Indeed, in ten provinces the figures are 5 per cent and less.

Similar variations are seen in the urban–rural dimension. It should be remembered that Turkey was and continues to be predominantly a rural country. According to the 1960 census, about 68 per cent of the population lives in localities having 10,000 inhabitants and less; and of the rural population, a substantial percentage (about 40 per cent) live in

---

[4] The statistics were taken from *Milli Egitim Istatistikleri Ilk Ogretim 1953–1960* (Türkiye Jumhuriyeti Bashbakanlik Devlet Istatistik Enstitüsü Bashkanligi, 1963), Yayin No. 431, p. 152; and *Milli Egitim Istatistikleri Orta Ogretim 1953–1960* (Türkiye Jumhuriyeti Bashbakanlik Devlet Istatistik Enstitüsü Bashkanligi, 1963), Yayin No. 437, p. 182.

villages of five hundred inhabitants and less. Although, during the Ottoman period and the first years of the republic, many small towns and villages provided primary instruction, educational provision was largely concentrated in the urban areas. As late as 1935–36 there were fewer primary schools in villages than in cities and towns. In that year, only 26 per cent of village children of primary school age were attending schools, but among city children of the same age, 81 per cent did so. In 1957–58, however, the percentage of village children rose to 61, and that of city children, to 87.[5] By this time, a large number of village schools were constructed, largely as a result of a drive in the fifties. According to the National Commission on Education, there were 1,988 primary schools in towns and cities compared to 18,785 schools in villages.[6] In 1960, the estimated number of children attending primary schools in cities of 10,000 inhabitants and over represented 11 per cent of the total urban population (about 9 million); that of children in rural schools, 7·9 per cent of the total rural population (about 19 million).

As in over-all enrolments, there are urban–rural disparities, sometimes quite sharp, in the boy–girl enrolments. There has also been relatively little progress in the increase of the percentage of girls attending village schools in the last thirty years or so. Robinson has estimated that, of the total number of children registered in village primary schools in 1936–37, 31 per cent were girls; this percentage increased to 35 only in 1958–59. On the other hand, the percentage increase in urban schools during the same period was from 34 to 42.[7] In 1952, an American consultant found glaring variations in the percentage of village girls attending schools. Taking a sample of six provinces in different parts of Turkey, he estimated that, although in the province of Istanbul about 91 per cent of village girls attended schools, in that of Diyarbakir

[5] Maynard, *op. cit.*, p. 107. The same percentages were computed from figures given by *The Report of the Turkish National Commission on Education* (Istanbul: American Board Publication Department, 1961), p. 43. Hereafter cited as *National Commission Report*.

[6] *National Commission Report, loc. cit.*

[7] Richard D. Robinson, *The First Turkish Republic: A Case Study in National Development* (Cambridge, Mass.: Harvard University Press, 1963), p. 196.

only 17 per cent did so.[8] According to the latest figures available (1962–63), in only nine provinces is there a 45 per cent and over female pupil enrolment in rural elementary schools. In twenty-three provinces, the percentage of girls in such schools was 30 and less, and in three provinces (Adiyaman, Hakkâri and Mardin) it was less than 20. The average for Turkey as a whole was estimated to be 36 per cent.[9]

The sharpest urban–rural disparities, however, are evident in the orta schools and the lises. Almost all of these schools are located in towns and cities, and the students enrolled in them are predominantly urban in origin. In this study of the lise, 76 per cent of the boys and 92·5 per cent of the girls described themselves as 'urban' in origin. Not surprisingly, the percentages were higher for foreign-operated schools and lower for public lises (see Table VI). On another index, 91 per cent of the boys and 98 per cent of the girls indicated cities or towns as parental place of residence. Indeed 69 per cent of the boys and 87 per cent of the girls indicated 'this city or town' as parental place of residence (see Table VII). This means that the great majority of lise students come from localities of over 20,000 inhabitants, which represent only 18 per cent of the total population of Turkey. The heavy urban character of the lise student population is further evident by the fact that in 1962–63, about 38 per cent of total enrolments in public lises were in three provinces (Istanbul, Ankara and Izmir); and Istanbul alone provided about 18 per cent of these enrolments. Percentages are higher if other types of lises are included. Similarly, these three provinces enrol about 28 per cent of the total number of orta school students.[10]

In examining the growth of school enrolments, changes in vocational and technical education should also be considered. Table I shows that from 1923–24 to 1961–62 there was a twelvefold increase in the number of children attending vocational and technical schools of various kinds. The greatest spurt in the growth of this type of education clearly took place between the establishment of the republic and the accession

[8] Figures taken from Maynard, *op. cit.*, 108.

[9] Eastmond, *op. cit.*, p. 9.

[10] These percentages are based on figures given by Eastmond. *Ibid.*, pp. 37–40.

to power of the Democrats in 1950, particularly after 1935. This was largely due to a concerted effort by the government to strengthen technical and vocational training. Indeed, in 1942, 81 million liras were especially appropriated for that purpose. This, plus the fact that there was a liberal provision of government scholarships, explains the sudden increase from 24,000 students in 1940–41, to 54,000 students in 1945–46. After 1945, however, government scholarships were reduced and enrolments dropped, reaching a low of 49,000 in 1952–53, a figure which also included attendance in the teacher-training institutions. A renewed emphasis upon this type of education after 1955 resulted in substantial increases.[11] Nevertheless, in spite of the many government efforts to draw more students into vocational and technical institutions, progress in this direction has not been so encouraging as authorities had hoped. Relative to other types of post-primary education (the orta schools and the lises), progress in the technical and vocational branch of the educational system has lagged considerably.

EDUCATIONAL ATTAINMENT AND OPPORTUNITIES

Increases in over-all attendance give only part of the picture of a nation's educational enterprise and the progress, if any, that has been made over a period of time. Modernization or development and the establishment of a democratic, equalitarian polity, all of which have been explicit goals of Turkish leaders, are in some form or another related to several other facets of the educational system.

Students of modernization have, for example, identified level of educational attainment, in terms of amount of schooling achieved by the population, as an index of economic development and of stability in political institutions. Likewise, the extent to which opportunities for different amounts and types of education are available to all the youth in the society, regardless of their ethnic, geographical, and socio-economic

[11] See *Mesleki ve Teknik Ogretim Müesseseleriyle ilgili Rakamlar* (T. J. Milli Egitim Bakanligi [Ankara: Bengi Matbaasi, 1961]), p. 16; and *Milli Egitim Istatistikleri Meslek, Teknik ve Yuksek Ogretim, 1953–1960* (T. J. Bashvekalet Devlet Istatistik Enstitüsü, 1963), Yayin No. 438, p. 3. The inflated figures given by these two sources are explained by the fact that they include enrolments in the elementary teacher training institutions.

backgrounds, has been found to be associated with 'stages' or 'levels' of development. Finally, and equally important in modern democratic polities, a host of qualitative factors bear upon this and related problems. To what extent, for example, does the quality of instruction in the schools match, surpass, or fall short of amount of schooling? Does the school develop the spirit of inquiry, of free thought and expression, or a 'scientific' or rational way of looking at man, his environment, and nature? This section will deal with questions bearing upon the first two facets, namely, educational attainment and opportunities for education.

The previous figures on educational expansion belie the very crucial problem of the holding power of the schools. The rate of attrition or of drop-outs has been a persistent major problem in Turkish education. Statistical estimates in this, as indeed in most other aspects of education, must be approximate and liable to error. But there is high consensus that the rates of attrition are very high. From one of the earliest studies on school attendance, progress in the attrition rate in the primary schools during the first decade of the republic may be inferred. In 1927–28, 45 per cent of all children in primary schools were enrolled in the first grade; this percentage dropped to only 42 in 1934–35. The percentage ratios in each of the four other grades in the latter year were: second grade, 24; third grade, 18; fourth grade, 10; and fifth grade, 6·5.[12] Another study estimated that, of the students who were registered in the first grade in 1933–34, only 33 per cent graduated five years later, in the spring of 1938.[13] Looking at more recent figures,[14] the following estimates have been made: of the total number of students (572,905) registered in the first grade of public primary schools in 1953–54, only 45 per cent (255,978) were enrolled in the fifth grade in 1957–58, and only 40 per cent received a graduating diploma from a five-year school. For the same period, there were great rural–urban and boy–girl

[12] Donald E. Webster, *The Turkey of Atatürk: Social Process in the Turkish Reformation* (Philadelphia: The American Academy of Political and Social Science, 1939), p. 214.

[13] Maynard, *op. cit.*, p. 109.

[14] Percentages were computed from statistics given in *Milli Egitim Istatistikleri Ilk Ogretim 1953–1960*, *op. cit.*, pp. 88–9; and from figures furnished by the Research and Measurement Bureau (mimeographed).

disparities. For example, of the total number of boys in the first class in 1953–54, 52 per cent were enrolled in the fifth grade in 1957–58, but of the girls, only 34 per cent reached the same grade. In urban shools, enrolments in the latter year represented 69 per cent of the original cohort, but in village schools, only 35 per cent. Taking the period from 1956–57 to 1960–61, the attrition rate has decreased: of the first grade children in all public schools in 1956–57, 50 per cent were in attendance in the fifth grade in 1960–61; that is, within a nine-year period, there was an increase in school longevity of 5 per cent. Furthermore, the increase in school longevity for girls was slightly higher than that for boys (6 per cent compared to 4·5 per cent).

The figures above indicate substantial progress since the first decade of the republic.[15] Nevertheless, the drop-out rate remains seriously high in a society aspiring towards modernity. This is rendered even more acute, considering: (a) that only about two-thirds of the primary school age population attend school at all, (b) that attrition is considerably higher in the rural areas, and (c) that attendance figures themselves are inflated because a substantial number of students fail in their examinations and remain in the same class.[16]

High attrition rates have also been characteristic of orta schools and lises. Maynard has estimated that, of students registered in the first class of the orta schools in 1933–34, 55 per cent graduated three years later; twenty years later (1954–55), only 47 per cent of those enrolled in the first class three years previously had graduated.[17] Basing present estimates on enrolments in all orta schools (public and private), calculations reveal that, of those in the first class in 1957–58 (98,440), 57 per cent (55,812) were registered in the third class

[15] Another index of the progress in this area is the percentage of all primary-school students who are able to obtain a diploma. According to statistics furnished by the Research and Measurement Bureau, over the period from 1920–29 to 1960–61, there was an increase of 5·5 per cent. to 10·44 per cent. *Ilkokularda Ogrenji Sayisi* (Ankara: Test ve Arashtirma Bürosu, 1961), p. 9.

[16] According to a recent study, over 25 per cent of the students in all the primary grades remain in the same class. See Turkan Ozgüven, *et al.*, *Türkiyede Resmi Ilk ve Ortaokullarla Liserlerde Sinifta Kalma Durumu* (Ankara: Test ve Arashtirma Bürosu, 1962), p. 4.

[17] Maynard, *op. cit.*, p. 131.

in 1959–60.[18] The school longevity in the case of public orta schools dropped from 61·5 per cent during the period 1953–56 to 57 per cent during 1958–61, but increased again to 61 per cent during 1959–62. However, the percentage of those who actually receive an orta school graduation diploma is considerably lower than the enrolments in the last orta class. For example, although 57 per cent of the 1957–58 cohort were enrolled in the third class in 1959–60, only 41 per cent of the original group actually received a diploma; and today, although approximately 60 per cent of first-year students may be able to reach the third orta grade, a smaller number do in fact earn a diploma.[19]

More so than in the primary schools, the attrition rate is lower among girls in the orta schools than among boys. For example, of the boys in the first class in 1959–60, 60 per cent were registered in the third class in 1961–62; but of the girls, 71 per cent reached the same level. The main reason for this variation could be that the socio-economic background of girls is generally 'better' than that of boys; hence, girls are able to stay at school longer, assuming, of course, that failure rates are the same for both sexes.

The drop-out rate is even higher in the lises. Maynard has estimated that, during the three-year periods (the normal lise course) from 1934 to 1943, the average percentage of first-year lise students who managed to pass the olgunluk examinations at the end of the third year of the lise was 42. Taking the period 1956–59, he calculated that only 36 per cent of the 1956–57 cohort passed the 'lise completion examination' in 1958–59.[20] As might be expected, a larger number of first-year students manage to reach the third lise class; but even so, the holding power of the public lise is low. For example, of the students enrolled in the first class in 1959–60 (27,928), only 50 per cent (14,179) were registered in the third class three years later. The figures were considerably higher among girls

[18] Percentages for middle schools were computed from statistics given in *Milli Egitim Istatistikleri Orta Ogretim, 1953–1960, op. cit.*, p. 4; and from tabulations of the Research and Measurement Bureau (mimeographed).

[19] Eastmond and his associates estimated that during the period from 1959 to 1962, 56·2 per cent 'graduated' from the orta schools. Eastmond, *op. cit.*, p. 14.

[20] Maynard, *op. cit.*, pp. 289, 304.

(3,777, or 67 per cent of the original group) than among boys (10,402, or 47·6 per cent),[21] perhaps for the same reasons as in the case of girls in the orta schools. Taking the same three-year period, Eastmond and the Research and Measurement Bureau have calculated that 45 per cent of the 1959–60 group 'graduated' (i.e., received a diploma) in 1961–62. Furthermore, in this study glaring variations were recorded from province to province: figures ranged from 100 per cent in the provinces of Mardin and Artvin, to 26·8 per cent in the province of Hatay. Indeed, in at least twenty-one provinces, the percentages were 40 and less, and no student has as yet graduated in the province of Diyarbakir.[22]

The foregoing analysis of the holding power of the schools is only one facet of educational attainment. On this index alone, the situation, although serious, does not seem to be hopeless, and the progress attained during the republic must not be underestimated. But the picture of educational opportunities and the extent to which children are able to ascend the educational ladder does not seem to be so encouraging, at least from the point of view of modernization, democratization, and development.

Today, somewhere between 65 and 75 per cent of all children of primary school age are enrolled in school. According to the Report of the Turkish National Commission on Education submitted in 1959, about one million, or about one-third, of the children of primary school age were not provided with 'schools and teachers'. The figures for village children were even higher (about 40 per cent).[23] Moreover, there were—and continue to be—great variations from province to province. There are regions, for example, where less than 30 per cent of the children attend schools. In 1962–63, an estimated one-third of all Turkish villages (35,537) were without any schools whatsoever.[24] Clearly, when this index and the previous one

[21] These percentages were computed from figures furnished by the Research and Measurement Bureau (mimeographed).

[22] Eastmond, op. cit., p. 15. No figures are given for the province of Diyarbakir. The lise in that province is a recent creation.

[23] National Commission Report, op. cit., pp. 43–4. The figures given by the Research and Measurement Bureau indicate that in 1960, 36·4 per cent of the children aged 6–10 were not attending school.

[24] Eastmond, op. cit., pp. 3, 33–5.

are taken into consideration, the constitutional provision that 'primary education is compulsory for all citizens, male and female',[25] seems to be more a dream than a reality.

Educational opportunities beyond the primary stage are even more limited. In the year 1959–60, the percentage of children of middle school age actually enrolled in middle-level schools was somewhere between 15 and 20 per cent; and in the same year, only 13 per cent of all children of secondary school age were enrolled in schools of corresponding level. From the approximate figures for 1963–64, it can be stated with a reasonable degree of accuracy that these percentages have remained constant.[26]

In Table VIII, numbers and percentage ratios of primary school graduates who entered orta schools and vocational schools at different periods since 1934–35 are given. Although a substantial proportion of such graduates entered middle-level institutions in 1935–36, in 1951–52, there was a considerable decrease.[27] By 1961–62, the percentage of primary school graduates who entered orta schools increased to 51 for boys, and 29 for girls. Unfortunately, exact figures for those who entered vocational and other schools for this year are not available. The National Ministry of Education gives the following data for 1959–60: 45 per cent of the boys and 25 per cent of the girls entered orta schools; 4 per cent of the boys and 6·5 per cent of the girls entered vocational and technical schools; and the rest entered 'other schools' or 'did not continue their education'.[28] Since 'other schools' does not include much, it could be concluded that the overwhelming number in the last category 'did not continue their education'.

Table IX shows numbers and percentages of orta school graduates who entered lises and lise-level vocational or technical schools over a period of time. In the mid-thirties, about 70 per cent of such graduates continued their education in the

[25] *Constitution of the Turkish Republic*, trans. Sadik Balkan, Ahmet E. Uysal, and Kemal H. Karpat (Ankara, 1961), Art. 50, p. 13.

[26] *1959 Istatistik Yilligi, op. cit.*, p. 157; Eastmond, *op. cit.*, pp. 23, 36.

[27] See also Richard D. Robinson, 'An Analysis of Turkish Education' (International Bank for Reconstruction and Development, a working paper for the 1950 Economic Survey Mission to Turkey [typewritten, Ankara, 1950]), p. 21.

[28] *Mesleki ve Teknik Ogretim Müesseseleriyle ilgili Rakamlar, op. cit.*, p. 18.

lises and most of the rest, in other types of schools. In 1958–59 however, about 52 per cent entered lises and 25 per cent, vocational and technical schools. On the basis of rough estimates, the proportions today are even less.

The decrease in enrolments at different age and class levels may be illustrated in different terms. In the year 1959–60, 92 per cent of the six-year-old children were enrolled in the first primary grade, 19 per cent of the eleven-year-olds were enrolled in the first orta class, 10 per cent of the fourteen-year-olds attended the first lise class, and only 3 per cent of the sixteen-year-olds were registered in the highest lise class.[29] Once a student has managed to complete the lise successfully, it is virtually certain that he will continue his education in an institution of higher learning. Educational opportunity beyond the primary stage may be summarized in terms of the following estimates:

(a) Of 100 primary school students, about 10 can expect to enter an orta school, or about 13 can expect to enter an orta or another middle-level institution.

Of 100 primary school students, less than 3 can expect to enter a lise.

Of 100 primary school students, about 1 can expect to enter a university.

(b) Of 100 orta school students, about 26 can expect to enter a lise.

Of 100 orta school students, about 14 can expect to enter a university.

(c) Of 100 lise students, about 55 can expect to enter a university.

Of 100 lise students, about 86 can expect to enter an institution of higher learning.[30]

A Minaret Pattern of Educational Opportunity

Graphically, the Turkish system of educational attainment and opportunity may be likened to a minaret-shaped pattern: enrolments diminish steadily and substantially from the pri-

[29] *Ilk ve Orta Derejeli Okullarda Ogrenji ve Ogretmen Sayilari ile Ilgili* (Ankara: Test ve Arashtirma Bürosu, 1961), p. 7.

[30] These estimates were based on tabulations given by the Research and Measurement Bureau for the year 1961–62 (mimeographed). It is important to note that the proportion of children continuing their education in 1961–62 did not differ significantly from those ten years earlier, except in the number of children entering middle schools. Cf. Robinson, 'An Analysis of Turkish Education,' *op. cit.*, p. 21.

171

mary school to the university levels, and they are dramatically peaked and constricted at the summit (also see Figure B, Appendix A). A child's chances of continuing his education are clearly lowest at the primary–middle rung of the educational ladder and highest at the lise–university one. One of the main reasons for this discrepancy lies in the urban–rural differences in educational provision and the socio-cultural variations associated with them. Middle schools and lises are essentially urban schools. The large number of village school children find it difficult to avail themselves of any opportunities for a middle school education. Many such children live in very isolated villages away from towns or cities and without any frequent or easy means of transport to and from places with middle schools. Leaving the village to go to a town or city presents the peasant child with almost insurmountable obstacles. More often than not, such a child comes from a very poor home, which means that neither he nor his parents can afford the luxury of sending him away to school. In the first place, they may not even have the money for his fare, let alone for his support; and in the second, they may not be able to afford to forego the economic benefits of an extra hand on the land. Studies of Turkish villages indicate that child labour is an important aspect of the economic activity of the village. Boys become 'helpful elements' at the age of seven, and by the time they are nine or ten years old they start working by themselves; girls do so at ten or twelve.[31]

Important as such constraining factors are they do not, in and of themselves, provide a sufficient explanation for the relatively small number of village children who continue their education beyond the primary level. Observers of the Turkish scene have frequently commented on the villagers' lack of appreciation for an extended period of schooling or for any schooling at all. In his study of Hasanoglan, an unusual village in terms of level of literacy and economic activity, Ibrahim Yasa wrote that the poorer peasants scorned at the intangible results of schooling. 'According to such families,' Yasa observed,

[31] Nermin Erdentug, *A Study of the Social Structure of a Turkish Village* (Ankara: Ayyildiz Matbaasi, 1959), pp. 45–7; and Ibrahim Yasa, *Hasanoglan: Socio-Economic Structure of a Turkish Village* (Ankara: Yeni Matbaa, 1957), p. 145.

'the boys will sooner or later learn to read and write in the army, and the girls need not know at all.' He added that 'most of the village families are not yet aware of the meaning of education. To them, gardening, digging a ground toilet, ploughing a field are activities which have nothing in common with education.'[32] Another writer, well acquainted with Turkish village culture, noted that 'village children have little motivation to go into town to school. It is not within the village pattern of behavior for them to do so. Normally, the village child graduates from a primary school in his or a neighboring village and then reverts to the traditional pattern of village life. In village eyes, he is "educated". That is enough.'[33] Maynard quotes the answer given a member of Parliament who had asked the inhabitants of a village what they wanted from the government most. The villagers' reply was, 'Sir, take this school away from our village, and we will ask nothing of you. Because of it, our cows go astray, and our work does not progress.'[34] Yet, as Maynard quickly adds, there are cases where villagers are anxious to build schools and provide more opportunities for the education of their children, but are handicapped by the costs involved and by the limited facilities of existing educational establishments.

In contrast to village children, those in urban areas have considerably better opportunities to continue their education. Although data on the social composition of orta school students is lacking, it could be inferred with good reason that the greatest majority of such children come from towns or cities, and that, socio-economically, they are a select group. Turning to the lise students, it was found that they are overwhelmingly urban in origin, and, even within the 'urban' category, they are recruited from relatively large towns and cities. As to the socio-economic background of this group, the study revealed some noteworthy characteristics, which are presented in greater detail in Chapter X. Suffice to mention here that about 40 per cent of the students in the public lises and about 52 per cent in the private Turkish lises have fathers classified as professional, high technical, managerial, high and low administrative,

---

[32] Yasa, *loc. cit.*
[33] Robinson, 'An Analysis of Turkish Education,' *op. cit.*, pp. 21–3.
[34] Maynard, *op. cit.*, p. 63.

and clerical; and yet these occupational categories constitute only 5·6 per cent of the male population of Turkey! This shows that the lise group is not only urban; it is also a rather socially select group. Furthermore, over 30 per cent of the students in all four types of lises are drawn from the categories of private traders, small business men, small farmers, fishermen, and the like, who constitute over 70 per cent of the male labour force. This indicates that, although the lise is a socially selective institution, it is by no means exclusively an elite school. Yet, taken in conjunction with the urban–rural variable it also shows that the children of urban traders, small business people, and such, have decidedly greater chances for a lise education than their rural counterparts.

Literacy and Educational Level of the Population

In concluding this section, it is relevant to refer to two other aspects of the Turkish educational enterprise, namely, (a) literacy, and (b) the educational attainment of the population at large.

When Turkey attained nationhood in 1923, its population was overwhelmingly illiterate. According to the earliest available statistics, 89·4 per cent of the total population could neither read nor write in 1927. Illiteracy was higher among women than men (96·0 per cent in the case of women), and in localities with less than ten thousand inhabitants. Increase in the rate of literacy since that time has been a major objective of the republic and was one of the motivating factors behind Atatürk's reform of the alphabet, the expansion of elementary education, and the several other programmes aimed at elevating the general educational level of the people. A population literate in 'Turkish' was considered necessary for building the new nation and developing a new national consciousness. Hence, a major preoccupation of the Turkish educational reformers has been to show statistically that more and more children were attending schools, and by implication, that more and more people were literate.[35]

By 1935–36, the literacy rate had almost doubled that of 1927 and stood at 20·4 per cent of the population. But the progress in subsequent decades, although significant in relation

[35] Robinson, 'An Analysis of Turkish Education,' p. 13.

to what it had been, has by no means been spectacular. In 1945–46, the proportion of literates was increased to about 30 per cent, and in 1955–56, to 40 per cent. But according to the latest census, it actually dropped to 39·6 in 1960.[36] The 1960 figures not only show that Turkey's level of literacy is low—and apparently declining from the peak reached in 1955 —they also reveal glaring disparities which have important implications for social, political, and economic development. Three such disparities are noteworthy: sex, urban–rural, and regional. As in the past, literacy is higher among males than females and among urban dwellers than among rural ones. For example, the estimated percentages, based on the 1 per cent sample in the 1960 population census, were as follows: among males, 54·5 per cent were classified as literate, compared to only 25·2, among females; of the percentage of literate males, 21·9 resided in localities having ten thousand or more inhabitants and 32·5, in places with less than ten thousand inhabitants; but of the percentage of literate females, only 12·2 resided in urban centres (i.e., places with ten thousand and more inhabitants). Stated differently: of 100 literate persons, 69 are male and 31 female; of the 69 literate males, 28 are urban and 41 are rural; but of the 31 literate females 15 are urban and 16 rural. These figures become more meaningful when it is remembered that about 70 per cent of the Turkish population is rural.

Glaring disparities are evident when literacy according to province is considered. In the province of Istanbul, the most literate of the sixty-seven provinces, 73·4 per cent of the population six years of age and older was able to read and write; but in the province of Hakkâri, only 11·5 per cent of this age group had equivalent literacy skills. Twenty-eight provinces, including all of those in the south-east region and most of those in the Black Sea and the east central regions, had literacy rates of less than 30 per cent in the age group six years and above. Indeed, the provinces of the south-east region

[36] The figures for 1960 are taken from Jefferson N. Eastmond, *Educational Attainment in Turkey* (Ankara: Research and Measurement Bureau, 1964), pp. 3–12; and *1960 Genel Nüfus Sayimi (1960 Population Census of Turkey: Estimated National Totals Based on 1% Sample;* T. C. Devlet Istatistik Enstitüsü [Ankara, 1962]).

registered a literacy rate of less than 20 per cent. Only the province of Istanbul had a literacy rate of over 58 per cent; and only sixteen provinces have registered any increase in literacy since 1955, such increases being quite insignificant.

The level of literacy might also be looked at in terms of variations among age groups. A comparison between the 1955 and the 1960 Census Reports shows that there was a general decrease in literacy in every age group, except that between fifteen and twenty-four years of age (this group registered an increase from 50·8 per cent in 1955 to 53·1 per cent in 1960). At the other extreme, the six-to-fourteen age group—the most important school-age group—registered the greatest decline (48·7 per cent in 1955 as against 43·3 per cent in 1960). The most literate male age group in Turkey is that between the ages of twenty and twenty-four (of 100 persons in this group, about 70 are literate). Among females, on the other hand, those between the ages of ten and fourteen were the most literate. Looking at all age groups, there was a consistently higher ratio of literates among urban dwellers than among rural ones. One of the main reasons for the only increase since 1955, namely, that of the male population between the ages of fifteen and twenty-four and the relatively high number of literates in the twenty to twenty-four age group, might be sought in the literacy training programmes in the armed forces. Military service in Turkey has been, and continues to be, an important avenue among the population, especially the rural one, for the development of basic literacy skills and for social and occupational mobility.

Although literacy figures in Turkey indicate progress since the beginning of the Turkish Republic, they highlight a state of affairs which, for purposes of development and the proper functioning of democracy, is 'shocking and calls for immediate and emergency action'.[37] This situation is rendered more serious when it is remembered that literacy in Turkey is gauged from answers given to the question 'Can you read and

[37] Eastmond, *Educational Attainment in Turkey, op. cit.*, p. 11. Although empirical data are lacking, impressionistic accounts and personal observations suggest that there is a relationship between the level of literacy and indices of modernization. This statement is also based on conversations with members of a group which has recently completed an extensive study on the Turkish villages.

write?' Often a person who is able to scrawl his name is considered 'literate'. Hence, even the low ratios presented above must be interpreted as considerably inflated. An indication of a more meaningful level of literacy might be the educational level attained by the population. In 1950, Robinson estimated that the number of persons who had completed primary school could not have been more than two million, a figure which represented only about 15 per cent of the entire population. According to the same writer, the maximum estimate that could be made for those who were literate 'to a point which makes any difference to themselves or to their community' was probably 20 per cent.[38] The 1960 figures show that this percentage had not changed over the ten-year period. Taking Turkey as a whole, 15 per cent of the population completed five years of schooling; and a bare 2 per cent of the total population had eight years of schooling. As in the case of the 'read and write' criterion, there were glaring variations from province to province on the five-year schooling index: these ranged from 29 per cent in Istanbul, to just 1·0 in Yozgat. At least thirty provinces registered percentages of 10 and less! Of the economically active population, only about 32 per cent of the males and 8 per cent of the females had completed an elementary school.[39]

TURKEY AND OTHER COUNTRIES: SOME COMPARATIVE FOOTNOTES

This chapter has focused mainly on the quantitative aspects of education in Turkey. Some of these facets of the Turkish educational enterprise will now be viewed in comparison to other countries which represent various stages of development and cultural background. Since Turkey has identified itself with nations classified as Western and 'democratic', comparisons with such nations become particularly meaningful in assessing the extent to which Turkey has approached Western standards. Moreover, since Turkey has adopted modernization and industrialization as its goal, comparisons with modern and

---

[38] Robinson, 'An Analysis of Turkish Education,' op. cit., p. 18.
[39] Eastmond, Educational Attainment in Turkey, op. cit., p. 4; and 1960 Genel Nüfus Sayimi, op. cit., p. 33.

industrialized societies also help to evaluate the success of the Turkish policy. Accordingly, comparisons will first be made only with advanced societies. England, France, and the United States have been chosen as representative of Western, advanced, democratic countries, and the Soviet Union and Japan, as non-Western, industrial, advanced nations. Data have been drawn from UNESCO sources to ensure uniformity; but it should be pointed out that they are liable to error, as are most statistics furnished by Ministries of Education.[40]

Of the six countries examined (the five above and Turkey), Turkey has registered the greatest increase in primary school enrolments (ages five to fourteen) during the period 1930–34 to 1959–60. The percentage increase in Turkish enrolments was 400, while that of the other countries was: France, 17; United States, 34; USSR, 44; and Japan, 18. Turkey, as well as the Soviet Union, also registered the greatest increases in 'enrolment ratio' (i.e., the estimated mean population five to fourteen years of age over actual average school enrolments from 1930–34 to 1950–54). In the United States, France, and Japan, although over-all enrolments increased, there were slight decreases in enrolment ratios. These findings, however, should not be at all surprising—Turkey started almost from scratch, whereas the expansion of primary education in countries like the United States, England, and Japan took place prior to 1930. Moreover, although the enrolment ratio in Turkey increased substantially, only 33 per cent of the children of the five-to-fourteen age group were actually enrolled in a school; that of all the other countries was over 60 per cent.

Although the UNESCO figures for secondary school enrolments are not so uniform as those of primary schools, some observations on the relative trends in the six countries can still be made. Between 1930 and 1960 over-all secondary school enrolments have increased more than 50 per cent in all these countries, with Japan and Turkey clearly registering the highest per-

---

[40] All the data for this part of the comparative analysis are drawn from *World Survey of Education*, Vol. II, Primary Education (UNESCO, 1958); *World Survey of Education*, Vol. III, Secondary Education (UNESCO, 1961); and *Current School Enrollment Statistics* (UNESCO, September, 1962). Full tabulations are presented in A. M. Kazamias and B. G. Massialas, *Tradition and Change in Education: A Comparative Study* (Englewood Cliffs, N. J.: Prentice-Hall, Inc., 1965), pp. 145 ff.

centage increases (Japan, 776 per cent, and Turkey, 736 per cent). Likewise, during the period 1930–57, enrolment ratios in all countries increased, with Japan, France, and the United Kingdom showing the highest increases. Educational provision was lower in Turkey than in any of the other countries, more so in secondary than primary education. The enrolment ratio for Turkey—the estimated total age group (ages fifteen to nineteen) over actual enrolments—was only 12 in 1955–57; in Japan it was 98; in England, 88; in the United States, 73; and in the Soviet Union, 36.

Turning to the relative distribution of female students in the total school population, Turkey lags considerably behind any of these countries. According to the UNESCO figures, although most of the other countries have attained parity of educational provision between sexes at the primary level, female enrolments in Turkey stood at 38 per cent in 1959–60.[41] In secondary schools, the figures for Turkey were even lower: only 25 per cent of the total secondary school population was girls in 1957; all other advanced societies had achieved parity of educational provision. Indeed, according to the same source, there has been no increase in the boy–girl ratio in the secondary schools of Turkey since 1930.

The differences in educational provision between Turkey and the more advanced countries are also reflected in the levels of literacy attained by the population. According to the 1963 figures, literacy rates, expressed in percentages of people fifteen years and over, were between 35 and 40 for Turkey, but they were almost 100 for all the above-mentioned countries.[42]

In his study, *Political Man*, Seymour Martin Lipset found that there is a positive relationship between stable democracies and such variables as urbanization, literacy, and the numbers per thousand of persons enrolled in various levels of educational establishments. The questions of stability in democracies and the level of political modernization are very complex matters, and statements should be made with a great deal of caution. In order to assess more precisely 'political modernity'

[41] This proportion was slightly higher than Tanganyika and approximately the same as Egypt, but definitely higher than Iraq and Afghanistan.

[42] *Population Information for 127 Countries* (Population Reference Bureau, Information Service [Washington, D.C., October, 1963]).

and 'democratic stability' reliable data are needed on such questions as popular political involvement, the extent to which decision-making is based on rationality, 'structural differentiation', the degree of political consensus and the mechanisms through which change takes place, the existence of an opposition, and so on. Yet, if European stable democracies are compared with Turkey on the basis of Lipset's indices, Turkey seems to have a long way to go to attain anything approximating a stable democratic polity. On the index of urbanization, in European stable democracies, 43 per cent of the population resides in cities of twenty thousand persons and over; in Turkey, only 18 per cent does so. Also, in the former, 38 per cent lives in metropolitan areas; in Turkey, only 11 per cend lives in comparable localities. Turning to education, Lipset found that in European stable democracies enrolment per 1,000 persons was as follows: primary, 134; post-primary, 44; and higher education enrolment, 4·2. In 1960, the estimated Turkish figures were: primary, 100; post-primary, 15; and higher education, 2·2. Regarding literacy, for the European stable democracies it was 96 per cent, but for Turkey it was 39·6.[43]

The editors of a recent study on *Political Modernization in Japan and Turkey* give statistical socio-economic indices and, viewing the two countries in qualitative terms, suggest the hypothesis that there is approximately a forty-year gap—and in a number of instances a gap of more than forty years— between 'the performance characteristics of the two polities'. One instance of a more-than-forty-year gap is the enrolment ratio of school children and the percentage of university students per 1,000 persons. As far back as 1918, 98·8 per cent of Japanese children of school age were enrolled in school, but in 1959, only 42·0 per cent of the Turkish children of comparable age were attending schools. And in 1920, the proportion of Japanese students attending universities was 39 per 1,000 of the population; in 1960, only 2·3 per 1,000 of Turks did so.[44]

[43] Seymour Martin Lipset, *Political Man* (New York: Anchor Books, 1963), pp. 37–8. The computations for Turkey were made from figures already cited.

[44] Robert E. Ward and Dankwart A. Rustow (eds.), *Political Modernization in Japan and Turkey* (Princeton: Princeton University Press, 1964), pp. 436–7.

In *Education, Manpower, and Economic Growth*, Harbison and Myers provide us with a list of 'indicators of educational development' in most of the countries of the world, which forms the basis of an analysis of relationships between education and economic development. Some of these 'indicators' or 'measures', which characterize different countries at various 'stages of development', are particularly relevant here. One such measure is the enrolment ratio at the first level of education (i.e., the total primary school enrolments as a percentage of the estimated population between the ages of 5 and 14). Other relevant indicators are: (a) enrolment ratios (adjusted) for first and second levels of education, that is, for primary and secondary schools, (b) per cent of estimated population aged fifteen to nineteen enrolled in secondary-level educational establishments, and (c) per cent of estimated population aged twenty to twenty-four enrolled in higher educational institutions. Turkey, according to these indices, falls within the 'partically developed' category, namely, the Level II countries on a four-level classification (under-developed—Level I; partially developed—Level II; semi-advanced—Level III; and advanced—Level IV). On all four measures, Turkey is far below the five 'advanced' societies mentioned earlier. On two measures (primary and primary-plus-secondary enrolment ratios), it is even lower than the mean of twenty-one countries classified as 'partially developed', which include, among others, Iran, Lebanon, Iraq, Pakistan, Tunisia, Ghana, Libya, Peru, and Jamaica. The means for all twenty-one countries are: first level enrolment ratio, 42; first and second level (adjusted), 45; second level (adjusted) 12·4; and third level, 1·6. The enrolment ratios for Turkey are 37, 42, 14·2 and 2·6 respectively. On all four indices, Turkey is below Cuba, Egypt, Greece, Italy, Chile, Portugal, Yugoslavia, Thailand, and others, all of which are classified as Level III (semi-advanced) countries.[45]

There are some other facets, examined in this chapter, of the Turkish educational enterprise which would help place the findings within an international context as furnished by

[45] Frederick Harbison and Charles A. Myers, *Education, Manpower, and Economic Growth: Strategies of Human Resource Development* (New York: McGraw-Hill Book Company, 1964), pp. 24–48.

Harbison and Myers. These writers found that: in 'partially developed' socities, there is high wastage or attrition at the various rungs of the educational ladder; educational provision in rural areas is more restricted than in urban areas; and enrolments in academic secondary schools are disproportionately higher than in other schools of equivalent level.[46] As shown earlier, the Turkish educational system exhibits similar characteristics. On the other hand, Turkey's post-primary enrolment ratios seem to be relatively higher than the ratios of other countries at comparable 'levels of advancement'. In the past five years or so, there has been a sudden upsurge in enrolments in middle and secondary schools, one which is relatively greater than that in the elementary schools. If, therefore, the index of relative increase in school attendance is taken, the problem in Turkey is not so much a question of quantitative provision (although compared to the more advanced societies this is also the case), as a question of qualitative improvement, and a more balanced distribution in terms of school types and curriculum training.

In this chapter evidence, mostly of a quantitative nature, has been marshalled on the developments and present status of the Turkish educational enterprise. Turkey has also been placed within some sort of comparative framework. But it should be stressed that the relation between education and general modernization or economic development involves more than quantitative expansion or educational provision. The qualitative dimensions of this process must also be examined, namely, the quality of instruction, the learning outcomes, the ideological, social and psychological factors which regulate, constrain, or facilitate the processes of change, and so on.

The following chapters will take up some of these questions.

---

[46] *Ibid.*, pp. 78–81.

THE SCHOOLS AND ASPECTS OF SOCIO-CULTURAL CHANGE

PART THREE

THE SOCIOLOGICAL ASPECTS OF SOCIOCULTURAL CHANGE

CHAPTER VIII

THE SECULARIZATION OF EDUCATION
AND THE LAICIZATION OF RELIGION

IN THE Ottoman period, the Islamic religion was a unifying element in society and the very basis upon which the Ottoman State rested. Accordingly, religious schools and religious instruction in schools were unquestioned premises in the Ottoman theocratic ideology. Even Ziya Gökalp, the intellectual apostle of the new Turkish order, envisaged Islamic education as a basic ingredient of the education of Turkish youth. On the other hand, Atatürk and his fellow revolutionaries conceived of such an education as a stumbling block in the modernization of the new nation and as an integral part of the old order that must be stamped out. By a series of bold strokes, the theocratic edifice of the state had collapsed and with it all the supporting paraphernalia. In 1923, the Ministry of Education took over the administration and control of all religious schools and all their means of support (endowments and funds). In the same year, the teaching of religion was proscribed in all state schools. The abolition of the caliphate in 1924 was followed by the closing of all medreses and other separate religious schools, by the elimination of the august office of sheyhülislâm, and by the replacement of the Ministry of Religious Law with a Presidency of Religious Affairs under the prime minister. In 1928, Article 2 of the first Constitution of the Republic of Turkey, which had made Islam the state religion, was amended, providing for disestablishment; and in 1937 the principle of secularism was incorporated in the Constitution. In the meantime, the jurisdiction of the courts of the Sheriat had been taken over by lay, Western-modelled courts, and a Turkish Civil Code, a virtual replica of the Swiss Civil Code, had replaced the orthodox private Mohammedan laws. By 1930, what few secondary schools for religious leaders had survived went out of existence, and by 1933, the foundering Faculty of Theology of Istanbul University was also abolished.

As time passed, the new government took other steps to undermine religion in the society and its influence in education. In 1925, the wearing of the famous fez, a headgear originally borrowed from the West which had become an important symbol of the Moslemness of the Turk, was prohibited, and all men were compelled by law to wear European-type hats; at the same time, a ban was proclaimed against the wearing of religious garments or insignia by any person who did not hold a religious office and against the famed dervish orders. In 1934, the wearing of religious vestments of any kind by any member —including clergymen—of any faith was proscribed except when such persons were in holy places or were conducting religious ceremonies.

One of the most revolutionary and far-reaching steps towards the religious reorientation and re-education of the people was the 'language reform', namely, the change in the alphabet from Arabic to the Latin script. The romanization of the alphabet had pedagogical, cultural, nationalistic, and religious implications. Arabic was the language of the Koran, and the Arabic script symbolized the people's holy attachment to the Mohammedan religion. It was also the symbol which united the Moslem world and distinguished it from the world of the 'infidels'. To the revolutionaries, it was a potent medium which chained the minds of the people to the old order, to superstition, alien beliefs, and reactionary tendencies. Moreover, it was a cumbersome vehicle for purposes of instruction, especially for the re-education of the entire nation. The change in the alphabet was followed by a systematic attempt to expurgate the language of all Arabic and Persian accretions and to develop a purely Turkish medium of communication. An intensive campaign to instruct the nation in the reading and writing of the new script followed, and Atatürk himself became the 'chief instuctor of the School of the Nation'. In 1929, Arabic and Persian were prohibited as subjects in the curriculum of the secondary schools; and history books were rewritten, with major emphasis placed upon the ethnic background of the Turks and with exaggerated and dubious theories about their origins and influence in the world.

The Turkicization of the language and the laicization of religion were part of the general process of modernizing the society and of developing a sense of national belonging among the people. Every single aspect of reform was justified on nationalistic grounds and as a concerted effort to indicate that the Turks were, or had the potential to be, as cultured as any other nation of the world. Thus, for example, according to Atatürk, the fez 'sat on the heads of our nation as an emblem of ignorance . . . fanaticism and hatred of progress and civilization'; the various kinds of garments worn were neither 'national', nor 'international', nor indeed 'civilized', but the hat and other types of dress (boots, trousers, shirts, ties, jackets, etc.) were civilized, and their adoption would demonstrate to the world that the Turks were as civilized as others; the older laws, customs, and beliefs were 'the most insidious enemies of the revolutionaries'; and Turkish letters, instead of Arabic as well as their teaching, was 'a patriotic and national duty', and the best way by which 'our rich and harmonious language will now be able to display itself'.[1]

There is no question that the changes effected almost overnight were dramatic. In outward form, the face of the nation was almost totally transformed; a tradition and a structure reaching far back into the Middle Ages all but disappeared. But to what extent Atatürk had succeeded completely in secularizing the new nation, or indeed education and the minds of the people, is today not so clear as it may have seemed during the heyday of religious reform.

The issue of religion or the role of Islam in the new state was quite dormant until the forties. With Turkey's transition from a one-party to a multi-party system (from 1946 to 1950), religion again emerged as a political and cultural issue. The process of liberalizing restrictions on religion, imposed during the Atatürk regime through positivistic secularist policies, has continued up to the present. In the past twenty years or so, Turkey has been groping with the problem of readjusting its

[1] *Atatürk' ün Söylev ve Demechleri* (Ankara: Türk Tarih Kurumu Basimevi, 1959), II, 212–13.

democratic ideology and policies to the pressing demands for a more positive approach to Islam as an educational and social institution. Not unexpectedly, of course, the liberalization of religion became a political slogan for vote-getting, as religion was still an important part of the lives of the people, especially the villagers. Indeed, part of the strength of the Democratic Party, which was voted into power in 1950 and remained so until the Revolution of 1960, lay in its promises and policies concerning religion in schools and in the lives of the people. However, the revival of interest in religion was part of an ideological reaction against the strict secularism of the republic by a diverse group of individuals who felt that the moral basis of the society was being corroded and that the youth were being brought up in a moral vacuum. In a society which had deep roots in an Islamic past, it was natural that there would be open criticism of the restrictions imposed by the government once the lid was lifted and a more pluralistic approach to politics was being charted.

The form which the revived issue took varied. There were those who had a fond yearning for the religious and simple life of the past, and who felt that the modern secular society had lost some of the spiritual moorings so necessary for its survival. The intellectuals in this group claimed that Islam was not reactionary, that it was supportive of science and modern institutions. In language reminiscent of the position taken by advocates of the value of religious instruction in secular societies of the West, the 'conservatives' in Turkey have argued that Islam would elevate the moral standards of the youth and of society. For, after all, is not the ultimate aim of any educational system the creation of moral and responsible human beings? Moreover, this group has argued that religion would more effectively combat any 'leftist' tendencies in the society, and it would restore the strong family ties which were characteristic of Turkish society.

Another, more 'moderate', position has been espoused by people who wanted to liberalize religion by making it a matter of individual conscience and rights, without any planned proscriptions by the government. At the other extreme were the staunch secularists who stuck to the republican ideology, not because they opposed Islam, but rather because Islam went beyond matters of faith by regulating many other activities of the individual in the social and cultural domains. Islam was too dogmatic and reactionary as an institution and, hence, was inimical to the modernization and development of the country.[2]

The stands of the political parties on the issue of religion varied. The National Party adopted a pro-Islamic position and openly advocated religious instruction in schools; the Democratic Party favoured the moderate view; and the Republican Party, the party of Atatürk and the party in power until 1950, modified its traditional secularist position by accepting certain changes.

One of the first openly discussed questions was that of religious education. After a full-dress debate in the Grand National Assembly, in 1949, courses in Islam were permitted in the fourth and fifth classes of the elementary schools. At first, the courses in religion were to be optional and only for those children whose parents had requested such instruction. Since most parents had indeed asked for such courses, they soon became compulsory for all Moslem children in the fourth and fifth classes, except in cases where parents would ask in writing that their children be excused from attending them. For other children in the lower classes, such instruction remained optional. By 1950, the great majority of primary school children took the course in religious education.[3]

Two other developments in religious education during this period were significant. In 1949, a Faculty of Divinity was opened at the University of Ankara, under the control of the Ministry of Education. Government scholarships were provided for a large number of students. At about the same time, secondary schools for the training of religious leaders (imam hatib okullari) were re-established, with a six-year course following the elementary schools. By 1961–62, there were nineteen middle-level religious schools enrolling 4,400 students, seventeen lise-level schools with 1,200 students, and one higher Islamic institute with 220 students.

[2] For a fuller discussion of these viewpoints, see Kemal H. Karpat, *Turkey's Politics: The Transition to a Multi-Party System* (Princeton: Princeton University Press, 1959), pp. 271–8.

[3] Robinson informed the author that he had visited many villages in which no religious lessons were being offered; in every case they were Alevi or Shiite villages.

There have been several other indications of a religious revival since the post-war period. More mosques were built and attendance in them increased considerably. After the Democratic Party came to power, it allowed the *ezan* (the Moslem call to prayer) to be read in Arabic instead of Turkish, and excerpts from the Koran to be read on the radio. Arabic inscriptions from the prophet's sayings appeared in shops, cafés, and other public places; several religious pamphlets and books were published; the tombs of sultans, which, closed in 1925, were reopened; and a greater number of Moslems made the annual pilgrimage to Mecca. There was even some relaxation in the wearing of religious garb: religious functionaries were allowed to wear the beret, a social equivalent of the turban. More ominous in the eyes of some was the re-emergence of the mystical and popular *tarikat* (religious brotherhood), especially the order of the dervishes. In the field of education, acrimonious debate in the press and in the Shura raged around the inclusion of courses in religion in the middle schools, the lises, and other schools. In 1956, a one-hour weekly course in Islam was introduced into the first and second classes of the middle school, and religious instruction was allowed in the 'normal schools'. Since 1950, there has been a dramatic increase in special courses of approximately a year's duration in the reading of the Koran.[4]

Explanations and assessments of the renewed interest in religion and of its possible future significance, have been made with a great deal of caution. From the political standpoint, some see the movement for the liberalization of religion as a natural consequence of the development of 'democracy' and the multi-party system. This, together with what seemed to be a genuine interest to reform Islam itself by 'purifying' and 'modernizing' it, would be a salutary sign and would not jeopardize the progress towards modernization. Yet, as Karpat points out, the liberalization of Islam may have been premature, in view of the fact that secularism had not as yet penetrated deeply into the lives and thoughts of all the seg-

[4] For more details on these signs of an apparent religious revival see Bernard Lewis, *The Emergence of Modern Turkey* (London: Oxford University Press, 1961), pp. 410–18. See also Richard E. Maynard, 'The Lise and Its Curriculum in the Turkish Educational System' (Ph.D. dissertation, The University of Chicago, 1961), pp. 71–3.

ments of the population.[5] Others seem to discount the significance of this religious interest for the social and political
development of the country. Staunch secularists feel that the
religious movement was fanned by survivors of the Ottoman
past who had a sentimental attachment to tradition. They
argue that when this generation disappears, so will any reactionary religious tendencies. Bernard Lewis rejects this viewpoint, arguing that, despite some of the policies of the revolutionary government of Atatürk and the adoption of laicism
as one of the elements of the ideology of the republic, Islam
has continued to be deeply imbedded in the minds and lives
of the people, especially among the peasant masses. According
to Lewis, 'the deepest Islamic roots of Turkish life and culture
are still alive, and the ultimate identity of Turk and Muslim
in Turkey is still unchallenged'. Under such circumstances,
Lewis hopes that the Turks will find a workable compromise
between Islam and modernism; otherwise, if the reactionaries
gain ascendancy, there will be a regression and Turkey 'will
slip back into the darkness from which she so painfully
emerged'.[6]

There is some other evidence on the question of religion in
Turkey which might cast more light on any speculations about
the future or on statements concerning the progress of modernization. The few studies on Turkish villages that are available
indicate that among villagers, Islam continues to be a powerful
force in regulating the activities of life and in the system of
beliefs about reality, the family, the individual, education, and
even the state. In his detailed study of the social structure of a
central Anatolian village, Paul Stirling observed that 'villagers
refer directly to religious authority to support almost every
social rule'; that the state or the government 'is still thought of
as the ultimate religious authority'; and generally, that 'almost
every aspect of the social organization . . . is related directly
or indirectly to Islam'. Stirling concluded: 'It was my impression that for the villagers the most important characteristic
of their society, and the one most resistant to innovation was

[5] Karpat, *op. cit.*, pp. 288–9.
[6] Lewis, *op. cit.*, pp. 417–18. See also Frederick W. Frey, 'Turkey', in
Robert E. Ward and Dankwart A. Rustow (eds.), *Political Modernization in
Japan and Turkey* (Princeton: Princeton University Press, 1964), p. 223.

their allegiance to Islam, and since their beliefs cover so wide a social field, they constitute a powerful support for the whole social order.'[7] Pierce, an American cultural anthropologist, echoed the same idea: 'The villagers do not make a distinction, common to Americans and Europeans in general, between the religious and the secular. Islam is a way of life and is the dominant factor in the making of any decision, no matter how slight, in the mind of the villager.'[8]

On the other hand, some observers have found that, although there is still a strong attachment to Islam, there is also an acceptance of innovation, social change, machines, secular schools, and so on, and that the possibility of a religious conservative reaction to the secular state is doubtful. Rather, Robinson observed, the Anatolian 'was beginning to reposition his religion so as to be relevant to the modern world'.[9] Another writer reported that in Hasanoglan, the authority and prestige of the imam has diminished considerably in the past thirty years.[10]

In assessing the political or social significance of Islam among villagers, it must be remembered that this large segment of the Turkish population is still a 'non-mobilized' mass. Strong bifurcations still exist between the rural peasant group and the urban dwellers, and between an educated urban elite and an illiterate village population. Although the peasant groups possess the right to vote, and indeed a large percentage has voted in recent elections, the distance between the 'rulers' and the 'ruled' is still great, the latter for the most part accepting the policies and directions of the former, as in previous periods. Consequently, the future of Islam depends to a large extent on the attitudes of the urban population—the intelligentsia—and the elites: The situation of these segments of the population

[7] Paul Stirling, 'Social Structure of Turkish Peasant Communities' (mimeographed). On the influence of religion in regulating life in the villages, see also Mahmut Makal, *A Village in Anatolia*, trans. Sir Wyndham Deedes (London: Vallentine, Mitchell & Co., 1954).

[8] Joe E. Pierce, *Life in a Turkish Village* (New York: Holt, Rinehart and Winston, 1964), p. 87.

[9] Richard D. Robinson, *The First Turkish Republic: A Case Study in National Development* (Cambridge, Mass.: Harvard University Press, 1963), pp. 201–6.

[10] Ibrahim Yasa, *Hasanoglan: Socio-Economic Structure of a Turkish Village* (Ankara: Yeni Matbaa, 1957), p. 166.

also seems to be rather uncertain. Throughout the period of the republic, urban classes have been exposed to greater amounts of education and the positive-secularistic campaign of the revolutionary government. Since education has been used to sustain the revolutionary ideology, a stronger attachment to secularism among the urban (more particularly the urban educated classes), a weaker hold of orthodox Islam on their lives, or a synthesis between Islam and modernism might be expected. Unfortunately information on the religious attitudes of these groups is rather limited. But on the basis of what is available, it could be said that at least among the more highly educated urban groups, especially in cosmopolitan centres like Ankara, Istanbul and Izmir, the secular ideology of Atatürkism has taken strong roots. In a survey on the value systems of students in lise-level institutions (ages 15 to 18), Frey, Angell, and Sanay found a strong secularism. According to them, this important school population refers most readily 'to the tenets of the revolution and its conceptions of modernity, very seldom to religious values and principles'. For example, only 2 per cent of the sampled students would, as parents, try to teach religious values to their children; only 7 per cent mentioned religion as an activity which would satisfy them most; and a religious career was ranked very low in terms of prestige. The only time that the students showed pro-religious interests was when about 69 per cent of the group indicated that they felt 'some form of religious belief [was] necessary to a fully mature approach to life'.[11] Taking an even more select group (students at Robert College, Istanbul, and at the Faculty of Political Sciences of the University of Ankara), Hyman, Payaslioglu and Frey found an even weaker attachment to religious, in contrast to nationalistic, values. Only 1 per cent of these university students mentioned accomplishments in the area of religion as something that would bring them the greatest pride; an even lower percentage stated that they would consider 'loss of religious faith' as one of the two worst things that could conceivably happen to them; and religion ranked the lowest—lower than 'amusement and local citizenship activities'—on a rating of the importance of six sectors in life. Hyman and his associates found that 69 per cent

[11] Frey, op. cit., p. 226.

of the sampled students indicated that they considered some form of religious orientation or belief necessary for the attainment of 'a fully mature philosophy of life'. Particularly revealing, however, was that even among such a highly select and highly educated group, 14 per cent gave kismet as the person's probable cause of death, this answer being one of the top three reasons given. The authors resolve this seeming paradox by saying that 'some of the central precepts or philosophical content of traditional religion could well persist', even though certain religious *practices* 'might well conflict with other values'. Nevertheless, comparing the responses of Turkish university youths in these two institutions with Gillespie and Allport's findings among youths of other countries,[12] they concluded that 'the Turkish students are only slightly more religious than Americans, and considerably *less* religious than German and Italian youth. This in the last home of the Caliph!'[13]

Part of the recent study conducted by the present writer is also relevant to attitudes of the Turkish youth concerning religion. In a sample of over 5,000 students in four types of lises (public, private Turkish, minority and foreign) 'religious leader' was ranked very low (less than 1 per cent) as the 'most preferred occupation'. The ranking was lower (·3 per cent) among students in foreign-operated lises, and about the same in public and minority lises (1·2 and 1·3 per cent respectively).

As another index of the relative position of religious leaders, students were asked to rank several occupations in terms of 'prestige' and 'respect'. Only 2 per cent of the students in the public lises and 2 per cent in the private Turkish lises ranked 'religious leader' as the highest in prestige. The percentages of those in the minority schools and in the foreign schools was 3·5 and 1·3 respectively. Interestingly enough, even such low percentages were still higher than those of 'local government official', and 'business executive or official'. On the same question as that asked in the Frey survey, namely, as parents what lessons they would like to teach their children, only 1·4

---

[12] James M. Gillespie and Gordon W. Allport, *Youth's Outlook on the Future: A Cross-National Study* (Garden City: Doubleday & Company, Inc., 1955).

[13] Herbert H. Hyman, Arif Payaslioglu, and Frederick W. Frey, 'The Values of Turkish College Youth', *The Public Opinion Quarterly*, XXII, No. 3 (Fall, 1958), 285–6.

per cent of the lise group indicated values associated with religion. This percentage was lower than that of the 1959 survey. It could be speculated that the Revolution of 1960 (by which the Democratic Party was forced out of office and declared illegal and some of its leaders executed) may have had an effect upon the values of youth by drawing them even closer to the secularism of the Atatürk era. A very frequent answer in this study, as in the two mentioned above, concerning values to be taught to children, fell under the category of 'ethics and morals' (48 per cent of the total number of students chose values in this category). However, the responses were expressed in ethical or moral rather than religious terms.

On the 'paradox' of kismet the author's survey was even more revealing than that of Hyman and his associates. Students were asked to 'agree' or 'disagree' with the following question: 'When a man is born the success he is going to have is already "in the cards", so he might as well accept it and not fight against it.' Of the total number of students in the four types of lise, 24 per cent answered in the affirmative. The highest percentage of 'agree' responses was registered in the public lise sample (24·5 per cent), and the lowest in the foreign-operated lise group (14 per cent). Except for the students in the foreign schools, these figures are significantly higher than those in the Hyman survey of university students. However, a breakdown in terms of students in the three lise classes (first, second, and third) revealed that there was a decrease of 'agree' responses in the second class and a further decrease in the third. The percentage of 'agree' responses among the third year lise students dropped to 14·5, which is almost identical to that in the Hyman study. Apparently, therefore, as students acquire more formal education, they also change their attitudes concerning the role of kismet in shaping their lives and their future. On the other hand, the fact that, even among the most highly educated groups in Turkey, some central precepts of traditional Islam (e.g., 'fatalism', 'submission', etc.) still persist, cannot be discounted. This acquires added significance when questions of modernizing or developing the society are considered, especially when it is examined in conjunction with certain other values traditionally associated with Islamic societies.

Orthodox Islam encompassed more than just matters of religious dogma; it also had political, social, and cultural connotations. It was both a religious and a social philosophy, and it minutely regulated even the interpersonal relations of the members of the society. The Kemalist Revolution substituted a secular state for the traditional Islamic theocracy, and curbed the power of religion as an institution by fiat. Moreover, Atatürk sought to inculcate a spirit of independence, a rational 'scientific' approach to life, and a positive feeling that the individual is capable of shaping his own destiny and combating the vicissitudes of his existence. The followers of Atatürkism are still too entrenched in positions of political power for any religious reaction to take place; and since 1923, a new generation of Turks has been educated in secular schools and 'socialized' in nationalism and 'laicism'. Nevertheless, although there may be no foreseeable danger to upset the secular state, the persistence of traditional Islamic attitudes and values slow the pace of modernity.[14] In addition to kismet, and to certain attitudes of the large village population, the study of lise students also reveals that certain traditional patterns of authority and family relationships seem to persist even among such a selected and highly educated group.

The traditional Ottoman Islamic society was based on an authoritarian normative pattern. This was reflected in the relationships between the individual and the 'government' (the sultan, the officials, the village elders), between man and woman, husband and wife, father and son, older and younger brother, and so on. In all interpersonal relationships, there was the same deferential attitude by those of 'inferior' to those of 'superior' status. These patterns of relations were regulated in no small degree by the Islamic religion. Through several reforms, Atatürk sought to substitute a democratic regime for the Ottoman political absolutism and to break down authoritarianism. It is well known, of course, that, although political institutions were changed, an absolutistic pattern of govern-

[14] For more details on the relationship between Islamic attitudes and habits of mind and modernity, see Daniel Lerner, *The Passing of Traditional Society-Modernizing the Middle East* (Glencoe, Illinois: Free Press Paperback Edition, 1964), pp. 43 ff.

ment (Atatürk, or the one-party system) continued until the emergence of the multi-party system in the forties. Even after that, and in view of another revolution and several abortive coups d'état in the sixties, whether democracy has taken roots in the Turkish republic is not clear. More will be said about this later. On the question of authoritarianism, it has quite probably been weakened by the many social changes, the new views about education, the content of the curriculum, and the aggressive campaign to introduce Western modes of thinking and behaving as well as Western symbols. Research in this area, however, is extremely limited, and the extent to which patterns of authority have changed has not been adequately determined. The few inconclusive studies that are available suggest that changes may indeed have taken place since the establishment of the republic. Contrasting what he calls the n-Achievement levels as gauged from children's stories in Turkey and Iran, McClelland found that Turkey ranked higher than Iran. Considering that the two countries have essentially similar background characteristics (especially the fact that they are both within the Islamic tradition) and that Turkey has attained a higher level of economic development, McClelland adduces 'concern for high achievement' as a possible explanation for the differential rates of growth between the two countries. He reasons: since low n-Achievement among sons has been found to be correlated with authoritarian fathers and since, according to Islamic tradition, Islamic societies are strongly dominated by the father, then the explanation for the differential levels of n-Achievement between Turkey and Iran must be sought in the extent to which the authority of the father has been maintained or has been undermined. McClelland then asserts that certain institutional and ideological changes carried out in Turkey since the revolution have indeed undermined the strong domination of the Turkish father. Thus he explains the differences between the two countries. Some of the institutional changes, which helped break down the strong male domination, were the abolition of the fez, 'traditional symbol of male dignity', the separation of church and state—consequently the replacement of Islamic law by civil law which altered the legal status of marriage—and the granting of rights to women. Furthermore, the organization of the new army and the establishment of village institutes[15] emancipated the boys from the control of their autocratic fathers. Under ideological changes, McClelland includes: (a) patriotism, which meant a shift in loyalty from father to nation or the 'generalized other'; (b) modification of the traditional theme of trickery 'in the direction of positive achievement', which undermined the belief that people cannot be trusted and that 'everybody is out to get you'; and (c) modification of people's perceptions of government authority or of how society affects one's life, which resulted in perceiving authority in more positive rather than negative terms.[16]

McClelland's approach to the analysis of national characteristics (what he calls 'content analysis of organized verbal or artistic symbol systems') and its application to problems affecting modernization and economic development is quite novel and intriguing. But his analysis of the Turkish situation must be looked at with a great deal of caution and largely as a hypothesis that still needs to be substantiated. McClelland's approach and study pose several questions. To what extent do children actually internalize the values which are found in the 'moral' of children's stories, and to what extent do they actually bring about changes in children's perceptions of authority? What evidence is there that the institutional and ideological changes during the republican period did indeed undermine the domination of the male and/or the father, or contribute to a higher concern for individual achievement? For example, McClelland's assumption that the abolition of the fez undermined traditional 'male dignity' might be questioned. The fez was more of a religious symbol signifying the 'Moslemness' of the Turks. The present-day European hat is as much a male symbol as the old fez! Also, the separation of children from their families for service into the army was as much a characteristic of the Ottoman Islamic past as it is of the Turkish

[15] The village institute (köy enstitüsü) was a type of institution established by law in 1940 for the training of village teachers, technical leaders, and advisers. In 1954, however, the village institutes were closed and converted into regular teacher-training colleges. See Alexandre Vexliard and Kemal Aytach, 'The Village Institutes in Turkey', *Comparative Education Review*, VIII, No. 1 (June, 1964), 41–7.

[16] David C. McClelland, 'National Character and Economic Growth in Turkey and Iran,' in *Communications and Political Development*, ed. Lucian W. Pye (Princeton: Princeton University Press, 1963), pp. 152–81.

present. Further, the actual effect of the village institutes is difficult to assess. For one thing, their duration was short (less than fifteen years); for another, the number of students who attended them was relatively small (in total, 17,162 diplomas were awarded), and all in all such institutions existed only in twenty-one villages. Although the village institutes represented an important experiment in the attempts to elevate the cultural level of the villagers and to bridge the gap between an educated elite and an uneducated populace, and although they provided an avenue for social mobility among the village youth, statements about their role in breaking down traditional patterns of authority must perforce be speculative. Finally, the different kinds of 'morals' that McClelland finds in the Turkish and Iranian stories and his assumption that the Iranian tales are representative of the Islamic tradition or that they correspond to the Ottoman Turkish tradition might be questioned. In other words, for his interpretations, assuming they are correct, to have any validity, the stories to which Turkish children were exposed during the pre-revolutionary period (i.e., during the period of male autocracy and authoritarianism in the society) must also be examined.

McClelland concedes that the ideological and institutional changes in Turkey may have been more effective in cities rather than in villages, although he maintains that the new norms were known nationwide. However, impressionistic accounts and some empirical studies of this aspect of village culture reveal that basic value patterns among the masses of the population have not altered to any substantial degree. In the much publicized *A Village in Anatolia*, Mahmut Makal, a young village teacher who was trained in a village institute, painted a dismal and discouraging picture of village culture. This document gives the impression that the people of Nürgüz, in central Anatolia, are mere modern shadows of the bucolic and 'primitive' Ottoman Anatolian peasant. Almost all the traditional modes of thinking, behaving, and feeling seem to have been totally unaffected by the ideology of modernity. The same fatalism, the same patterns of authority, the same suspicion about the 'outsider' and the government official, and the same customs and superstitions of pre-republican days still exist.[17]

[17] Makal, *op. cit.*, pp. 11, 64, 68.

Pierce observed that 'status is acquired primarily by growing older'. He writes:

'All men over 50 years of age ordered everyone else around, except men of their age or older, and I never saw anyone refuse to follow the orders. Old women ordered all of the other women around, but usually restricted their ordering of men to those quite young. All of the middle-aged men and women were able to order the young adults around, and so on down the line. As a matter of fact, anyone could give orders to anyone younger than himself of the same sex, but men could order women around who were older than they were.'[18]

And Stirling noted that existing patterns of authority between the sexes are justified on religious grounds.[19]

Admittedly, such places do not represent the whole of rural Turkey, nor all of the villages of central Anatolia. Robinson, for example, reports that when he visited Alishar in 1949, he noticed many 'physical changes' since 1932.[20] And Daniel Lerner's Balgat changed from a 'traditional' peasant community to a suburb of Ankara in four years! Yet Balgat cannot be taken as typical or as reflecting a country-wide change for the simple reason that it is so close to a fast growing metropolitan centre which is also the capital of Turkey. Nor does Robinson's Alishar represent 'physical' let alone 'normative' changes in the country as a whole. Indeed, while pointing to the quick transformation of Balgat, Lerner also notes that the 'traditionals' in Turkey far outnumber the 'moderns' and the 'transitionals'. According to him, they compose 'well over half' (about 60 per cent) of the Turkish population 'even today'. And his description of their 'psychic traits' as well as their outlook on life, is not substantially dissimilar from Makal's observations. Their institutions, Lerner writes, 'usually are authoritarian, patriarchal, changeless; the values they enjoin are loyalty, obedience, inertia. The whole complex forms a "courage culture", in which absence of curiosity is a primary component ("theirs not to reason why, theirs but to do or die").'[21]

Turning to an urban and highly educated group, the Hyman

[18] Pierce, *op cit.*, p. 78.
[19] Stirling, *op. cit.*, p. 7.
[20] Robinson, *op. cit.*, pp. 126–7.
[21] Lerner, *op. cit.*, p. 133.

and Frey surveys depict the Turkish youth as 'quite authoritarian'. Using the Gillespie and Allport item to gauge authoritarian values (viz., 'the world is a hazardous place, in which men are basically evil and dangerous') the Hyman survey showed that 39 per cent of the respondents in the Ankara University group expressed agreement. This figure is higher than what Gillespie and Allport found in other national groups, except in countries like South Africa, Mexico, and Egypt. The writers conclude that 'while that aspect of the value constellation involving political absolutism seems dissipated in the present Turkish group, the authoritarian aspect seems to have persisted'.[22] Although, on the same item, the Frey survey also indicated a high degree of authoritarianism among lise students, the author expresses doubt that such students were as authoritarian as the general population. Furthermore, according to him, although authoritarianism is characteristic of the political culture, 'it tends to be counteracted by a strong sense of solidarity and by a growing ideological commitment to democratic forms, also inculcated by the school system'.[23]

In the survey conducted by the present writer, at least four items were included to explore the extent to which traditional values bearing on authoritarianism and attachment to the family still persist among students in the academic lises. The first item was identical to that in the Hyman survey, which for purposes of abbreviation will be called 'hazardous world'. The percentage of 'agree' or 'slightly agree' responses was slightly higher among the lise students than among those at Ankara University. Of the total sample in the study, 40 per cent expressed agreement with the question that 'the world is a hazardous place' and that men are 'basically evil and dangerous'. There were, however, some significant variations among students in the four types of schools. The lowest percentage of students who expressed strong agreement was registered among the 'foreign' lise group and the highest among the 'minority' group. On a four-choice scale (agree, slightly agree, slightly disagree, disagree), the 'agree' responses in the four types of lise were: public, 6 per cent; private Turkish, 6 per cent; minority, 10 per cent; and foreign, 4 per cent. On the other

[22] Hyman, Payaslioglu, and Frey, *op. cit.*, p. 286.
[23] Frey, *op. cit.*, pp. 224–5.

hand, the highest percentage of 'disagree' responses was registered with the public lise group (44 per cent) and the lowest with the 'minority' group (31 per cent). Similarly, these two groups indicated the sharpest contrast with respect to 'agreement' (agree and slightly agree) responses (35·5 per cent in the public lise group, and 48·5 in the 'minority' group).

In interpreting some of the inter-school variations in these findings, it would be helpful to state that the 'minority' lises, all located in Istanbul, recruit their students almost exclusively from the non-Moslem population of Turkey, and they are mostly schools belonging to the Christian minorities (Greek and Armenian). In contrast to these schools, the public and the private Turkish lises are almost exclusively Moslem in terms of the religious composition of the student body. The foreign lises (American, English, Austrian, French, etc.) are heterodox in their religious composition, but still predominantly Moslem. Looking at the figures, the most unusual single group is clearly the students in the minority lises. Since this is largely a Christian group, the argument of Islam as a conditioning factor in the existence of any authoritarianism is somewhat blunted—but not that of the persistence of a traditional pattern of authority, nor indeed that of 'religion'. The non-Moslem minority groups in Turkey, especially in Istanbul, are not recent newcomers. They have always lived there, and they are as much heirs of the Ottoman absolute and authoritarian tradition as are the Moslem Turks. Conceivably, the force of the religion of these groups may be as great as that of Islam, if not greater. Another explanation of the variation among the minority groups is that they are fearful of the world and of other people precisely because they *are* a minority group, and Christian at that, in an overwhelmingly Moslem country. Some of these minorities, especially the Greeks and the Armenians, have had open conflicts with the ethnic Turks. Moreover, two episodes in recent Turkish history involving minority groups may have exacerbated the feelings of suspicion and insecurity among this segment of the Turkish population. The first episode was the infamous *varlik vergisi* (capital tax), an emergency fiscal measure in force during 1942–43, by which a capital levy was imposed on property owners, businessmen, large farmers and others. Much controversy has surrounded this measure. The significant point here is that the methods by which this law was applied bore heavily upon the minority groups, many members of which were ruined financially or punished severely by the exorbitant taxes they were called upon to pay. A person's religion and nationality seemed to be the real important factors in determining the tax assessments.[24] As a consequence of this measure, which is considered a sad affair by the Turks themselves, old suspicions and fears about discrimination were revived. Similar feelings were aroused in 1956, by the riots in Istanbul in which mobs destroyed property belonging to the minority groups and, according to some observers, committed all sorts of other condemnable acts. This second episode was also condemned by the Turks themselves and was indeed one of the prosecution's arguments against the Menderes regime (which was overthrown in 1960). But the point is that whether or not it was instigated for political (the Cyprus issue), for nationalistic (the alleged bombing of Ata-türk's birthplace in Salonica), or for social reasons (a disconnected, deracinated, lower class striking at the more affluent minorities),[25] it heightened suspicions and feelings of insecurity among the non-Moslem population. The recent anxieties among the Greeks (the largest minority group and the one that provides the greatest number of minority schools) resulting from the Cyprus question could be added to these two episodes.

The second item relating to authoritarian values was also based on the Gillespie and Allport F-scale. It read, 'People can be trusted', and students were asked to choose from the same four alternatives as the 'hazardous world' item. Of the total sample, 45 per cent expressed disagreement. The responses in the four types of schools ranged from 42 per cent of public lise students to 49 per cent of the students in minority schools. Here again, although the difference is not as large as the 'hazardous world' question, the minority group registered the highest 'disagreement' scores. In both of these items, the public lise group scored the lowest on choices which indicate degrees

[24] For more details on the varlik vergisi, see Lewis V. Thomas and Richard N. Frye, *The United States and Turkey and Iran* (Cambridge, Mass.: Harvard University Press, 1952), pp. 95–8. See also Lewis, *op. cit.*, pp. 291–5; and Karpat, *op. cit.*, pp. 114–17.

[25] Karpat, *op. cit.*, p. 422n.

of authoritarianism (35·5 per cent on the first question and 42 per cent on the second).

Assuming the validity of the instrument and of the questions, namely, that they do indeed measure values which exhibit degrees of authoritarianism, it might be concluded that a relatively high degree of authoritarianism among students in the academic lises persists. It also seems likely, as Frey argues, that authoritarianism among this highly educated and mostly urban group is less than among the general population. Although authoritarianism persists, the *majority* of the students chose responses which do not indicate authoritarian values (60 per cent in the 'hazardous world' item and 55 per cent in the 'people can be trusted' item).

Furthermore, the responses of the highest lise class showed that authoritarian attitudes diminish as the student climbs the educational ladder. On the 'hazardous world' item, only 36 per cent of all the third-year students expressed agreement, in contrast to 44 per cent of all the first-year students. On the 'people can be trusted' question, the comparative figures (i.e., those who expressed disagreement) were 42 and 48 per cent. These findings suggest that as students receive more education, authoritarian attitudes diminish. If, therefore, this observation is extended beyond the lise groups to the society and the population at large, the question of the role of education and Turkish modernization might be reasoned as followed: (a) amount of education seems to be related to degree of authoritarianism among Turkish youth; since the revolution, the amount of education of such people has increased; therefore, there is less authoritarianism among the Turkish youth now than during the pre-revolutionary period; and (b) since the sampled group constitutes one of the most highly educated segments of the general population, the degree of authoritarianism among the lise students is lower than that of the population at large.

At least three other items were included in the survey to explore attitudes concerning social relationships. Apparently, the often-mentioned Turkish trait of deference to age[26] persists even among such a select group as the lise students. Students were asked simply to 'agree' or 'disagree' with the following

[26] See also Nermin Erdentug, *A Study of the Social Structure of a Turkish Village* (Ankara: Ayyildiz Matbaasi, 1959), pp. 50–1.

statement: 'Respect is due an older person *no matter what kind of person he is.*' Of all the respondents, 73 per cent agreed, the largest percentage being among the public lise group (83 per cent) and the smallest among the 'foreign' lise population (58 per cent). There was no significant difference between the other two groups (77 per cent in the private Turkish lises, and 78 per cent in the minority schools). It is difficult to interpret these findings, or to make any comparisons with youth of other cultures since comparable information is not available. However, responses among youth in America or England, for example, might well be quite different, and age in and of itself would not seem to be a determining factor in the respect accorded an individual. The relatively high percentage of 'agree' answers among the public lise group may be due to the fact that the patterns of social and geographical recruitment into such schools are more varied than in the others: more public lise students are rural than urban (hence, perhaps, more attached to traditional values), they come from less-educated home backgrounds, a larger number of their parents are engaged in primary occupations, and so on.[27] The high consensus shown by all groups except the foreign lise students suggests a strong persistence of a value associated with tradition. The relatively lower percentage registered among students in foreign-operated schools suggests that children of highly educated parents (about 41 per cent had an education beyond the secondary level, this being by far the highest percentage among the total group), who are overwhelmingly urban (about 95 per cent, again the highest of all groups) and who are exposed to a more 'modern' type of educational environment, are less inclined to regard age as a criterion for 'respect'.

The other two items sought to explore the extent to which Turkish youth had a strong attachment to their families. One of the questions read: 'When the time comes for a boy to take a job, he should stay near his family, even if it means giving up a good job opportunity away from his family'; and the other, 'Nothing in life is worth the sacrifice of moving away from your parents'. The alternatives of the first were 'agree', 'disagree', and 'undecided'; and of the second, 'agree', and, 'disagree'. The percentages of 'agree' responses to the two questions

[27] For more information on patterns of recruitment, see Chapter X.

were 20 for the first, and 28 for the second. Significantly, on the 'job opportunity' item, 20 per cent were undecided.

Such findings, however valuable they may be in *exploring* certain values among Turkish youth, must be examined and interpreted with a great deal of caution. In seeking to measure or assess attitudes and values in developing societies through the application of instruments validated in Western, culturally and politically different societies, there is a danger of drawing hasty conclusions or reading the same meanings into the responses as those made in Western settings. This caveat must be entered particularly in the case of the afore-mentioned answers by the Turkish youth on items pertaining to authoritarianism, insecurity, and so on. The relatively high incidence of authoritarian responses among Turkish youth, as indeed among youth in other developing societies, may reflect *ideological* rather than *personality* factors or characteristics. A verbal response by a Turkish youth to a questionnaire item, which in another cultural setting might be interpreted as a psychological trait produced by a certain pattern of family relationships or as manifested in actual behaviour, might indeed represent a standard superficial reaction to a persistently advocated idea. Moreover, what in a society like the United States is interpreted as 'authoritarian', and hence undesirable, may be quite an acceptable way of thinking in a country like Turkey and may not necessarily affect an individual's behaviour. In some cases (as, for example, in that of the students in the *minority* schools), responses which elsewhere would be interpreted as manifestations of authoritarianism might indeed reflect a *realistic* appraisal of the situation in which such individuals find themselves. It is hoped, however, this exploratory investigation into such attitudinal areas as authority, distrust, piety, and the like, will spur further research on the cultural-psychological aspects of education in Turkey and in other transitional societies.

CHAPTER IX

EDUCATION AND
PROBLEMS OF POLITICAL CULTURE

THE school system is related in several ways to the political system and to the general political culture of a society. In the first place, schools are regarded as important agencies for the inculcation of social attitudes and behaviours which are deemed essential for membership and participation in the body politic. The 'politicizing' of youth in this sense is not restricted to formal instruction through organized content on the political traditions and governmental institutions of a country; it also covers more general attitudes and values (e.g., attitudes towards authority, peer relationships, distribution of power, legitimacy, and so on). This political significance of formal education is known as 'political socialization'. In addition, the school system selects and trains people for certain occupations and social roles, both of which may be politically important. Attending or graduating from certain schools, for example, may be an important determinant in the social placement of the individual as well as in his political participation. In many societies, education is an important agency of social mobility and political ascendancy. Furthermore, the whole range of skills (intellectual and otherwise) and knowledge attained at school, and the total 'school climate' may affect a person's future political views and behaviours. Clearly, the range of problems suggested by 'education and political culture', even if limited to Turkey, is too great to be adequately treated here. Accordingly, this chapter will be confined to problems for which there is some information or about which some reasonably valid statements can be made.

EDUCATION AND TURKISH POLITICAL ELITES

Interest in political elites, or in that special group in the polity demarcated from the rest of the population in terms of certain characteristics, especially in terms of political power, dates back to antiquity. A very important modern development has been the application of empirical methods and techniques and a shift in emphasis away from the normative types of questions—the 'should' questions—to what actually happens, namely, how the political process functions and what the political behaviour actually *is*. Moreover, a rather extensive branch of this empirical type of political science research has focused on the social characteristics of political leaders, on what has been termed 'social background analysis'.[1] In this connection, political scientists have sought to establish certain non-psychological, and relatively general, social attributes (past and present) of individuals occupying key positions in the political hierarchy, in order to establish regularities or relationships of political behaviour. In inquiries of this nature, the educational background of political leaders, together with such other social attributes as sex, age, occupation, race, religion, class, wealth, income, club membership, and so on, have been examined.

The significance of 'social background studies' has been amply justified by several social scientists and political philosophers. A basic assumption of such studies is that political attitudes and behaviours are functionally related to certain prior experiences of the individual. Another assumption is that it is possible to infer certain generalizations concerning political behaviour and to make judgments concerning the nature of the polity on the basis of certain common background characteristics of its leaders.

The relevance of such a concern is further strengthened by the following considerations which pertain particularly to Turkey. As indicated in the first part of this book, education played an important part in attaining elite status during the major part of the Ottoman period. Indeed, educational back-

---

[1] For an excellent account of the development of 'elite analysis' in general, and of 'social background analysis' in particular, among political scientists, see Frederick W. Frey, *The Turkish Political Elite* (Cambridge, Mass., pre-publication dittoed copy).

ground was a crucial differentiating factor between the ruling elites and the masses and, with certain qualifications, within the elites themselves, between religious 'traditionalists' and 'modernists' (this being particularly true since the nineteenth century). Education was, in a large part, the single most fundamental variable of social differentiation and social stratification. In an overwhelmingly illiterate society, as the Ottoman society was, the few people who went to school or possessed some knowledge were accorded higher prestige by their contemporaries, and the longer one went to school or the more knowledge he possessed, the higher the people's deference towards him. In the analysis of the Ottoman background, the changes and variations in the types of education and the associated value placed upon them were discussed: how, for example, the type of education received in the Palace School qualified one for certain offices in the military and civil bureaucracies, and a medrese type of schooling, for the ecclesiastical branch of the polity; how, later, when the empire sought to modernize its institutions and way of life, educational establishments like the military academies, the Mülkiye, the Galatasaray lise and others provided a different type of training for military and civic leaders and, in varying degrees, played a part in the movement towards modernity.

The significance of education in building the new nation was repeatedly stressed by Atatürk and by all other modern Turkish thinkers and political leaders. A cardinal tenet of the revolutionary ideology and of the new Turkish nation-state has been to create a cadre of new Turkish leaders who would initiate and carry through changes in order to transform traditional patterns, beliefs and practices, and to establish a modern, democratic, and secular state. The educational system, particularly certain types of schools, were assigned the major task of training such 'new Turks'. Far from undermining the significance of education for political ascendancy and social differentiation, the policies of the republic carried forward and indeed strengthened this feature of the Ottoman legacy.[2] The difference between the Ottoman and the republican periods, insofar as this aspect of the school-society relationship was

[2] For a more detailed examination of the bifurcations in the modern Turkish society drawn in large part on educational lines, see *ibid.*

concerned, lay not in the role assigned to education for social mobility, class differentiation, and more pertinently, leadership status; rather, as will be shown below, they lay mostly in the kind of educational or professional specialization that facilitated access to positions of political leadership, and in the types of institutions and the occupational categories from which political leaders were recruited.

This topic will be approached mainly from three interrelated dimensions: (a) the amount and level of formal education of political elites, (b) the types of institutions in which they received their formal education, and (c) their educational or professional (occupational) specialization. The deputies of the Turkish Grand National Assembly and, to some extent, the civil bureaucracy, will be included under political elites; and education will be restricted to mean formal schooling.

A recent comprehensive study by Frey furnishes the most valuable detailed information on the educational characteristics of the deputies of the Turkish Grand National Assembly from 1920, when it was first established, to 1957. The study covers the first ten of the eleven assemblies prior to the 1960 coup d'état.[3] The first and most striking feature of the educational profile of the deputies in the Turkish national legislature is the consistently high level of formal schooling attained by them. In the First Assembly (1920–23), about 70 per cent of these political leaders had a university education; in the Tenth Assembly (1954–57) the percentage of deputies with such an education was even higher (77 per cent). Taking the total number of deputies (2,210) throughout the entire thirty-seven-year period, Frey found that over 60 per cent had some sort of university education. The distribution of all the known members of the ten assemblies in terms of highest educational level attained was as follows: university, 73 per cent; lise, 12 per cent; middle school, 10 per cent; primary school, 2 per cent; private school, 2 per cent; and medrese, 1 per cent. It was also found that on a four-level formal

[3] I am greatly indebted to Professor Frey, who was kind enough to allow me to examine a copy of the volume before it was published and to use some of the findings. I am also indebted to him for several other ideas bearing on the problem of political leadership in Turkey. All figures on the social characteristics of the deputies of the Turkish National Assembly are taken from Frey.

leadership classification (cabinet ministers, top leaders, middle leaders, and back-benchers) the four leadership groups were differentiated in terms of formal educational attainment: the cabinet group was clearly the 'most educated', and the back-benchers, the 'least educated'. For example, in the Tenth Assembly (1954–57), the percentage of deputies with a university education in the four groups was as follows: cabinet ministers, 97 per cent; top leaders, 95 per cent; middle leaders, 92 per cent; and back-benchers, 71 per cent. On the three leadership groups (the cabinet ministers were included in the 'top leaders') throughout the thirty-seven-year period, Frey has concluded:

'Of all the social background characteristics which we have examined . . . education distinguished most clearly and consistently between the designated leadership levels in the Assembly . . . At its highest levels, Turkish political life is still dominated by relative intellectuals in Turkish society.'[4]

In modern Turkey, the amount or level of formal education has clearly been a crucial prerequisite for the attainment and sustenance (in terms of parliamentary longevity) of high political leadership positions. Assuming for a moment that people with a university training are an intellectual group, and assuming further that political ascendancy through education represents a form of occupational placement based on achievement rather than on ascriptive criteria, it would appear that modern Turkey exemplifies a sort of *meritocracy*, similar in these respects to the early Ottoman *meritocracy* discussed in the first chapter. This situation would also make a strong prima facie case for a polity that displays features which are believed to be characteristic of the more advanced democracies. Furthermore, what better guarantees are there for political prudence, stability, and good government than placing the most educated people at the helm of the statecraft? And, finally, what better recourse does a transitional society like Turkey have than to entrust her destinies to a group of intellectuals exposed to Western knowledge, skills, and modes of thought? These are complex questions, and they cannot be fully answered here. But comments on the significance and

[4] *Ibid.*, pp. 390, 416 (in pre-publication copy).

implications of some of the material thus far presented will be relevant and appropriate at this stage.

The educational level of the Turkish deputies becomes more meaningful if it is first examined against the background of the educational level of the Turkish population at large. Taking literacy first (see Table II), although the great majority of the Turkish population were totally illiterate (i.e., could *neither read nor write*), the great majority of the deputies were university graduates or had university training. In 1955, about 44 per cent of the male and 76 per cent of the female population was classified as *illiterate*;[5] yet in the Tenth Assembly (1954–57), 77 per cent of the deputies had *university* education. Looking at literacy among age groups, in 1955, *over 75 per cent of the population* between the ages of 45 and 64 or of the population 45 years old and over *could not read or write*,[6] but *over 75 per cent of the deputies*, most of whom would fall within the 45-years-old-and-over age category,[7] *were university trained*. Clearly, in relation to the general population and to the comparable age group of this population, the Turkish political elites are not only a very highly educated group, they are also recruited from a relatively small segment of the Turkish society. This is most apparent when the educational background of the deputies in relation to the level of formal education attained by the population is examined. Although there have been over-all increases in school and university enrolments since 1923, the percentage of children of school age population who have actually attended schools becomes progressively lower as the educational ladder is ascended (see also Tables I–III). The percentage of students attending universities has been consistently the lowest and has never exceeded the 2 per cent mark (actually, the number of people with some university training has been closer to 1 per cent). Figures for the year 1960 show that *only 1 per cent* of the total Turkish population 25 years of age and older is university graduates, and a meagre

---

[5] *1955 Genel Nüfus Sayimi* (T. J. Bashvekalet Istatistik Umum Müdürlügü [Ankara, 1957]), No. 372, p. 25.

[6] Jefferson N. Eastmond, *Educational Attainment in Turkey* (Ankara: Research and Measurement Bureau, 1964), p. 14.

[7] Frey has estimated that the average age of the deputies at the time of the first meeting of the Tenth Assembly was 46·7. See Frey, *op. cit.*, p. 295a (in pre-publication copy).

·7 per cent have had eleven years of schooling.[8] Thus, restricting the base to even the small 'educated' group, the Turkish political leaders are recruited from the most educated in their midst; they are, as it were, the super elites (in terms of education) of a larger elite class. 'Educationally,' according to Frey, 'these deputies were about as atypical as they could be.'[9] Some may argue that political leaders are 'atypical' even in stable democracies like England and the United States. In Turkey, however, not only are the *rulers* 'atypical'; equally important, the *ruled* are as well. The very fact that the leaders are so highly educated, and the led are educated to a much lesser extent, if at all, creates a chasm bridged by very few lines of communication. Moreover, there is no convincing evidence that a society ruled by the most educated is a well-governed or a better society. Factors besides amount and level of education are also important, namely, consensus among the entire body politic concerning the legitimacy of the political institutions and the mechanisms of political change, political participation of all the people, accountability to popular will, responsibility for the general welfare, quality of education received by the rulers, and so on.

Are the Turkish political elites 'atypical' in regard to type of institution they attended and area of educational or professional specialization? Historically, as was shown earlier, certain specific schools or types of educational institutions, such as the Palace School and the famous medreses of Istanbul, were known to be recruiting grounds for disproportionate number of political, religious, and other leaders.[10] In the nineteenth century, military academies like the *Harbiye* (War College) produced many of the more activist leaders of the Young Turk Revolution. Information on the secondary educational background of political leaders during the republican period is at present lacking. One could speculate, however, that a large and

[8] Eastmond, *op. cit.*, pp. 6–7.

[9] Frey, *op. cit.*, pp. 131–2 (in pre-publication copy).

[10] During the Ottoman period certain schools of the minorities produced a large number of people who assumed high posts not only within the millets, but also within the Ottoman bureaucracy. For example, it was in the School of the Greek Orthodox Patriarchate (*He Megale tou Genous Schole*, today known as *Fener Rum Erkek Lisesi*) that many of the famous Phanariotes received their basic education.

213

disproportionate number of such leaders have received their schooling in select lises. One such school, the *Istanbul Erkek Lisesi* has been called *Vekiller Okulu* (Ministers' School). It has been particularly outstanding in the relatively large numbers not only of cabinet ministers, but also of high political personages who have received their secondary education in it.[11] From 1938 to 1950, there was an over-representation of deputies who had gone to the political science and the law faculties (i.e., to two types of institutions).[12] In the general category of civil bureaucrats, many of whom had reached positions as deputies and cabinet ministers during the First Turkish Republic (1923–60), more than half had attended the Political Science Faculty of Ankara University, and 23 per cent, the Law Faculty. Of the cabinet ministers during the same period, from 50 to 75 per cent had attended these same two faculties. It should also be noted that in Turkey appointments to high civil service posts (e.g., valis and kaymakams) presuppose attendance at universities, especially at the aforementioned two faculties. It is not surprising, therefore, that 99 per cent of this branch of the civil bureaucracy are graduates of the political science and the law faculties of Ankara University.[13]

The fact that a large number of deputies attended the political science and law faculties suggests that the type of professional training provided in such institutions would be related to their representation in the assembly. On the index of 'parliamentary longevity' (i.e., number of assemblies served), political science, military, and education training were ahead of literature, agriculture, medicine, law, economics, engineering and science, pharmacy, veterinary medicine, dentistry, and so on. In other words, deputies with a professional background in political science, the military, and education were

---

[11] Frey, *op. cit.*, p. 119 (in pre-publication copy).
[12] *Ibid.*, p. 153.
[13] Richard I. Chambers, 'The Civil Bureaucracy: Turkey,' in *Political Modernization in Japan and Turkey*, ed. Robert E. Ward and Dankwart A. Rustow (Princeton: Princeton University Press, 1964), pp. 325–5. If these findings are viewed against those on the occupational destinations of the graduates of the Mülkiye (see Chapter IV), it could be inferred that, in this sense, the social function of the Political Science Faculty has not changed from what it was in the nineteenth century.

'favoured groups with a high election rate'. compared to the other specialties most of which are called *serbest meslekler* (free professions). However, regarding numerical representation in the assembly, the picture did not uniformly correspond to that of 'parliamentary longevity': law was over-represented and education, from which one could infer educational specialty, under-represented. According to the *occupational* distribution of all the deputies from 1920 to 1957, law was at the top (18 per cent of the total group); government was second (14 per cent); trade, third (13 per cent); military, fourth (10 per cent); medicine and agriculture, fifth (9 per cent each); education, seventh (8 per cent); and religion, eighth (4 per cent). Reducing all the occupational categories into three major groups (official, professional, and economic), without including religion and journalism, the percentage numerical representation was estimated as follows: official, 33 per cent; professional (mostly law and medicine), 31 per cent; and economics, 24 per cent.[14]

University education was earlier concluded to be an important desideratum for political elite membership, for high officeholding within the political elite hierarchy, and for parliamentary longevity. Apparently, attendance at certain types of institutions, educational specialization, and occupational background are also significant factors in enhancing one's chances for high positions in the polity. The element of occupational background acquires added significance when the occupational distribution of the Turkish population at large is considered. Excluding the armed forces, throughout the republican period, the professional, technical, administrative, managerial, and government categories averaged less than 5 per cent of the total male population fifteen years of age and over. In 1955, these groups constituted about 5 per cent, and in 1960, about 5·5 per cent. In contrast, farmers, fishermen, hunters, or, generally speaking the 'agriculture' category, constituted over 60 per cent of the same male population (in 1955, it was 63·5 per cent and in 1960, 62·3 per cent). If the relative representation of these two occupational groups (that is, professional, etc., and 'agriculture') in the national legislature are compared, the disparities are obvious. Agriculture provided

[14] Frey, *op. cit.*, pp. 153–6, 175a (in pre-publication copy).

only 9 per cent of the deputies; the other, over 70 per cent.

Another point that merits further comment is the relative over-representation of people whom students of comparative politics have labelled 'specialists in persuasion'. In the NADIR studies, Harold D. Lasswell and his colleagues have found that high representation of 'specialists in persuasion', especially lawyers, journalists, and 'teachers' among political elites is a characteristic of pluralistic stable democracies of the Western variety like England and the United States, and their absence characterizes monolithic societies like the Soviet Union.[15] Turkey presents some interesting parallels to this phenomenon, and it also raises some equally interesting questions. Throughout the republican period, there has been a relatively high number of deputies with legal training, and since the Seventh Assembly (1943–46), there has been a steady increase. A 27 per cent high (the highest occupational representation) was reached in the Tenth Assembly (1954–57); and during the thirty-seven-year period (1920–57), 18 per cent of the deputies were classified in the category of 'law'. These figures compare very favourably with a country like England.[16] Clearly, the phenomenon of over-representation of the legal profession in the Turkish Assembly is an important departure from the Ottoman Islamic tradition and, as Bernard Lewis points out, an indication of the emergence of a new, Western elite group.[17] Also, limiting the argument to lawyers in the Turkish national legislature, a prima facie case could be made that Turkey is a stable democracy. Although a multi-party system was established after 1946, and in some subsequent elections (the 1950 election in particular), there were strong signs that democratic institutions were taking root, recent events seem to cast strong doubts on the development of democracy in Turkey: (a) the policies of the Menderes regime during the later years, (b) the

[15] See Harold D. Lasswell, Daniel Lerner, and C. Easton Rothwell, *The Comparative Study of Elites* (Hoover Institute Studies, Series B, No. 1 [Stanford: Stanford University Press, 1952]).

[16] In 1950, for example, 22 per cent of the newly elected Conservative M.P.s were classified as barristers and solicitors. For more details on the social background of English political elites, see W. I. Guttsman, *The British Political Elite* (London: MacGibbon & Kee, 1963).

[17] Bernard Lewis, *The Emergence of Modern Turkey* (London: Oxford University Press, 1961), p. 455.

military coup in 1960, which resulted, among other things, in the execution of some prominent political leaders, including Premier Menderes himself, and in the imprisonment of a host of others, including President Jelal Bayar, and (c) the two unsuccessful coups of 1962 and 1963. Even though the Turkish political elite is 'in the process of', and in some respects has taken, 'the same occupational hue as that of its models in the West',[18] there does not seem to be evidence of a stable democratic polity of the Western variety. Returning, therefore, to what was said earlier, it should be added that neither a highly educated elite (in terms of years of schooling) nor one that exhibits features in its social composition found in other countries is a sufficient condition for a modern (in the sense of Western), democratic polity. Yet, without venturing into judgments of this sort, but speaking merely of political elites as an aspect of political culture, it would be true to say that during the republican period, a significant change has taken place in the occupational background of this group. Examples of such social change are: (a) the emergence into political prominence of the free professionals (lawyers, doctors, engineers, and, to some extent, journalists); (b) the relative decline (from the First to the Tenth Assemblies) of 'government officials' and 'military leaders'; (c) the relative increase (comparing the First and the Tenth Assemblies) of 'trade' and 'agriculture'; and (d) the virtual disappearance of the occupational category of religion (from 17 per cent in the First Assembly to only 1 per cent in the Tenth).[19] Undoubtedly, these new Turkish elites as a whole have been recruited from occupational backgrounds different from their Ottoman counterparts, and variations have been taking place since the establishment of the republic. Regardless of what changes of this nature have been at work, one single element has remained constant: the *high level of formal education* which has characterized all members of the Grand National Assembly.

Historians of the Ottoman period, Turcologists, travellers, and other observers have often referred to a relative 'openness' in the patterns of social recruitment, selection, and occupational placement, and to a fluidity in the Ottoman-Turkish

[18] Frey, *op cit.*, p. 306 (in pre-publication copy).
[19] *Ibid.*, p. 305a (in pre-publication copy).

society. They have pointed to the absence of a 'caste' or 'aristocratic' system and to the several methods and instances in which people of low socio-economic backgrounds moved up the social scale and attained positions of power and high status. The picture does not seem to be so clear in the period of the republic. Some writers have claimed that the Ottoman 'mud-hut-to-palace' phenomenon, or vertical social mobility, was 'even more marked a characteristic of the Kemalist society', and that the Turkish society is 'essentially an open class society', meaning that people can move up or down the social scale without having to bolster or constrain such mobility movements on family or other 'ascriptive' grounds.[20] Others have talked about the pervasive influence of family background in access to education, occupational employment, and high political office-holding. Referring specifically to political party leaders, Kemal Karpat wrote:

'The party founders and leaders belong almost exclusively to the well-to-do landowners or intellectuals . . . Moreover, family background is of major importance. The present party leaders of Turkey, with only minor exceptions, belong to rich, or politically and socially prominent sections of the population. Many times individuals with little experience in public life and questionable educational background are catapulted into leading positions in the parties merely because of family background.'[21]

Certainly, there are many *individual* examples to support either of these claims.[22] However, statements about social mobility or social fluidity, about prestige, status, and the like, have mostly been impressionistic or based on individual cases. There has been a conspicuous absence of research on the various dimensions of this facet of Turkish culture. This study on the Turkish lise sought answers to some questions pertaining to social mobility, occupational prestige, and such, and some

[20] See, for example, Lewis V. Thomas and Richard N. Frye, *The United States and Turkey and Iran* (Cambridge, Mass.: Harvard University Press, 1952), p. 113.
[21] Kemal H. Karpat, *Turkey's Politics: The Transition to a Multi-Party System* (Princeton: Princeton University Press, 1959), p. 392.
[22] With certain qualifications, Frey takes a position which lies in between. He agrees with a Turkish writer that although 'a good family background' may be an advantage, 'a poor background' does not constitute a serious handicap. See Frey, *op. cit.*, pp. 248–52 (in pre-publication copy).

of the findings are analysed in Chapter X. In view of what has been discussed thus far, a caveat would be in order at this point. 'Openness' and 'closeness' are somewhat slippery concepts. It is quite possible, for example, to have an 'open' pattern of elite recruitment, but low aggregate mobility. This may occur in societies in which high status employment opportunities or elite positions are rather limited. As Foster rightly pointed out, such a situation holds true in many developing or new nations where expansion of the employment sector is slow, or where the modern sector of the economy is controlled by government agencies. Education is often linked to mobility and elite status, but those who 'make it' may be relatively few. This often leads people to assume a higher rate of social nobility and a high degree of 'openness' in the system. The Turkish situation displays similar characteristics. As in Foster's study of Ghana, 'few are chosen—but those that are chosen frequently provide dramatic instances of personal mobility'.[23] This also is essentially what 'openness' implied during the pre-revolutionary Ottoman period.

Finally, as in the Ottoman period, certain specific educational skills and other 'educational' activities seem to have persisted in facilitating access to high political office. One such 'skill' has been knowledge of a foreign language. Until the first quarter of the nineteenth century, members of the minority millets (e.g., the Greek Orthodox dragomans) were able to occupy high posts in the 'Sublime Porte', partly because of their linguistic proficiencies. In the nineteenth century, knowledge of French became a very valuable asset for entry into the civil bureaucracy and for promotion within its ranks. In addition, until the first years of the republic, knowledge of Arabic and Persian was an important prerequisite for eminence and status in certain branches of Ottoman life, especially in the religious and intellectual spheres.

Some sort of foreign language competence has been a significant factor in 'parliamentary longevity' during the republican period; and some knowledge of French a predominant linguistic

---

[23] Philip J. Foster, 'Secondary Schooling and Social Mobility in a West African Nation,' *Sociology of Education*, XXXVII (Winter, 1963), 165–6. See also James S. Coleman (ed.), *Educational and Political Development* (Princeton: Princeton University Press, 1965), pp. 26–7.

accoutrement of political leaders. As English gains a firmer foothold, however, the relative prominence of French is diminishing.[24] This is characteristic not only of the political elites, but also of the other elites (business, professional, educational, etc.). The change is apparent in all walks of Turkish life, and it is revealed in the age differentials of the educated classes. Persons over 45 years of age more often than not know French rather than English or any other foreign language; younger individuals, who received their education later in the history of the republic, especially after World War II, more often than not know English rather than French or any other foreign language. This reflects the growing influence of English-speaking countries, especially the United States, in the Westernization or modernization movement of Turkey as a whole. In some instances, such as education, knowledge of English or French is also associated with Americanophilia or Francophilia, and all the educational strengths and weaknesses such associations connote.

THE SCHOOLS AND POLITICAL IDEOLOGIES

Since the emergence of the idea of a Turkish national state, Turkish leaders have conceived of the schools as prime agencies in developing national consciousness, ideologies, values, and behaviours different from what had existed before and aimed at the over-all transformation of the political ethic of the country. As stated above, the idea of a Turkish nation-state was not even introduced until the latter part of the nineteenth century. But the idea of a *Turkish* secular nation with clearly defined physical boundaries, with a common culture, a common language, a common religion, and a common ethnic heritage was a twentieth-century and, for all meaningful purposes, a post-revolutionary phenomenon. To accomplish this task the schools were assigned a great deal of importance.

Foremost in the schools' responsibility for the political education of the Turkish youth has been the inculcation of nationalistic sentiments. Objectives such as the training of youth 'to feel the honour of being a son of the Turkish race',

---

[24] Frey, *op. cit.*, pp. 140–3, 301–14 (in pre-publication copy). English has already supplanted French as the predominant foreign language in the secondary schools and the universities.

to respect the national flag, to 'protect the esteem of the glorious Turkish history', to appreciate 'the great Turks whose services have made the great Turkish nation', to be bound by the principles of the Turkish Revolution, 'to preserve' as Atatürk put it, 'and defend the National Independence of the Turkish Republic', and so on, continue to be important goals of national education. All political parties in Turkey have proclaimed these as being central goals of formal education.[25]

Instruction in schools aimed at the development of patriotism and other Turkish nationalistic attitudes takes the form of both formal and informal activities, that is, courses in civics, history, and Turkish, and the observation of national holidays, national celebrations, and so on. An example of the more formalized aspect of nationalistic instruction is the content and emphasis of the lise course in history. In each of the three lise classes, special emphasis is placed upon the history of the Turkish Republic (the Revolutionary War, the establishment of the republic, the revolutionary ideology, the developments since 1923, etc.), and on the origins, migrations and empire-building of the Turkish 'race'. One of the explicit objectives of the history course is 'to prepare citizens with a national consciousness and feeling'.[26] In pursuing this objective, linking the development of the Turkish 'race' with that of the Turkish 'nation' is stressed. 'Racism,' according to one intimate observer of Turkish schools, 'is a strong element in Turkish nationalism'. In history textbooks, the word 'motherland' sometimes refers to Central Asia (with racial connotations, since the Turks originated in that part of the world) and sometimes to Anatolia, where the Turkish nation was born.[27]

Precisely how successful have the schools been in this aspect of political education or socialization of Turkish youth? From several observations and impressionistic statements, the Turkish youth as well as the Turkish people could be said to display strong nationalistic attitudes and beliefs. Turkish

[25] See, for example, the views of the Democratic Party in 1950, in Richard D. Robinson, 'An Analysis of Turkish Education' (International Bank for Reconstruction and Development, a working paper for the 1950 Economic Survey Mission to Turkey [typewritten, Ankara, 1950]), p. 12.

[26] Richard E. Maynard, 'The Lise and Its Curriculum in the Turkish Educational System' (Ph.D. dissertation, The University of Chicago, 1961), p. 331.

[27] *Ibid.*, p. 252.

nationalism is no longer the dream of a few visionary utopian intellectuals; it is an activating force pervading the entire fabric of the society and influencing the course of Turkish development. In the words of a Turkish political scientist: 'Nationalism is the foundation of the Republic and a basic tenet in the program of all the political parties ... In internal affairs, nationalism became the supreme force dominating all activities in the society, visualizing problems and moulding ideas in the light of its own conceptions.'[28] Turkish nationalism, like most of Turkey's modernization concepts and institutions, originated in the West; but like such concepts and institutions, it has been substantially transformed, in accordance with Turkish cultural and historical conditions and the revolutionary political ideologies. The concept is still undergoing change and adjustment. One particular characteristic of Turkish nationalism has been its self-centredness and its distrust of 'the outside world'. Largely because of Turkey's own peculiar historical background, it is marked by relative intolerance, or perhaps inflexibility, in accommodating anything that smacks of competition in loyalties or ideologies. Criticism of national heroes, of the revolutionary ideology, or of nationalism itself, is tantamount to rejection of Turkey itself; it is close to treason and hence not to be tolerated. In one respect, the history of Turkish nationalism has been a constant attempt to eradicate all 'foreign' elements which in any sense were felt to compete with *the one and only Turkish nationalism*. Many minority groups symbolized elements antithetical to Atatürk's concept of Turkish nationalism in the minds of the new Turks; according to the Turks, they still do; hence they have no place in Turkey. The excesses manifested in the treatment of certain minorities must in part be attributed to this monolithic and inflexible character of Turkish nationalism.

As for the role of formal education in the creation and development of this regulating ideology in modern Turkey, the only statement which can be made is that it exists among the youth. This is particularly true of many of the lise youth examined. It was manifested on several occasions and in varying forms. For example, to the question, 'As a parent, what two specific things will you try hardest to teach your children?'

[28] Karpat, *op. cit.*, p. 251.

answers such as 'love of country' and 'usefulness to the nation' were quite frequent. Similar responses were given to the question, 'What is the most important thing you have gained from your schooling up to now?' Statements such as 'because I [he] will be of greater service to my [his] country or to my [his] nation' were quite common in answers to several questions pertaining to preferred occupations and occupational ranking. But *none of the students in the minority lises* gave such, or similar, answers!

However, nationalistic attitudes, even if they are found to be strongly espoused by lise students, do not provide proof that the schools are responsible for generating them. They may exist before the students enter the lises, and they may be developed in the lower rungs of the educational ladder, in the family, the youth organizations, the extra-school activities, or somewhere else. This may indeed be the case with other attitudes pertaining to the political education of the Turkish youth.

In building the new nation, Atatürk and his followers envisaged a modern system of government with authority vested in a popularly elected national assembly, with broader citizen interest and involvement, and with the decision making process based on rational and secular procedures. In 1931, the Republican People's Party adopted six fundamental principles upon which the Turkish state was to be based: republicanism, nationalism, populism, *étatism*, secularism, and revolutionism, all of which were incorporated in the Constitution of 1937. The latest Constitution of Turkey, adopted after the 1960 coup d'état, stipulates that 'the Turkish Republic is a nationalistic, democratic, secular and social State governed by the rule of law, based on human rights and the fundamental tenets set forth in the preamble'.[29] Thus the polity towards which the Turks have aimed is a secular democracy governed by the principles of equality, freedom, and popular political participation. In the attainment of this goal, the schools have been

[29] The preamble states that the Turkish nation is 'guided by the desire to establish a democratic rule of law based on juridical social foundations, which will ensure and guarantee human rights and liberties, national solidarity, social justice, and the welfare and prosperity of the individual and society.' See *Constitution of the Turkish Republic*, trans. Sadik Balkan, Ahmet E. Uysal, and Kemal H. Karpat (Ankara, 1961), p. 3.

called upon to do several things, including the task of 'educating' the younger generation to accept and commit itself to such a political ideology. To what extent they have succeeded in the performance of this function is difficult to determine. Comments on the existence of a high degree of secularism among the lise youth have already been made, but, as with nationalistic attitudes, it is not certain that the lise has been responsible for student commitment to such secularism. Indeed, the high degree of consensus manifested among students at this level of education would suggest that, if the schools are at all responsible for this secular politicization, this is probably done at the lower levels of schooling. It may be done at home, or it may be the result of a variety of agencies. In addition to the many government reforms, teachers and parents were called upon to implant secular values in the children. In conversation with many Turks who received their basic education in the thirties, this writer was informed that there were explicit efforts made by parents, elders, and teachers to instil anti-traditional and anti-clerical beliefs and attitudes; attachment to the Islamic religion was inextricably associated with the stagnant and decadent Ottoman past.

Secularism in Turkey, however, is more complex than would appear at first sight. The lise youth represent a select group of students and, even in their case, expressed 'commitment' to an ideology must be distinguished from a personality characteristic. And the overwhelming mass of pupils in the villages, where the distinction between secular and religious is not clearly drawn, must be remembered. These distinctions and observations would also apply to other politically relevant questions as reflected in the expressed statements by the Turkish youth. Frey, Angell and Sanay have found that among the lise-age group there was expressed 'commitment' to certain democratic principles, that is, students emphasized participation 'by the people' and voting in national elections as basic democratic principles. However, as these writers quickly point out, although such answers are heuristically valuable in that they suggest attitudinal changes from traditional beliefs, they are by no means conclusive. The consensus displayed by the Turkish youth on democracy defined in terms of participation 'by the people' may mean that to such youth *voting* in national or other elections sufficiently defines their concept of participation. Moreover, although the political importance of an expressed ideological commitment should not be discounted, it does not automatically reflect a personality or behavioural trait.

There is no way of knowing what the ideological commitment to democracy among students is in other types of schools or among the population at large. It is known that a comparatively large number of the electorate has voted in national elections; but there are also strong indications that, among the peasant groups in particular, people did not know either the party or what they were actually voting for. Commenting on consensus or commitment to a democratic ideology unavoidably brings memories of the recent successful and unsuccessful military coups. The question is raised as to how successful the various agencies (including the schools) responsible for establishing such consensus or commitment have been. That substantial progress has been made since the Ottoman days would certainly not be denied, but the establishment of a viable, stable, and modern democratic polity in Turkey has yet to be attained.

CHAPTER X

THE LISE AND SOCIAL CHANGE:
A CASE STUDY

THE lise is centrally located in the educational, socio-economic, and power structure of Turkey. It is the school upon which the Turkish leaders, since the early years of the twentieth century, have relied for the development of the intellectual skills, the attitudes, and the necessary leadership for the nourishment and sustenance of their national and cultural aspirations. To the 'common man' a lise education will socially and culturally elevate his son and make him an efendi. In short, the lise is perceived to play an important role in Turkey's ongoing movement towards modernity. As such, it merits special attention which would go beyond the 'educational' functions discussed in a previous chapter. Accordingly, this last chapter will focus on certain *social* functions of the lise: how it is related to certain characteristics of the Turkish society, what the specific cultural attributes of the students attending them are, and what implications these have for Turkish social and political development.

Ideally, an inquiry of this nature would be more complete if there were sufficient data on the graduates of the lises: what jobs or positions they occupy after graduation, what their performance, role and normative patterns are, and how, in retrospect they perceive their previous education. Such information, now unfortunately lacking, would be valuable in several ways. In the first place, it would shed more light on the status spread of the aggregate of school products. This would be particularly relevant in assessing the role of specific schools or types of institutions in elite recruitment, a point referred to in the previous chapter. Merely looking at the educational background of political elites tells only part of the story concerning the political role of institutions. In the second place, as Foster aptly put it, 'Knowledge of the occupational activities of school-leavers is a prerequisite to any meaningful educational planning.'[1] And thirdly, information of this kind would facilitate more reliable statements concerning the changes that have taken place since the Ottoman days.

The examination of the social role of the lise will focus on the lise students themselves: who they are, what they aspire to in life, how they perceive certain aspects of the society, and what values they espouse. In seeking answers to such questions we shall draw mainly from the findings of a field study conducted by the present writer in 1962–63.[2]

SOCIAL BACKGROUND CHARACTERISTICS

As with the political elites, research into the social characteristics of school populations has been receiving increased attention from educationists, sociologists, political scientists, historians, and even economists. Education in general, and schools in particular, have always aimed at the moral and intellectual development of the individual and the society as well as at the transmission of a nation's cultural heritage. In addition, schools have performed selective functions; that is, on the basis of certain criteria, they have also acted as sieves, retaining and allowing some individuals to pursue educational paths different from those pursued by others, thus exposing them to different types of education and charting different career paths for those selected. This, naturally, results in differences in the part—political, occupational, family, or what not—which the selected individual will play in the society after attending or finishing school or a special type of educational institution. Selection has been characteristic of the

---

[1] Philip J. Foster, 'Secondary School Leaders in Ghana: Expectations and Reality,' *Harvard Educational Review*, XXXIV, No. 4 (Fall, 1964), 537. Some of the information in this chapter could easily be compared with similar data in Foster's studies on Ghanaian secondary schools.

[2] For a description of the research procedures, see Appendix C.

Turkish lise, as it has of comparable institutions in other countries. From its inception, the Turkish lise has been envisaged as a school for the potential elites—those few talented individuals who were destined to be the leaders or the 'builders', so to speak, of the new society and the new state—as well as the repository of Turkish culture and ideals.

That the lise should be selective in terms of intellectual criteria is a view which has persisted throughout the history of the institution. Whether the lises have indeed selected the most intellectually competent students is another question. Statements made at several periods of Turkish history indicate that to some, the lise was a school confined to the 'enlightened class', or, as Gökalp put it, 'to those who will make up the ruling class'. An official statement in 1932 reads, 'The first educational objective of our government is the education of children, the second the education of the people, and the third [which was to take place in the *lises*] of the enlightened class.'[3] It is not clear whether 'enlightened class' means a social group already considered 'enlightened', which would imply that the lise would also be a *socially* exclusive institution. As noted in the previous chapter, many people have claimed that the Turkish society has always been 'an open class society' with ample opportunities (a major one being education) to move up the social scale. Be that as it may, for an understanding of the evolution of the lise and of its place in present-day Turkish society, a look into certain *social* characteristics of the lise population is important. Accordingly, this study will focus on the social origins of students and such family characteristics as paternal occupation, parental education, parental place of residence, and some other rough indices of the students' socioeconomic background.

Father's Occupation

Students and observers of Turkish society have often commented on the importance of occupations in status differentiation and social distinctions. As Frey put it, 'A man's occupation is second in importance only to his education in determining

[3] For this and other statements, see Richard E. Maynard, 'The Lise and Its Curriculum in the Turkish Educational System' (Ph.D. dissertation, The University of Chicago, 1961), pp. 170–3.

his social placement in Turkish society.'[4] Moreover, father's occupation seems to be a crucial factor in the son's place in the status hierarchy. What then are the characteristics of the lise students in terms of this variable?

In the sample, the three major occupational categories most heavily represented in the lises were: (a) 'official' (government, administrative, and clerical, i.e., occupations whose primary association was with some state function); (b) 'trade and business'; and (c) 'professional' (free professions). The approximade percentages in each of these groups were: 23 for each of the first two and 22 for the 'professional' category (see Table XI). Combining the categories of 'official' and 'professional', about 44 per cent of the sampled students were drawn from 'white collar' occupations, in comparison to 17·5 per cent who were drawn from the ranks of skilled and unskilled workers, and 34 per cent from such economic groups as 'agriculture' and 'trade and small business'. The foreign and private Turkish schools draw most of their students from the professional category, the public lises, from 'farmers, fishermen, hunters, and the like', and the minority lises, from the trader and business groups.[5] Except for the minority schools, all three other types of lises recruit the largest percentage of their students from the 'white collar' category. This is more so the case with the foreign schools and less with the public lises.

These figures become more meaningful if they are interpreted against the background of the distribution of occupations in Turkey as a whole (see Table XII). It is patently clear that the professional and official occupational groups are over-represented, and the 'agriculture' category, under-represented. Although farmers, fishermen, and related groups constitute over 60 per cent of the entire male population, less than 10 per cent in the sample indicated that their fathers were engaged in such occupations. On the other hand, 44 per cent of the

[4] For this and other statements on the social importance of occupations, see Frederick W. Frey, *The Turkish Political Elite* (Cambridge, Mass., pre-publication copy), pp. 165–72.

[5] In the case of the minority schools, this is not shown in the Table. Breaking down the category of 'skilled workers and craftsmen' into the two constituent groups results in the following representation: craftsmen, 23 per cent; and skilled workers, about 11 per cent.

229

students indicated that their fathers belonged to the official and professional groups, yet such occupations constitute only 5·5 per cent of the male population of the country. Clearly, on this basis alone, there are inequalities of access into the academic lises in Turkey. However, the variations among the four types of schools should be examined before elaborating this question. Dividing the occupational categories into white-collar and others, the foreign and the private Turkish schools are seen to recruit the *majority* of their students from the white-collar group (59 per cent in the former, and 52 per cent in the latter). The representation of the white-collar group is high in the public lises (about 39 per cent); but, in relation to the private Turkish and the foreign schools, so is that of 'others', more particularly, of the agricultural group. Viewed against the occupational background of the Turkish male population, the following statements could be made: (a) in all four types of schools, the 'white-collar' occupations are over-represented, and agriculture is under-represented; (b) the white-collar over-representation is higher in the foreign and private Turkish schools than in the public or minority schools, and it is highest in the foreign and lowest in the minority; (c) within the white-collar category, the representation of the *professional* group is highest in the foreign schools, and lowest in the public schools, but that of the *official* group is highest in the public schools and lowest in the minority schools; (d) the representation of the 'agriculture' group is highest in the public schools and lowest in the foreign schools; (e) the representation of skilled workers and craftsmen is higher in the minority and public schools, about equal in the private Turkish schools, and lowest in the foreign schools, the highest representation being in the minority lises; and (f) private traders and small businessmen are over-represented in all types of schools, but more so in the minority schools and less so in the public schools.

The last finding points up an interesting characteristic of Ottoman and Turkish culture. In general, there is a relatively heavy representation of 'middle' social strata, namely, minor administrators, clerks, private traders and small businessmen, particularly the last two, the 'business' groups. Within these groups, the largest concentrations are in the minority and the foreign schools. This should not be unduly surprising, especially in the case of the minority representation. Traditionally, the Greek, the Armenian, and the Jewish minorities were mostly engaged in careers in business, commerce, industries and crafts. This traditional occupational pattern continued during the early decades of the republic, and, to a large extent, it still characterizes the small remaining Greek and Armenian minorities of Istanbul. The ethnic Turkish elites, on the other hand, have traditionally been engaged in administrative and military occupations; and the overwhelming majority of the masses (over 75 per cent) has been engaged in 'agriculture' and 'services'. It is not surprising, therefore, that three-fourths of all the students who came from 'clerical backgrounds' should be in the public or private Turkish lises, that is, in schools which are almost completely Turkish in ethnic composition. Such an occupational characteristic of the Turks would also explain the relatively high representation of agricultural occupations (small farmers, fishermen, hunters, etc.) in the public lises, and the relatively low representation of these groups in the minority and foreign schools.

Considering paternal occupation as a criterion of access into the lises, there are differences in the chances a child has to enter a lise. Assuming that the professional and the official categories also represent the more prestigious or the elite groups (a point to be supported later), the lises are, in general, 'socially elitist', this being more the case with some types (e.g., the foreign and the private Turkish) and less with others (e.g., the public and the minority). On the basis of this argument alone, it could be said that the socially elitist nature of the lise has persisted, since the Ottoman lise was indeed an elite institution. However, the data also indicate that the lises, especially the public ones (which are more numerous and, in the Turkish society, perhaps the most significant), are by no means socially exclusive institutions. The *majority* of the students in the public lises are drawn from the non-white-collar occupational groups. About 23 per cent are drawn from what might be called primary occupations, about 20 per cent from such groups as skilled, semi-skilled, and unskilled workers and craftsmen, and about 14 per cent from private traders and small business people. Also, the 'economic' (not including professional, official, and agriculture) groups are fairly well

231

represented in all types of lises. It would seem, therefore, that the lise is not an elite school in the sense that certain of its nineteenth-century European counterparts were,[6] nor in the sense that the sultanis were during the Ottoman period. The number of students from the less affluent segments of the society or from the 'lower social classes' attending the lises does not seem to represent a 'mere trickle', although this may indeed be the case *in some specific schools*. The public lise, in particular, appears to be as much a 'popular' school as it is the school of the memur and the professional classes. This in itself signifies an important development in the selective function of the lise.

Distribution According to Sex

We have already commented on the privileged position of the male in the Ottoman and Turkish cultures. During the Ottoman period, only girls from the urban higher classes received any schooling; even among such classes, the number of educated women was quite small. The policy of the republic was to extend educational opportunities for women and to provide the same type of education as for boys.[7]

Although there have been increases in female enrolments during the republican period, girls' education continues to lag behind that of boys. As expected, there were more boys than girls in the aggregate sample, and the same imbalance was found in the several occupational categories. The findings also show that, in general, girls came from higher occupational groups than boys. While *one-third* of the girls were drawn from the three uppermost groups (professional, higher technical, managerial and higher administrative), less than *one-fourth* of the boys came from the same groups. The sharpest deviations were in the 'agriculture' and the 'higher professional' categories: there are more girls and fewer boys than expected whose fathers are higher professionals; but there are fewer girls and

---

[6] Foster has made the same observation about the recruitment patterns of Ghanaian secondary schools. See Philip J. Foster, 'Secondary Schooling and Social Mobilty in a West African Nation,' *Sociology of Education*, XXXVII (Winter, 1963), p. 163.

[7] See Hasan Ali Yüjel, *Türkiyede Orta Ogretim* (*Secondary Education in Turkey* [Istanbul: Devlet Basimevi, 1938]), p. 26.

more boys than expected whose fathers are small farmers, fishermen, hunters, and the like.

Parental Education

Education in Turkey, as already stated, has been one of the most important, if not the most important, single factor in determining a person's social placement. It has been described as the 'hallmark of the elite', and it has been found to be the crucial criterion underlying social distinctions among the Turkish people. As Daniel Lerner has observed, education differentiates the Turks into moderns, traditionals, and transitionals, thus performing 'a critical function' in the modernization process.[8] Education has been, and is still perceived to be, an important condition for social mobility and occupational placement. Studies of other societies have also revealed that level of education is related to the desire for more education, and that one of the criteria for recruitment and selection in the schools is educational background of parents. For these reasons, it is necessary to examine the composition of the student body in the Turkish lise in terms of this crucial variable.

More than half of the students had fathers with a secondary (middle, technical, lise) or higher education, and about one-fourth had fathers with an elementary education (see Table XIII). The educational level of the mother was lower, but not substantially so: about 46 per cent of the students indicated that their mothers had attended and/or completed a secondary school or an institution of higher learning; and about 28 per cent, that their mothers had gone to an elementary school. In the case of both father's and mother's education, the highest percentage was in the secondary school category; that is, taking a four-tiered structure (no education, elementary, secondary, and higher), the largest number of the students' parents had attended or finished an orta school, a lise, or a vocational school. Viewed against the educational background of the Turkish population at large, the figures show clearly (see Table XIV) that the majority of the lise students are drawn from relatively well-educated segments of the Turkish society.

[8] Daniel Lerner, *The Passing of Traditional Society: Modernizing the Middle East* (Glencoe, Illinois: Free Press Paperback Edition, 1964), pp. 47 ff.

About 38 per cent of the students had fathers who had *completed* a secondary or higher educational institution; and yet, among the Turkish population between fifteen and sixty-four years of age, *only 7 per cent* had the equivalent in formal schooling. Among the Turkish *female* population of the same age range, less than 1 per cent had, in 1960, completed a secondary or higher school, but more than 30 per cent of the students in the four types of lises indicated that their mothers had comparable amounts of schooling.

The data, therefore, show that the educational background of the parents is an important factor in gaining access into the lises. Stated differently: relative to the educational level of the Turkish population, the lise students are recruited from a small and comparatively well-educated class. A combination of family education with family occupation suggests that children of well-educated parents, who also belong to the 'white-collar' occupational groups, have greater chances for a lise type of education than non-educated blue-collar or other groups.

The relationship between occupational and educational background on one hand, and student representation in the lises on the other, might be illustrated further by examining other relevant data. In the 1960 Census estimates, the majority of the 'economically active male population' (over 60 per cent) had not completed elementary school, and only about 1 per cent had completed an institution of higher learning). This population group includes people engaged in agriculture, commerce, industry, and the like. In contrast, the 'white-collar' workers are the most educated segment of the Turkish population. Cross-tabulations of the two variables (occupation and education) in the lise study reveals the following variations: of those students with fathers engaged in the professions (1,073, representing about 22 per cent of the total number who responded), close to 70 per cent indicated that their fathers had a lise or higher education; only 1·5 per cent had fathers with no education and 10 per cent, with elementary education. Of the white-collar group, close to 60 per cent had fathers with lise or better education. In contrast, of those respondents with fathers engaged in agriculture and related occupations, less than 5 per cent indicated that their fathers had a lise or higher education; about 36 per cent had no education, and an additional 45 per cent, an elementary education. Of all students whose parents had a university education, close to 85 per cent indicated that their fathers belonged to the white-collar group, and a mere ·4 per cent, to the 'agriculture' group; but of the students whose parents had an elementary education and less (1,680, representing about 34 per cent of the total sample), 7 per cent belonged to the white-collar category and 42 per cent, to 'agriculture' plus skilled and semi-skilled vocations. Of all students whose parents had completed a university (about 16 per cent of the total sample), about 91 per cent also belonged to the white-collar category and only ·25 per cent, to 'agriculture'; of all students whose parents had no education, about 59 per cent belonged to agriculture and skilled–unskilled categories, but only 8 per cent to the white-collar group. In short, students with parents in the white-collar category also had well-educated parents, those in the blue-collar categories had less-educated parents, and so on. However, the aggregates and the variations within the four types of schools warrant some additional comments and qualifications.

In a society in which the majority of the people are totally illiterate or possess very little formal schooling, the very fact that 20 per cent of the fathers and 29 per cent of the mothers are drawn from an educationally 'disadvantaged' group is particularly noteworthy. A look at the students in the *public* lises reveals this important variation in the social recruitment pattern with greater clarity. About one-third of this group (see Table XIV) had fathers who had no formal education or had attended, but not completed, an elementary school; and the percentage was much higher (58 per cent) when mother's education was given. Indeed, among the public lise students, about 17 per cent indicated that their fathers had no formal education whatsoever (Table XIII). Apparently, therefore, when education is taken as the social background characteristic, public lises in Turkey are not exclusively elite institutions. Elitism in this sense is more apparent in the private Turkish lises and most apparent in the foreign schools (for example, more than 60 per cent of the students in the foreign schools had parents who had completed a secondary or higher institution;

and *more than one-third* indicated that their parents had completed a *university or equivalent higher institution*).

The educational background characteristics of the minority lise students lend themselves to some interesting comparisons with those of the students in the other lises.

The figures show that a substantial percentage (surpassed only slightly by the students in the public lises) of the minority school pupils had fathers with no education or very little formal education. But within this category, only about 6 per cent of the fathers and about 9 per cent of the mothers had 'never attended school', the comparable percentages for both the public and the private Turkish lise students being higher. The educational level of the majority of the parents of the minority lise students does not go beyond the lise level, and about 21 per cent (the highest single figure) of such parents completed a middle school (orta) or a lise. In general, the educational level of the mothers of these students is higher than that of the mothers of the public lise students, but lower than that of the 'foreign' and the private Turkish pupils.

Finally, it is quite obvious that the majority of the lise students have already reached a level of education considerably higher than their parents. These students are also overwhelmingly desirous of continuing their education in an institution of higher learning, a level attained only by a very small percentage of the Turkish population; and further, they aspire to careers which are ranked high in the prestige hierarchy.

Educational Distribution According to Sex

The findings on the educational background characteristics of boys and girls lend further validity to the observations made concerning the occupation variable. Generally, the parents of female students are better educated than those of the males. Cross-tabulations have shown significant relationships between sex and paternal education ($\chi^2 = 330 \cdot 45$; D.F. $= 11$; significant at $\cdot 001$ level), and sex and maternal education ($\chi^2 = 452 \cdot 11$; D.F. $= 11$; significant at $\cdot 001$ level).

The 'emancipation' of the Turkish woman has been an avowed policy of the Turkish modernizers. Turkish writers speak with pride about the progress that has been made. Some of them, however, tend to exaggerate. One such writer eulogized:

'But most important of all are the thousands of Turkish girls who crowd the high schools and the universities in competition with men. Moreover, these are the daughters of rich and poor, educated and illiterate—ordinary Turks—all equally eager for schooling . . . In the flow of Turkish life, their joint desire to educate their daughters, and their amusement, together on holidays, dramatizing the dissolution of the patriarchal family into a conjugal unit, is vastly more meaningful than any outstanding performance by a handful of barristers, politicians, or educators.'[9]

This study casts doubt at such an encomium of progress in female education. Although today's lises include more girls than ever before, although more illiterate parents than before may send their daughters to 'high school', the fact remains that in the lises, girls with illiterate parents represent only a 'trickle' of the total population even in the urban centres. The more educated the parents are, the better a girl's chances are for a lise education and for higher education.

Regional and Urban–Rural Variations
The lise was and continues to be a city school. The two largest cities of Turkey (Istanbul and Ankara) contain *one-quarter* of the total public lises; and Istanbul alone contains about half of the private Turkish lises, all of the minority schools, all but two of the foreign schools, and 16 per cent of the public lises. The private schools (Turkish, minority, and foreign) are overwhelmingly big city schools; the public lises are more evenly distributed. Even these latter schools are heavily concentrated in the big cities; and the others are in cities or towns which are the capitals or centres, and therefore the largest localities, of the provinces.

Under these conditions, it would be natural to expect that the majority of the students attending lises would be 'urban' in origin, and that the majority would be overwhelming in the private schools. The findings, as noted earlier, corroborate this statement (see Tables VI and VII). Furthermore, taking paren-

[9] Nuri Eren, *Turkey Today and Tomorrow: An Experiment in Modernization* (New York: Frederick A. Praeger, 1963), p. 181.

tal residence as the index, it was found that: (a) less than 7 per cent of the aggregate of students indicated that their parents lived in a village at that time, the figures being higher for boys than for girls, and for public lise students than for those in the other schools; (b) the overwhelming majority of the respondents (86 per cent) listed parental place of residence as being 'in this vilayet', the figure being lower among boys than girls, lowest among foreign lise students, and highest among the minority ones; (c) two-thirds of the public lise students and over three-fourths of the students in each of the other types of schools stated that their parents lived 'in this city or town in which I am going to school', the total percentage for girls being higher than for boys; and (d) the lowest percentage of students whose parents lived in places outside 'this vilayet' was recorded among the minority lise students, and the highest percentage of students whose parents lived in a city or town outside 'this vilayet' was recorded among the foreign lise respondents. On the basis of these findings, it could be generalized that the Turkish lise is not only an urban school; it is also a *local* school in that it recruits most of its students from the town or city in which it is located and from nearby places. The minority lises, as might be expected, are the most urban and the most local; and so are the girls vis-à-vis the boys.

On another index, namely, how the students consider themselves, the overwhelming majority (82·0 per cent) described themselves as 'urban', the percentage being higher among girls, lowest among public school students, and highest among the respondents in the foreign schools.

These findings, taken in conjunction with the previous ones (occupational and educational background), suggest the following generalization: urban, white-collar children, whose parents are also well educated, are over-represented in the lises, while other children, who constitute the great bulk of the Turkish population, are under-represented. Or to put it another way: children whose parents live in cities, and the largest cities at that, are engaged in white-collar occupations, and are well educated in terms of formal schooling attained, have greater chances for a lise education than other children. This generalization is supported by other tabulations. Taking the second index mentioned above, (a) urban parents are also the more highly educated parents, and (b) 'white-collar' parents are also the more urban parents. And it has already been concluded that: (a) most students have urban fathers or consider themselves as urban, (b) they have well-educated fathers in relation to the population, and (c) they are, to a great extent, recruited from white-collar occupational categories. To reiterate, there are some variations, especially in the case of the public lises and the minority lises: in the public lises, in particular, 17 per cent of the students stated that their fathers lived in villages, and 39 per cent described themselves as 'rural'. And among students in these groups, there are significant proportions whose parents have had very little or no education, and did not belong to the white-collar groups. It would seem, therefore, that the public lise, in comparison to the other Turkish, and predominantly Moslem, schools is also more of a 'people's school'.

FATHERS, GRANDFATHERS, AND SONS

Reference has already been made to the various viewpoints concerning 'fluidity' or 'openness' in the Turkish society. It was pointed out, however, that information on such questions as social mobility, occupational prestige, and the like, is rather impressionistic in nature. The analysis of the recruitment pattern of the lises has shown an over-representation of certain occupational groups, but also a certain fluidity in the system in terms of the inflow of students from a variety of occupational and educational backgrounds. In order to assess better questions of mobility and social status, and this facet of social change, information was secured on generational changes in the occupational background of the students in the four lise types. Admittedly, this sample of the Turkish population is a rather select one, as already indicated. The lise is one, *but not the only one*, avenue of opportunity and of mobility; other institutions, such as the teacher-training colleges, the village institutes, and the several educational programmes of the army, have always been important agents of social mobility, especially among the village populaton, or at least among those who have taken advantage of them. But the lise occupies a pivotal position in the whole process of social advancement. It is virtually the only avenue for admission into the universities and thereby into the professions, the high offices in the bureaucracy, and the political hierarchy.

In view of the significance of father's occupation as an indicator of social status, information was sought on the following variables: grandfather's and father's occupation, and student's occupational aspirations and expectations. Answers to these questions would facilitate a better understanding of certain changes that have taken place during the republican period and what the outlook for the future seems to be. Moreover, students' perceptions concerning the occupational structure, occupational accessibility, and opportunity for advancement bear upon development and modernization in many countries of the world.

Taking aggregates first, Table XV shows substantial changes in the professional (high professional, professional, and high technical) and the agricultural categories: the percentage of *professional* fathers is almost *double* that of professional grandfathers, but the percentage of *agricultural* fathers has been reduced to about *half* that of grandfathers. The majority of the lise students (58·5 per cent), on their part, aspire towards careers in the professions, and more particularly, the high professions (medicine, engineering, law, etc.). Relative to fathers and grandfathers, the difference in this connection is most marked: *about 48 per cent* of the respondents indicated that, if they had their own choice about a job after finishing their education, they would like to become high professionals or engage in one of the so-called 'free professions'; yet only 6 per cent of the grandfathers and 12·4 per cent of the fathers belonged to this category. In contrast, *virtually no students* aspired towards 'agricultural' careers, which represent the largest single occupational characteristic of grandfathers and, to a degree, even of fathers. Likewise, relative to fathers and grandfathers, a very small percentage of students aspired towards careers in trade or business.

Similar disparities between grandfathers and fathers, between grandfathers or fathers and students, and generally between 'fathers' and 'offspring' are apparent in each of the four types of schools. With few variations, especially in the foreign schools, the pattern is the same: more professional fathers than grandfathers, and less agricultural fathers than grandfathers;

substantially high *professional* aspirations on the part of lise students; and substantially *low* aspirations for agricultural, trade, and business careers.

The data reveal some other interesting points. Relative to fathers, fewer students aspire towards careers classified as 'managerial and high administrative' (high-ranking business administrators, high-ranking members of the civil bureaucracy, e.g., valis, kaymakams, etc., high military officers, generals, large landowners), as 'minor administrative', and, excepting the minority group, as 'clerical' (memurs or minor government officials, teachers, non-commissioned officers, etc.).

Another important finding, as indicated in the same Table, is the variation or disparity between *aspirations* and *expectations*. Following a question on 'job toward which they aspired', students were asked: 'Of course, we cannot always have the job we would like best of all. Looking realistically at your future, what job do you think you will get?' The tabulated answers speak for themselves. The most dramatic change was registered in the case of the free professions. The group as a whole registered a *decrease of more than one-half* in the percentage of 'aspired' and 'expected' responses; and the percentage decrease was even greater among public school students. Increases, on the other hand, were registered in the case of clerical and 'trade and business' occupations. No significant differences between 'aspired' and 'expected' were found in the case of most of the other occupational categories.

Before any assessments on the significance of these findings are made, some other information pertaining to aspirations and expectations and to the students' perceptions of the occupational structure of Turkey would be relevant. Within the category of 'free professions', boys aspire towards careers as engineers more than towards any of the kindred free professions: *about one-third of the total number of boys marked 'engineering' as the job they would most like to have,* but only half of them *expected* to become engineers; and 19 per cent of the boys aspired towards careers in medicine, law and the like, but only about 9 per cent expected to become doctors, lawyers, dentists and so on. Preference for the free professions was also evident when students were asked to choose and to rank five occupations which, in their opinion, it would be 'most desirable to have'. Over 45 per cent of the total group chose and ranked highest 'free professional' as their preference. When asked to choose one of ten occupations (free professions and big business) as their first preference, about 25 per cent chose 'engineer' (not including architects), the percentage in favour of this occupation being higher among public lise students (30 per cent) and lowest among minority lise students (about 20 per cent). As in the item on 'job aspired', about 34 per cent of the *boys* chose 'engineering' from these occupations. But there were some interesting variations in the responses to the 'most preferred occupation' items. For example, from a list of eighteen different types of occupations in Turkey, about one-fifth of the public, and an equal percentage of the minority, school students chose teaching careers (primary, middle, and lise teacher), the percentages in each case being higher for 'lise teacher'. In contrast, a relatively small percentage of public school students chose careers in business (either as employees or as self-employed); but over 9 per cent of the students in each of the other schools chose such careers. Turning now to the free professional category and big business (merchant, factory owner, contractor, etc.), although the highest single percentage in the case of boys was 'engineer', the next highest were: scientist (12 per cent), medical doctor (11 per cent), and big business (11 per cent); among girls, for some reason or other, the highest was 'chemist' (17 per cent), the next highest, architect (16 per cent), and the third, medical doctor (15 per cent).

How do the lise students rank occupations in terms of prestige? Students were first given a list of eleven occupational categories ranging from 'free professional' to 'skilled labourer' and 'farm owner'. Then they were asked to rank them (1 to 11) according to the prestige and respect which in their opinion 'people in Turkey' accorded them. Here is how the students ranked as *number one* the various occupational clusters:

Occupational category	Highest prestige ranking (in per cent)	
	All students	Boys
Free professional	43	47
Diplomat (ambassador, consul, cultural attaché)	27	24
Education (teacher, principal, etc.)	6·6	7

Occupational category	Highest prestige ranking (in per cent)	
	All students	Boys
Business man (big)	6	7
Military officer	5	7
Religion	2	3
National government official	2	2
Farm owner	1	less than 1
Business executive or official (e.g., insurance company official, bank official, etc.)	1	less than 1

Following this, students were asked to do the same thing, that is, to rank according to prestige or respect, *specific* occupations under *four* selected clusters: free professional, government, education, and business-labour. Again only highest ranking (those marked as number one) is recorded. Regarding 'free professional', the results were as follows:

Free professional	Ranking (in per cent)	
	All students	Boys
Scientist	31	32
Engineer	29	33
Medical doctor	22	19·5
Lawyer	7	7
Pharmacist	3	2·4
Religious leader	2	2·5
Journalist	1·8	2
Dentist	1	1

Asked to rank eleven occupations having to do with the national and local government, the students' answers were:

Government (official)	Ranking (in per cent)	
	All students	Boys
Diplomat	33	29
Deputy in Assembly	31	35
Vali	14	17·5
Judge	7	7
Military Officer	3	3·7
Kaymakam	2·3	3·5
National Government Official	1·0	1·1
Müdür	1·0	1·3
Non-commissioned officer	·3	less than 1
Muhtar	·3	less than 1
Nahiye müdürü	·31	0

243

To point out some inter-school variations: (a) the percentage of students who ranked assembly deputy as possessing the highest prestige was lower among the minority school students than among those in the other three types of schools; (b) the figures for diplomat were lowest among the 'public' students and highest among the foreign school students; (c) the percentages for vali were highest among public and lowest among foreign lise students; and (d) figures for 'military officer' were higher among the public lise students than among the students in the other types of schools.

Regarding occupations classified under 'education', the majority of all the students (58 per cent), and of both the boys and the girls (57 and 67 per cent respectively) ranked 'university professor' highest in prestige. The occupation which received the next highest number of 'one' votes by all the students and by the boys was *milli egitim müdürü* (national education director); 'elementary school teacher' came third for the group as a whole (9 per cent) as well as for the boys (10 per cent); and 'lise teacher', quite surprisingly, was fourth (6 per cent of all the students). Some of the inter-school variations are noteworthy: (a) the percentages for 'professor' were highest among foreign (75 per cent) and lowest (51 per cent) among public lise students; (b) the figures for 'elementary teacher' were lower among minority and foreign lise students (7 per cent for each) than among those in the public and private Turkish schools (12 and 10 per cent respectively); (c) likewise, more public and private Turkish lise students ranked 'national education director' highest than minority and foreign students; but (d) more minority and public school respondents ranked 'lise teacher' highest.

Finally, turning to occupations classified under 'business and labour', the results were as follows:

Business and Labour	Ranking (*in per cent*)	
	All students	Boys
Manufacturer	47·6	50
Merchant (*tüjjar*, i.e., importer, exporter, etc.)	16·0	16·6
Building contractor	9·6	11·6
Independent large farm owner	6·5	9·0

Business and Labour	Ranking (in per cent)	
	All students	Boys
Mechanic	2·8	4·0
Private business executive or official		
(müstakil ish yeri müdürü)	2·0	3·0
Bank official	1·6	1·6
Small farm owner	·9	1·0
Agricultural worker	·9	1·0
Factory worker	·5	less than 1
Small merchant (küchük tüjjar)	·3	less than 1
Accountant, bookkeeper (muhasib)	·1	·0

As in the previous clusters of occupations, there were some interesting inter-school variations: (a) the percentages for 'manufacturer' ranged from 42 in 'minority' schools to 59 in foreign lises; (b) the range for 'merchant' was from 12 per cent in the public to 27 per cent in the minority schools; (c) figures for 'large farm owner', 'business official', and 'agricultural worker' were lowest among the minority group; and (d) more public and private Turkish lise students ranked 'large farm owner' highest in prestige than 'minority' or 'foreign' students.

The data presented in this section are perforce limited in that attention has been focused on one select segment of Turkish society. Also, in seeking to establish some sort of 'objective' ranking of occupations, only the students' highest rankings have been recorded. Nevertheless, on the basis of what has been presented, certain changes that have taken place during the period of the republic can be discussed, and statements about 'implications', and such, for the future course of 'development' can be ventured.

FATHERS AND SONS: FURTHER COMMENTS AND SOME
IMPLICATIONS FOR DEVELOPMENT

Discussion of the existence, in some cases the *persistence*, of certain 'bifurcations', 'dichotomies', or 'social distinctions' in the Turkish society is not meant to give the impression of a society which is stagnant or in which social categories, classes, and the like, are clearly demarcated and relatively stable. The application to transitional societies like Turkey of concepts which have been found to be relevant in Western industrial and advanced societies must be made with a great deal of caution. This is brought out with unusual clarity in the data on the lise students.

The findings, limited as they are, suggest important changes taking place in the occupational structure of modern Turkey, or at least of urban-modern Turkey. They suggest not only occupational and social 'mobility', but also the emergence into prominence of different occupational categories, as well as a changing pattern of occupational prestige. Assuming that the students' grandfathers and fathers represent pre-republican and republican eras, occupational movement is seen from rural-agricultural and 'unskilled' pursuits to 'white-collar' (professional and official) and skilled careers. Within the 'white-collar' category, the rise to prominence of the professional and high technical groups is particularly important, an observation most saliently manifest in the students' expressed aspirations, expectations, occupational choice, and occupational ranking. Within the same group, there is also an increase in 'minor administrative' and 'clerical' occupations from grandfather to father, but a relative stability in the 'managerial and high administrative' category. In contrast, a smaller (although still relatively high) percentage of sons aspire towards occupations in the former category, and a much smaller percentage towards those in the latter. Considering 'aspirations', it would seem that, as occupational background of fathers changed in favour of 'white-collar' and skilled occupations, the sons' *aspirations* also changed dramatically in favour of professional and high technical careers. In view of what has been said about the Ottoman period, this phenomenon highlights a shift away from the traditional Ottoman careers in the military, religious and bureaucratic spheres, an observation also reflected in the prestige ranking of the various occupational clusters.

The index of student aspirations, coupled with (a) the education which these individuals already have, and (b) the very high level of education towards which they aspire, suggests a high degree of opportunity for occupational and social advancement or mobility. Nevertheless, when *expectations* are being considered, there is a large measure of 'realism' among the lise group concerning their occupational chances. For example, although the overwhelming majority of the students

(77 per cent) aspire to some sort of 'white-collar' job, fewer (57 per cent) expect to enter such careers; and although slightly less than half aspire towards the high professions, only 23 per cent expect to become free professionals. On the other hand, more students expect than aspire to enter the clerical groups (memurs, teachers, etc.). To reiterate the point made earlier, considering the Turkish occupational structure, the over-all rates of upward social mobility are considerably low. Only a very small proportion of the population *and of the lise students* ever achieves, or is likely to achieve, positions of high status. Certain high status posts in the government (e.g., vali, kay-makam, assembly deputy) presuppose high levels of education (beyond the lise) and competitive examinations. University training is also a precondition for entrance into the prestigious 'free professions'. Considering these factors, as well as more 'ascriptive' ones (family background, 'pull', etc.), and the over-all rate of growth of the relevant sectors, it is almost certain that even the lower percentages registered for expectations reflect a great deal of 'wishful thinking' on the part of the lise students.

Foster's observations and comments on Ghanaian education would apply to Turkey as well.[10] Historically, a sultani or lise education enabled students to attain high status positions, or at least it fulfilled their educational and occupational aspirations. Until quite recently, the relatively stable increase in enrolments did not seem to create major problems of unfulfilled hopes, unemployment or under-employment. But since 1961, the increase in lise enrolments has been quite dramatic (from 68,000 to over 90,000), and according to the projections in the 1963–67 Five-Year Development Plan as well as in 'Turkey's Manpower Requirements and Educational Targets (1962–1977)', there is every indication that there will be an over-abundance of lise graduates.[11] Already there are visible signs of a drop in the 'occupational worth' of a lise education, which will certainly become more exacerbated in the coming years. The foreseeable

[10] Foster, 'Secondary School Leaders in Ghana,' *op. cit.*, pp. 538 ff.

[11] See *Five-Year Development Plan of Turkey* (Prime Ministry of the Republic of Turkey, State Planning Organization [Ankara: September, 1962]); and *Turkey's Manpower Requirements and Education Targets, 1962-1967* (Prime Ministry of the Republic of Turkey, State Planning Organization [Ankara, May, 1962]).

imbalanced expansion of school outputs in relation to antici-
pated employment opportunities, coupled with the persistence
of high aspirations, could have serious repercussions; it could
create frustration, unemployment or under-employment. As in
Ghana, however, students may ultimately 'reconcile themselves
to the changed occupational currency of their education'. The
expressed expectations noted in this study would suggest that
this is already happening. Although there is no comparable
data, it is hypothesized that Foster's generalization for Ghana
would hold true of Turkey.

'From the viewpoint of the secondary school graduate . . . there
has to be a rapid readjustment and downgrading of vocational expectations. It can be contended that this has everywhere been the
inevitable sequel of educational expansion; the vocational currency
of a given level of education declines at the same time as the formal
educational requirements for a given occupation tend to rise.'[12]

Lise Students and Careers in Business, Trade, and Industry

The occupational categories of business, trade, and industry
are not only significant for Turkey's economic and social
modernization, but also the subjects of considerable interest
and controversy. The Ottomans, as so often stated, perhaps
too simply but not inaccurately, were primarily soldiers and
administrators; commercial, business and industrial enterprises
or occupations were virtually the monopoly of the non-Moslem
minorities and foreigners, a state of affairs which was strengthened after the middle of the eighteenth century by the privileges
associated with the famous system known as 'capitulations'.
The economic activities of the large Moslem population were
limited largely to the tilling of the soil, the raising of livestock,
to handicrafts, and so on; these were carried out through
primitive methods; hence, they were unable to compete with
industries supported by foreign capital and employing better
trained individuals. By the end of the nineteenth century,
according to one writer, even the fez was largely manufactured
abroad.[13] The Ottoman Moslem elite looked down upon occupations in business and industry and more so upon the bucolic

---

[12] Foster, 'Secondary School Leaders in Ghana,' *op. cit.*, p. 549.
[13] W. S. Monroe, *Turkey and the Turks: An Account of the Lands, the Peoples,
and the Insituttions of the Ottoman Empire* (London: G. Bell & Sons, 1908),
p. 153.

activities of their peasant co-religionists; hence, perhaps, the proverbial disdain with which the Turks are said to have viewed careers in these areas of economic activity, and the relative lack of interest in education concerned with economic affairs.

With the political changes following the revolution of the Young Turks, there was a concerted effort to stimulate economic growth by encouraging industrial development. But not until after the Revolution of 1923 were thorough attempts made to transform the social and economic basis of the society. The basic facts concerning the economic policies of the Atatürk period are well known and discussed in great detail in several sources. Such policies included the abolition of capitulations, the development of railways, the establishment of the *Ish Bankasi* (Work Bank), and, finally, the introduction of *étatism* (the assumption by the state of major responsibility in the planning, direction, and guidance of the country's economy).[14] In addition, the political aftermath of the Revolutionary and Greco-Turkish wars had important repercussions in the economic development of the country. The compulsory, and to a lesser extent 'voluntary', emigration of large numbers of non-Moslem minority groups denuded the Turkish industrial and business enterprises of skilled personnel and men with business experience and entrepreneurial spirit, in short, of what Schumpeter has called the 'creative minority'. The Turks had to rely on their own manpower resources, which, as heirs of the Ottoman Islamic legacy, did not amount to much in terms of skills, business acumen, or outlook conducive to economic progress. The progress made in this connection has been a topic debated by several students of modern Turkey, but a full evaluation of it falls outside the scope of the present study. Here only certain *social* and *cultural* changes believed to bear upon the economic sector, and what light the lise study throws on them, will be considered.

[14] On the economic policies of the Kemalist Republic, see Richard D. Robinson, *The First Turkish Republic: A Case Study in National Development* (Cambridge, Mass.: Harvard University Press, 1963), pp. 93 ff.; Robert E. Ward and Dankwart A. Rustow (eds.), *Political Modernization in Japan and Turkey* (Princeton: Princeton University Press, 1964), pp. 164–73; and Bernard Lewis, *The Emergence of Modern Turkey* (London: Oxford University Press, 1961), pp. 275–87.

In discussing social change in modern Turkey, several writers have referred to the growth, albeit a slow growth, of a new class of Turks, a 'bourgeois' business middle class with different education and different attitudes towards business and the government. Bernard Lewis put it as follows:

'Perhaps more important than the economic achievements were the social changes which, unintended and probably undesired, followed in their wake. The economic activities of the Turkish government may have been incompetent and misdirected; they did, however, create new openings and new careers, and initiate the process which in time gave Turkey something she had never had before—a Turkish middle class of business men, managers, and technicians . . . These new Turkish business men and managers were self-confident, self-reliant, and ambitious; they were becoming resentful of the controls and restrictions imposed upon them by what they had begun to regard as the dead hand of officialdom. The civil servant was falling from the dizzy eminence that he once occupied in the Turkish social hierarchy.'[15]

Likewise, recent research on the business classes in Turkey speaks of the 'emergence' and the 'rise' of an 'entrepreneurial group'. Although it is geographically limited to certain regions (particularly the Aegean), and still hampered by traditional beliefs and the family structure, such a group, to quote Bradburn, is 'capable of creating and running modern business enterprises'.[16] Moreover, it seems apparent that the void resulting from the elimination of the 'creative minority' is gradually being filled by an 'indigenous minority'. However, another aspect of this problem is also of paramount importance. The apparent emergence or creation of a business or entrepreneurial class is a significant aspect of social change in modern Turkey; yet, as Robinson argues with good reason, 'the economic growth of an underdeveloped-backward country . . . rests heavily upon *social* and *personal* development' (italics mine). Hence, the same writer continues, 'to talk in terms of

---

[15] Lewis, *op. cit.*, pp. 465–7.
[16] Norman M. Bradburn, 'The Managerial Role in Turkey: A Psychological Study' (Ph.D. thesis, Harvard University, April, 1960), p. 59. On the increase of the business class, see also Kemal H. Karpat, *Turkey's Politics: The Transition to a Multi-Party System* (Princeton: Princeton University Press, 1959), p. 113; and A. J. Mayer, *Middle Eastern Capitalism: Nine Essays* (Cambridge, Mass.: Harvard University Press, 1959), pp. 38–9.

long-range economic development in Turkey is ill-conceived unless close attention is likewise given the education, culture, and health of the people'.[17] Moreover, economic change is largely regulated by such factors as the social and political structure, as well as by the ways business enterprises are actually run. When these historical, cultural, psychological, and sociological aspects of the problem are considered, the picture of change in Turkey is somewhat different.

Before interpreting this study's findings and those of others, concerning people's attitudes towards business and related occupations, it would be helpful to describe some features of the present-day Turkish economy in general terms. Turkey was, and continues to be, primarily an agricultural country. According to the latest estimates, in 1962, over three-fourths of the labour force (77 per cent) were engaged in the agricultural sector, which contributed about 44 per cent of the Gross National Product; about 10 per cent was engaged in industry, and about 13 per cent in various services.[18] The policy of *étatism* resulted in government monopolies on such products as alcohol, matches, tobacco, and gunpowder, and on control of business enterprises and such establishments as the Karabük Iron and Steel Enterprises. In addition to this public sector, there is a private sector. In certain enterprises (e.g., textiles and shoes), the state and private firms compete with each other; but in others (e.g., food, soap, flour, etc.), private enterprises dominate. Many of the industrial plants are very small. Bradburn noted that 'approximately 50% of the textile plants in the Istanbul area employ over four to ten workers while only about 2½% of them employ over 1,000 workers'.[19] Furthermore, the entrepreneurial pattern in most of the small and medium-sized enterprises is the family firm or a one-man company with tight control vested in the hands of the 'owner-manager'. This pattern prevails in most Islamic Middle Eastern countries, and with it, all the associated problems. According to

[17] Robinson, *op. cit.*, p. 95.
[18] *1963–67 Plani Hazirlik Chalishmalari: Türkiyede Insangüjü Ihtiyachlari ve Egitim Programlanmani* (T. J. Bashbakanlik Devlet Planlama Teshkilati Müshtesarligi, Ekim, 1962), p. 12. The 1960 figures based on the 1960 Census (1 per cent sample) were: for agriculture, 80·1 per cent; industry, 8·5 per cent; and services, 11 4 per cent. See *Turkey's Manpower Requirements and Education Targets 1962–1977*, *op. cit.*, Table 1.
[19] Bradburn, *op. cit.*, p. 53.

Meyer, 'In most businesses the family, with its myriad problems of inefficient management, still survives . . . In short, the basic loyalty of the businessman is still probably to his family, only secondarily (if that) to his firm. Thus the creation of rational capitalist enterprise becomes difficult indeed when it conflicts with the noble Oriental tradition of taking care of one's family.'[20]

What about attitudes towards careers in business? Has the emergence of a business class or an entrepreneurial group and the relative growth of business and industrial enterprises brought about any changes in the prestige or respect which people accord to business and related careers or in people's vocational aspirations and outlooks? The available information on this problem is rather limited and inconclusive. Bradburn's conclusion, drawn from questionnaires and interviews of Turkish junior executives and 'potential school administrators', is stated as follows:

'. . . while there may have been considerable increase in the relative prestige of business as a career, in that it is now accepted as something which Turks may do and as something which may even lead to a high social status under some circumstances, i.e., if one is a big businessman, it is still not accepted as one of the highest prestige occupations. Turkey appears to be moving toward an occupational prestige hierarchy similar to that described by Inkeles and Rossi as characteristic of industrial countries in which business ranks fairly high but is outranked by the higher government offices and certain professions.'[21]

The findings of this study, based on a larger stratum of the Turkish society, shed considerable light on the problem. First of all, it is necessary to point to the variations in careers classified under the general rubric of 'business'. The Turkish word tüjjar may mean either a big business man (importer, exporter, etc.) or a small business man (a shop-keeper, a retail small merchant, etc.), and the difference between the two, more often than not, is immense. Likewise, the difference between a 'business executive', in the sense of a director of a big bank (a high government official), and a müstakil ish müdürü who, more

---

[20] Meyer, *op. cit.*, p. 39. On the problems associated with this pattern in Turkey, see Bradburn, *op. cit.*, pp. 77 ff.

[21] Bradburn, *op cit.*, p. 53.

often than not, is the owner-manager of a very small 'firm', is great. And the term muhasib connotes not a highly specialized accountant, but a mere bookkeeper. It is not, therefore, surprising that *some* business careers have been accorded high prestige, but others were ranked below 'agricultural labourer', for example! But even when 'big businessman' was placed against 'free professional', 'diplomat', 'education', and such, the percentage of all students and of boys who ranked it at the top was comparatively small; indeed, in relation to 'free professional' and to 'diplomat', it was extremely small, although by no means totally insignificant. *As many boys ranked 'military officer' and 'educator' highest as they did 'manufacturer, contractor, importer, exporter, etc.'* Some of those respondents who placed 'diplomat' or 'free professional' or 'educator' at the top, gave as their reasons, 'knowledge', 'needed in our country', or 'service to people'; or as a boy from a private Turkish lise put it: 'first of all because he [an ambassador] is chosen in the name of Turkey; other nations will show us the respect due to our nation'. It could be speculated that to the nationalistically minded Turkish lise youth, the benefits accruing from business careers are not as easily observable for their country's welfare and 'name' in the world as those from other occupations. The comparatively low 'respect' for careers in big business, trade, and the like, is also revealed rather clearly by the fact that very few of the respondents indicated that they *aspired towards or expected to enter* such sectors of Turkish economic life. And again, among the public lise students, in particular, only 2·5 per cent chose 'big business' as their 'most preferred occupation'.

Of course, it could be argued that the academic lise is the wrong place to look for favourable attitudes towards business. Yet business careers ranked very low, and free professions very high, in another study which included a wider variety of youth, namely, students in *commercial* lises, and secondary level teacher-training institutions. Indeed, there was very little, if any, difference in attitudes between the academic lise students and those in other institutions.[22] Apparently, therefore, if there

[22] Frederick W. Frey, George W. Angell, Jr., and Abdurrahman Sh. Sanay, *Ogrenjilerin Meslek Gruplarina Bagladiklari Degerler* (Ankara: Test ve Arashtirma Bürosu, 1962).

is a high motivation to enter careers in business, trade, and such, it must reside elsewhere than in the schools, or it must develop after graduation. Further, what interest *has been shown* may indeed signify an important change; and the interest among the non-public lise students was quite noticeable, especially on the 'most preferred' occupation item (9 per cent of the private Turkish lise group, and 10 per cent of the 'foreign' group).

Attitudes towards careers in business and vocational aspirations do not by any means define the social, cultural, or personal factors influencing or bearing upon development. On several other indices, students of Turkey seem to agree that, although opportunities have expanded and progress has been made since the proclamation of the republic, powerful social, cultural, and psychological constraints which hinder or perhaps slow down the pace of development still persist. Some of these constraints were referred to in a previous chapter, in which McClelland's concept of 'need for achievement' and the authority patterns in the Turkish family and the Turkish society were discussed. The following could be added here: (a) what Robinson called 'the partial divorce of two processes long thought by Western economists to be indissolubly married—industrialization and urbanization';[23] (b) what Bradburn found in many forms to be a tight central control by one individual, often 'the owner-manager', and a system of recruitment of business personnel based on ascriptive rather than achievement criteria;[24] and (c) what this study found to be a certain timidity or overconcern for 'job security' on the part of the lise students, which was reflected in some of their answers.

The foregoing analysis suggests that the social significance of the lise, and what this connotes in the area of modernization and development, lies *less* in its conceivable contribution toward the creation of an entrepreneurial group and *more* (perhaps much more) towards the preparation of the professional-official class of Turkey. The lise, being the major avenue for higher studies necessary for entrance into high posts in the government and into the free professions, occupies a central position in the selection of that crucial elite component

[23] Robinson, *op. cit.* p. 117.
[24] Bradburn, *op. cit.*, pp. 76 ff.

of the middle class, namely, the intellectuals and the high professionals. Being also a major source of supply for the bureaucracy, especially for the large number of 'minor officials', it occupies a pivotal place in the preparation of the Turkish 'intelligentsia', interpreted here to mean the broad 'white-collar' class, that is, those who are not engaged in manual occupations. In a sense, this has always been the main function of the lise, beginning with the Mektebi Sultani at Galatasaray. However, in its development through the years the lise has also undergone important transformations. For one thing, as has been shown, there has been a greater social diversification of the students attending the lises; for another thing, the dizzy level which positions in the civil and military bureaucracies occupied in the minds of the lise recruits has given way to the professions and the intellectuals; and thirdly, although the lise has been Western-oriented and secular from the start, in the Ottoman period it was not (as it has developed to be today) an integral part of the Turkish culture, and, perhaps more importantly, of that part of the Turkish culture upon which so much of the future course of Turkey's efforts to develop and to modernize its values and institutions depends. For good or for ill, modern Turkey, to paraphrase a common saying, has put all its leadership potential in one educational basket. This leadership potential reflects the emergence of a new elite, a social change of the utmost importance, and influences the future course of such a change. Who these people are, what type of education they get, what values they hold, what hopes and frustrations they have, are, therefore, equally important questions. Most of them have already been discussed. This case study will conclude with a short account of some of the findings concerning the lise students' views about education in general, and their own lise education in particular.

THE STUDENTS' VIEWS OF THEIR OWN EDUCATION

A comment frequently heard in discussions about education in Turkey and other countries is that schools, teachers, and people in general place heavier emphasis upon theoretical than practical matters, and that they stress memorizing and the accumulation of knowledge rather than 'ability to reason'.

Admittedly, the lise students do not represent the educational thinking of Turkey. Also, their opinions might not reflect what actually takes place. Nevertheless, it was felt that the views of this highly select group of Turkish youth would tell something more than the usual impressionistic statements on this subject. The students were asked to express agreement or disagreement with the following statements: (a) 'Schools should concentrate on practical skills rather than on theoretical and intellectual matters,' and (b) 'Memory is more important than reason in becoming well-educated.' On the first item, the majority (58 per cent) answered in the affirmative, 19 per cent disagreed, and the rest indicated they 'had no idea'; on the second, 37 per cent 'agreed', 50 per cent 'disagreed', and the rest 'had no idea'. Interestingly enough, on the 'memory-reason' item the figures for 'agree' among the students in the more 'Turkish' schools (public and private Turkish) were higher than those among the other students. On another item, which read, 'What in your opinion is the most important mark of an educated man?' the responses were as follows: (1) 'Ability to reason properly', 39 per cent; (2) 'good behavior and good way of talking', 27 per cent; (3) 'good character', 17 per cent; (4) 'good citizen', 5 per cent; and (5) 'a lot of knowledge', 4 per cent. Too much should not be read into these answers for the reasons stated above. But it would be rather instructive for someone to compare these answers with those given to similar questions by youth in the United States, for example, especially at a time when the schools are under heavy attack for not emphasizing intellectual matters and for concentrating 'on practical skills'.

Perhaps more significant for Turkey than the above, were the students' answers on 'favourite subjects' at school and 'useful and helpful subjects' after school. It was particularly revealing to this writer that *half* of the respondents indicated that they liked best mathematics and science (biology, geology, physics, and chemistry); *the percentage was even higher* (54 per cent) on the 'most useful and helpful' item. Although 12 per cent stated that they liked history and geography best, only 4·5 thought that these subjects would be most useful and helpful in their careers after school; 9 per cent specified foreign languages as their favourite subject, but 14 per cent marked that they would be most useful; and although 17 per cent gave

'Turkish' their 'vote' on 'most favourite subject', 13 per cent
cast it for 'most useful'. The mathematics-science preference
might be taken as indicative of many things: in the first place,
it reflects a changing curriculum emphasis; in the second place,
it accords with the students' perceptions of the differentials in
occupational rewards, prestige, and so on; and thirdly, it
could be ventured that the message of Atatürk, with its stress
on science, has taken a firm hold on this group of people.
Questions could be raised as to whether the over-emphasis on
mathematics and science is entirely salutary for any nation.

Another group of items sought to find some answers to the
general question of the preference for the lise vis-à-vis other
schools of the same level. According to the respondents, the
most important reason for going to a lise instead of to a vocational or technical school was, 'because I want to go to a university or a higher institution' (over two-thirds of the students);
about 13 per cent of the total sample gave as the most important
reason 'a broader general education (*genel kültür*); and only
8 per cent indicated 'a better job' as the reason. It must be
remembered, however, that going to a university means a
better job as well. On another, more general item, namely,
'Why in your opinion do people get an education?' 39 per cent
of the total sample marked 'because they will raise their social
status'; 21 per cent, 'because they will become powerful members of the community'; and 17 per cent, 'because they can get
a better-paid job'. Still another item read as follows: 'In general,
about how much schooling does a young man need to get along
well in life?' The answers were:

schooling	Responses (*in per cent*)		
	All students	Boys	Girls
None	·9	1·0	1·1
Primary school	·5	·7	·1
Middle school	2·5	3·2	1·2
Vocational school	5·7	6·3	4·6
Lise	12·3	23·8	9·4
University of higher institution	65·8	59·5	76·1
I don't know	6·3	5·5	7·5

A breakdown of the responses in terms of type of school shows
some variations between students in the private Turkish and

foreign lises as compared with those in the public and minority schools. About 70 per cent of students in the former categories considered university or higher institution as needed for a young man 'to get along well in life', but only about 59 per cent of students in the latter categories of schools did so. Similar differences were registered with respect to 'lise' and 'middle school': more public and minority school students than private or foreign felt that a lise or middle school education was sufficient for a young man.

On a similar item concerning schooling for a young woman, only 28 per cent felt that the fair sex needed higher education 'to get along well in life'; 42 per cent marked 'lise'; 11 per cent, 'vocational school'; and 8 per cent, 'middle school'. As might be expected, the girls, in contrast to the boys, thought that young women needed more education: about 86 per cent of the girls marked 'lise' or 'higher institution', but only 59 per cent of the boys did so.

Several comments could be made on the basis of these findings. Quite clearly, the lise youth consider schooling as of the utmost importance in what they envisage their future lives to be; but perhaps more important than this is *the type and amount of such schooling*. Since only a very small fraction of the Turkish youth as a whole can ever hope to attain the level considered necessary 'to get along well in life', the lise youth must regard themselves as a very privileged group. The inter-school variations, taken in conjunction with other findings on the socio-economic background of students, suggest that students coming from the upper classes, or generally from the white-collar groups, place a heavier premium upon amount of schooling for purposes of getting along well in life. But, in general, education beyond what these youth as a whole now have, and far beyond what their fathers or grandfathers had, appears to be considered necessary for a satisfactory life in modern Turkey, at least insofar as men are concerned. Of course, these references are to an already select group and, in relation to the Turkish population at large, a highly educated one; and the observation that educated people value education should perhaps not be surprising. Yet there is reason to believe that such attitudes are not limited to the lise population and that they are shared by the people at large. Unfortunately, there are no empirical data at present to support this contention. The findings of an extensive survey on peasant attitudes in Turkey have not yet been released. Since this study's questions on amount of schooling for a young man and a young woman were the same as those used in the questionnaire of the afore-mentioned survey, the hypothesis cannot be fully supported until this document appears. In conversation, however, with some of the members of the research team responsible for what is referred to as the 'Turkish Village Study', this writer was led to believe that, even among the Turkish peasant, a lise or higher education was felt to be necessary 'to get along in life'. It would appear, therefore, that a lise or university type of education is perceived to have a high functional value in the minds not only of the privileged Turks, but also of the general population. This is another indication of why students and parents prefer the lise to any other type of secondary education, and it partly accounts for the recent dispropor-tionate expansion of lise enrolment in comparison with that in the technical schools. The high value placed upon a great deal of education is also a reflection of the ideological change which has been taking place in the Turkish society, and this, as was shown previously, in spite of the fact that only a very small fraction of the youth can expect to attain what they and their parents think is necessary to satisfy their aspirations in life.

CHAPTER XI

MODERNISM AND TRADITIONALISM IN TURKISH EDUCATION: GENERAL CONCLUSIONS AND COMMENTS

MODERNISM through 'reformism' has been an activating ideal of the Turkish national state, which emerged after the Young Turk and the Kemalist Revolutions of the twentieth century. Yet, as is now generally recognized, the movement towards modernity has been going on since the latter part of the eighteenth century: it was traced to Sultan Selim III's 'New Order' (Nizam-i-Jedid); it gained accelerated momentum under Sultan Mahmud II and Sultan Abdul Medjid and during the period of the Tanzimat in the nineteenth century; and it continued even under the reactionary regime of Abdül-Hamid during the closing decades of that century. Whatever its starting point, its historical evolution, and its complexities may have been, one thing stands out as being of paramount importance: in the process of change whereby an Islamic, theocratic, and absolutistic empire was being transformed into a secular, constitutional, and national republic, education was assigned a prominent role. It was through reform in education, be it in the training of the military and the bureaucrats or in the setting up of new schools (military academies, the rüshdiyes, the Galatasaray Sultani, the Mülkiye, etc.) that the Ottomans sought to provide the skills and the leadership needed to accomplish their modernizing policies; and it was upon a modern, secular, national, and nationalistic system of schooling that Atatürk and the new Turkish leaders relied for the building of a viable republic. Indeed, one way the history of the modernization movement in Turkey could be viewed is through an examination of the modernization of education: (a) how an Islamic, essentially 'private', system of schools and an essentially Islamic content and mode of thinking were transformed into a state, secular system with emphasis upon modern subjects and a modern pedagogy; and (b) how the schools themselves were related to social change, both as reflectors and as active agents of such a process. The preceding chapters sought to illuminate Turkey's transformation or modernization by focusing on these two main aspects of the Turkish educational scene.

In seeking to modernize their institutions and modes of thinking and behaving, the Ottoman and the Turkish leaders looked to the West (France, Germany, England, and, lately, America) for inspiration and guidance. This was most saliently evident in the case of educational reform. For example, in the early period of 'defensive modernization', the main 'channel of transmission' of Western practices was instruction in military schools, many of which were themselves based on Western models; the comprehensive Code of 1869 was based on the French educational system, and the Galatasaray lise was 'borrowed' directly from the same source; and the organization and control, the curriculum, and many of the ideas and practices of the educational system under the republic not only had parallels in the West, but they drew directly from Western (French and, more recently, American) models and patterns. Moreover, Western languages (again, mostly French, but more recently, English) and other subjects introduced in the schools or studied elsewhere were, and continue to be, important vehicles of cultural and ideological transmission. Educational modernization, therefore, like the broader movement of which it formed an integral part, meant largely the *Westernization* of educational institutions, beliefs, and practices. This fundamental goal in Turkey's development, which has often resulted in indiscriminate borrowing of anything labelled 'Western', has led some educational writers to criticize certain Turkish educational institutions as mere replicas of Western models, as alien to Turkish values, and as being functionally unrelated to the needs and aspirations of the Turkish people. A case in point has been the lise, an institution originally based on the

French lycée. This study has shown that such contentions tend to ignore the important transformations in the place of this institution within the Turkish society and the meaning which it has conveyed to the Turks themselves. Although structurally it resembled European prototypes, as it still does, functionally it has come to be an integral part of the Turkish ethos and the Turkish culture. In other words, an originally Western institution was gradually translated into the emerging Turkish social system and body of beliefs. Today the lise is as much Turkish as the medrese was Ottoman Islamic.

In some respects, the modernization-Westernization process in Turkey, particularly as it was related to educational 'borrowing' or 'transfer', displayed similarities with other 'empire to nation' developments in countries of Africa, Asia, and the rest of the Middle East. To wit: Western educational institutions, ideas, and practices were introduced by the ruling elites for specific purposes (for example, the training of cadres of government officials); those who went through such institutions, or were exposed to Western ideas, reacted against the traditional state of affairs and called for reform; faced with a reactionary opposition, which would not accommodate their demands for change, these new elites initiated revolutions and assumed power; and upon their accession to power, they embarked upon programmes of reform and reconstruction. Indeed, the introduction of Western secular education into the nineteenth-century Ottoman society could be viewed as the start of the chain of events which led to the Young Turk and the Kemalist Revolutions. As a consequence of a 'modern' education, 'modern' elites were created, who vied with the traditional elites, mostly educated in the medreses (the religious schools), until they gained enough power to tip the balance in their favour. However, neat categorizations, clear-cut dichotomies, over-simplified explanations, and unqualified comparisons must also be guarded against. Turkey displayed its own peculiar characteristics, and the movement towards modernity, as well as its pace, was coloured by the particular cultural context in which it manifested itself.

Educational transfer, borrowing or innovation in the Ottoman Empire, unlike that of some ex-colonies in Africa, for example, was largely initiated by the indigenous elites themselves;

Western education was not superimposed by *external* agents. Added to this kind of 'transfer' was the fact that Western education was introduced into a society which had a long-standing tradition concerning the value of education, and some sort of 'high culture'. Learning and schooling enjoyed high prestige in the Ottoman Islamic world, so when Western education was introduced, it gradually inherited much of the prestige traditionally attached to Islamic learning, particularly in the minds of certain of the elite groups. Even among the conservative Islamic groups, powerful voices did not reject Western education outright, but sought to accommodate it or to translate it into their own world framework. On their part, the modernizers, although anxious to bring about change, were themselves circumscribed by the same historical past which they sought to supersede. All too often, such terms as 'traditionalism' and 'modernism' used to describe the dynamics of social change are thought of as all-inclusive entities and clear-cut stages where one ends and the other begins, and as states in societies which are all of one piece, where everything seems to fit into a complete whole, and where one is directly in conflict and/or irreconcilable with the other. In the development of Turkey, particularly during the Ottoman phase, the lines between the secular-modernists on one hand, and the religious-traditionalists on the other, were often not so sharply drawn as the terms to describe them seem to imply. This may be one of the reasons why the pace of modernization was relatively slow during this period.

During the republican period, the modernization-Westernization movement acquired new dimensions. It became an all-out attempt to wipe out everything that was associated with the Ottoman-Islamic past. The means used in pursuing this goal were often arbitrary and dictatorial. In the minds of the new leaders, there was no room for reconciliation, no ground for any syntheses; the older order must be replaced lock, stock, and fez by a new one. Education became a major instrument for what was to be Turkey's 'grand transformation', hence, a major focus of reform. First, since secularism was a cardinal tenet of the revolutionary ideology, education must be completely secularized; second, the new Turkish national state, bent as it was on changing the entire fabric of the society along modern Western lines, must possess a national system of public education controlled by the state, a graded and balanced system of schools from the primary to the university levels, institutions for the training of teachers and technical personnel, an administrative machinery at the central and local levels to co-ordinate the various educational activities, and a uniform means to support the entire educational enterprise. Third, a nationalistic state could materialize if education itself assumed the responsibility of politically educating the new generation in accordance with Turkish nationalism. Fourth, a 'populistic' system of government (i.e., one which extended political participation to all the members of the society), which was also to be dynamic, must ensure certain minimal levels of education, such as literacy, must provide educational opportunities for all the people, must eliminate glaring inequalities, and must create conditions whereby recruitment and selection into the various occupations were not restricted to self-perpetuating social groups. A major part of this study has dealt with these and related questions, and to reformulate the findings would be to repeat what has already been said. However, in view of the discussion on the interplay of tradition and modernity, some additional remarks are appropriate.

In certain respects, Atatürk's task of educational reform and reconstruction was facilitated not only by the groundwork that had been laid earlier (e.g., the various secular or 'quasi-secular' schools and the educational laws of 1869 and 1913), but, paradoxically, by certain pervasive elements in the tradition he inherited. The idea of the ruling elite initiating change by force was not uncommon in the annals of Ottoman history; nor was the elitist view of prime attention being given to the education of the governing classes. Under the empire, much of the educational activity was in the hands of the ulema, of individuals, and of voluntary bodies. In the nineteenth century, the central government assumed a share in the education of the people, but it was not until the republican period that all formal education became completely a state function and was placed under the control of the central government. However, although *education* was not centrally controlled during the Ottoman period, the *official* system was, and it was from this tight bureaucratic set-up that Turkish education under the

Atatürk regime grew. Hence, the rigidity and centralization that characterized the educational system after the revolution followed almost automatically.

In spite of its despotic and absolutistic nature and its great inequalities of wealth and power, the Ottoman society was also characterized by a comparative 'fluidity' or 'openness'; learning and education, as mentioned above, enjoyed high prestige and were important desiderata for occupational and social advancement. Atatürk's task lay not so much in creating an acceptance of the value of education as in transferring an existing ideology into new forms.

However, in other respects certain *given* cultural conditions affected the course of modernization, and, compared to Western societies and Japan, progress in that direction has been slow. First, the sharp divisions between rulers and ruled and between educated elites and illiterate masses allowed change to be initiated, but they also created difficulties in communication and in general political participation. The bridging of these gaps continues to be one of the major problems of Turkey. The expansion of education has been viewed as an instrument of eliminating existing social and cultural barriers; yet high educational requirements for political leadership, which only a small fraction are able to fulfil, tend to perpetuate such chasms. A second cultural 'given' is the fact that modernism in Turkey has depended on the transformation of an Islamic heritage. Islam, as often stated before, was an all-embracing religion: it covered theological doctrine, social organization, government, law, patterns of authority, ethics, and, generally, all aspects of man's thought and behaviour. Secularization has been a major aim of the Turkish modernizers, and in this the achievements have been many; yet secularization remains a major problem in Turkey. For secularization does not merely mean the disestablishment of religion, the abolition of religious schools, the proscription of religious instruction, the adoption of new laws, or the sweeping away of the traditional power of the religious elites; it also means change in the patterns of authority, in the general value-system of the society, and the ways in which individuals perceive themselves in a changing society. Furthermore, secularization means a more scientific or rational approach to life.

Another cultural 'given' was the attitudes which the Ottoman Moslems had towards careers and the occupational hierarchy. The analysis of the lise students' perceptions of the occupational structure revealed important changes, among which the most notable was the emergence into prominence of the free professions and the relative decline in prestige of careers in the military, in religion, and in certain areas of the civil bureaucracy. However, vestiges of the traditional Ottoman disdain for careers in business, commerce, and industry and for certain technological pursuits have lingered on and are evident even today.

In conclusion, 'traditional', 'modern', and 'Western' are 'loaded' concepts and are not devoid of value connotations. To be modernized or Westernized may be good or bad, depending on what values individuals or societies attach to such states or processes. In Turkey, modernization-Westernization has been viewed in the same sense as the Turks themselves have viewed it, namely, as social change which has been *desired* and *desirable*. Compared to what the situation was when the republic was proclaimed, advancement towards modernity, as this study has shown, has been quite remarkable. Yet in comparison with the models upon which she has sought to base her modernizing course, Turkey is still confronted with as great a challenge as she was when she emerged as a nation-state.

APPENDICES

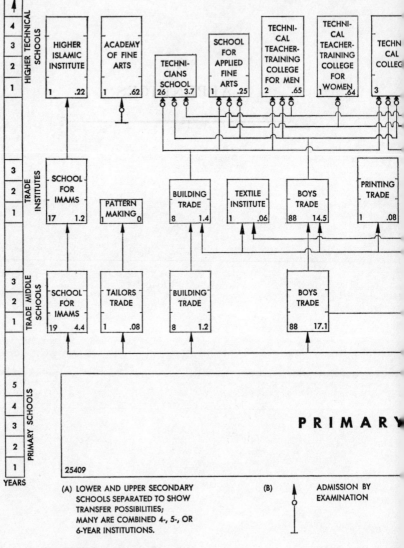

ORGANIZATIONAL DIAGRA
1961-

HIGHER ISLAMIC INSTITUTE 1 .22	ACADEMY OF FINE ARTS 1 .62	

TECHNICIANS SCHOOL 26 3.7

SCHOOL FOR APPLIED FINE ARTS 1 .25

TECHNICAL TEACHER-TRAINING COLLEGE FOR MEN 2 .65

TECHNICAL TEACHER-TRAINING COLLEGE FOR WOMEN 1 .64

TECHNICAL COLLEGE 3

HIGHER TECHNICAL SCHOOLS

SCHOOL FOR IMAMS 17 1.2

PATTERN MAKING 1 0

BUILDING TRADE 8 1.4

TEXTILE INSTITUTE 1 .06

BOYS TRADE 88 14.5

PRINTING TRADE 1 .08

TRADE INSTITUTES

SCHOOL FOR IMAMS 19 4.4

TAILORS TRADE 1 .08

BUILDING TRADE 8 1.2

BOYS TRADE 88 17.1

TRADE MIDDLE SCHOOLS

PRIMARY

PRIMARY SCHOOLS

25409

YEARS

(A) LOWER AND UPPER SECONDARY SCHOOLS SEPARATED TO SHOW TRANSFER POSSIBILITIES; MANY ARE COMBINED 4-, 5-, OR 6-YEAR INSTITUTIONS.

(B) ADMISSION BY EXAMINATION

TURKISH MINISTRY OF EDUCATION, EDUCATIONAL RESEARCH AND EVALUATION CENTER, ANKARA, 1962

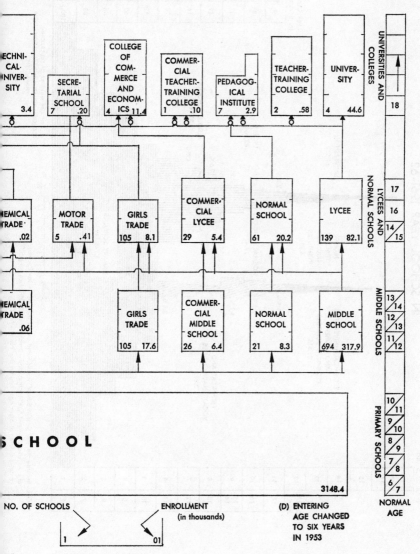

NO. OF SCHOOLS   ENROLLMENT (in thousands)   (D) ENTERING AGE CHANGED TO SIX YEARS IN 1953

1   .01

DISTRIBUTION OF TURKISH YOUTH POPULATION ENROLLED IN PUBLIC SCHOOLS
IN SCHOOL YEAR 1961-62

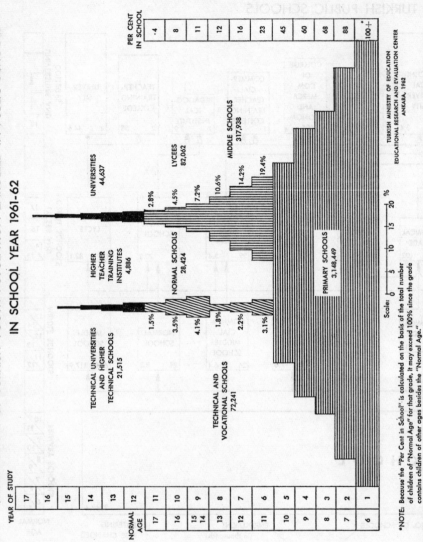

YEAR OF STUDY

17	
16	
15	
14	
13	
12	
11	
10	
9	
8	
7	
6	
5	
4	
3	
2	
1	

PER CENT IN SCHOOL

.4
8
11
12
16
23
45
60
68
88
100+ *

UNIVERSITIES 44,637

LYCEES 82,062

MIDDLE SCHOOLS 317,938

HIGHER TEACHER TRAINING INSTITUTES 4,886

NORMAL SCHOOLS 28,424

TECHNICAL UNIVERSITIES AND HIGHER TECHNICAL SCHOOLS 21,515

TECHNICAL AND VOCATIONAL SCHOOLS 72,241

PRIMARY SCHOOLS 3,148,449

2.8%
4.5%
7.2%
10.6%
14.2%
19.4%

1.5%
3.5%
4.1%
1.8%
2.2%
3.1%

%
20   15   10   5   0   %

Scale: 0   5   10   15   20

NORMAL AGE

17
16
15 14
13
12
11
10
9
8
7
6

TURKISH MINISTRY OF EDUCATION
EDUCATIONAL RESEARCH AND EVALUATION CENTER
ANKARA, 1962

*NOTE: Because the "Per Cent in School" is calculated on the basis of the total number of children of "Normal Age" for that grade, it may exceed 100% since the grade contains children of other ages besides the "Normal Age."

APPENDIX B

TABLE I

NATIONAL TRENDS IN SCHOOL ENROLMENTS, 1923–1962

Year	Primary	Orta	Lise	Vocational Technical and (Middle level) Institutions	Teacher Training (Elementary)	Institutions of Higher Education All Institutions	Universities
1923–24	336,061	5,905	1,241	6,547		2,914	
1930–31	489,299	27,093	5,699	9,296		4,331	
1935–36	688,100	52,386	13,622	9,231		7,227	
1940–41	955,967	95,332	24,862	20,264		12,844	10,310
1945–46	1,357,740	65,608	25,515	54,248		19,273	14,367
1950–51	1,616,626	68,187	22,169	52,177	16,301	24,815	18,405
	(1,602,198)[1]	(61,737)	(19,022)				
1955–56	1,983,086	131,450	33,412	63,117	17,629	37,192	26,822
		(126,227)	(30,675)	(72,675)[2]			
1959–60	2,564,195	253,474	58,954	69,775	21,216	52,060	34,304
	(2,528,401)	(229,875)	(54,812)	(98,010)[2]			
1960–61	2,785,039	277,566	68,600	72,241	23,494	62,872	41,114
1961–62	3,148,449	317,938	82,062		26,872		44,637
1962–63			97,337				
			(88,232)				

[1] ( ) enrolments in public schools.

[2] These are the figures give by the National Institute of Statistics. The difference in the enrolment figures is explained by the fact that the Institute includes enrolment in teacher-training institutions.

Sources: T. C. Başbakanlik Genel Müdürlüğü, 1959 *İstatistik Yıllığı*, Yayin No. 380, ph. 144–168; *İlk ve Orta Dereceli Okullarda Öğrenci ve Öğretmen Sayılari ile İlgili. Araştırma Raporu.* (Ankara: Test ve Araştirma Bürosu, 1961), p. 20, T. C. Başvekalet, Devlet Istatistik Enstitüsü, *Millî Eğitim İstatistikleri Meslek, Teknik ve Yüksek Öğretim, 1953–1960*, Yayin No. 438, p. 3, Maynard, *op. cit.*, p. 58. The figure for 1962–63 was collected by the present writer through a questionnaire.

TABLE II

POPULATION, SCHOOL ATTENDANCE AND LITERACY

Year	Total population of Turkey	Total school enrolments (full-time students)	Per cent of population in school			Literacy (Percentage of total population)
			Primary[1]	Secondary[2]	Total	
1927–28	13,648,270	497,300			3·7	10·6
1935–36	16,158,018	770,500	4·2	·43	4·7	19·2 (20·4)
1940–41	17,820,950	1,109,300	5·3	·74	6·2	22·4
1945–46	18,790,174	1,507,900	7·2	·71	8·0	29·0 (30·2)
1950–51	20,947,188	1,732,200	7·7	·65	8·3	34·6
1955–56	24,064,763	2,296,700	8·2	·88	9·5	40·0
1960–61	27,754,820	3,396,857	10·0	1·50	12·2	39·6

[1], [2] Percentages computed by the writer.

Sources: *1959 Istatistik Yıllığı, op. cit.,* p. 34; *Genel Nüfus Sayimi, 1945* (Ankara, 1950), p. 208; *1955 Genel Nüfus Sayimi* (Ankara, 1959), p. 2; *1960 Genel Nüfus Sayimi* (Ankara, 1962), p. 6; Frey, *op. cit.,* p. 218; Maynard, *op. cit.,* p. 142.

272

TABLE III

SCHOOL AGE DISTRIBUTION AND SCHOOL ATTENDANCE

Year	School Age Population			Percentage Attending Schools		
	Ages 6–11	Ages 6–14	Ages 6–18	Primary (Ages 6–11)	Primary *Orta* (Ages 6–14)	Primary–Secondary (Ages 6–18)
1935	2,492,412	3,367,897	4,273,893	27·6	22·0	18·0
1945	2,951,333	4,345,584	6,105,841	46·0	32·7	24·6
1950	2,861,204	4,265,691	6,359,633	56·4	39·4	27·2
1955	3,383,423	4,777,453	6,809,764	58·6	44·0	33·7
1960	3,932,247 (ages 6–10)	7,107,784 (ages 6–16)		63·6 (ages 6–10)	41·05 (ages 6–16)	
1964[1]	4,473,035 (ages 6–10)	8,748,439 (ages 6–16)		81·0 (ages 6–10)	48·2 (ages 6–16)	

[1] The figures for this year are only estimates.

Sources: *1959 İstatistik Yıllığı, op. cit.*, pp. 72–73. The percentages up to 1955 were computed by the writer, and the bases are the totals of the corresponding school age population. The figures for 1960 and 1964 were taken from Jefferson N. Eastmond, *Türkiyede Okulların Mevcudiyeti ve Yeterliği (Availability and Efficiency of Schools in Turkey,* No. 3), Ankara: Test ve Araştırma Bürosu, 1964), p. 23.

TABLE IV

DISTRIBUTION OF PRIMARY EDUCATION
BY PROVINCES

Province	Population (1960)	Elementary school (1959–60)	Percentage of total population attending primary schools	Literacy (Percentage of population 6 years of age and older)
Adana	760,803	82,803	10·9	40·5
Adiyaman	233,717	11,793	5·1	13·3
Afyon	459,115	47,182	10·2	36·0
Ağri	215,118	10,277	4·6	17·2
Amasya	258,281	26,9,87	10·4	39·0
Ankara	1,321,380	124,422	9·4	55·2
Antalya	516,130	42,655	10·3	38·8
Artvin	196,301	23,017	11·7	44·1
Aydin	467,341	52,179	11·1	43·4
Balikesir	670,669	69,241	10·2	45·8
Bilecik	145,699	16,966	11·6	47·0
Bingöl	131,364	7,947	6·1	17·0
Bitlis	128,966	6,678	5·4	16·1
Bolu	353,004	29,211	8·2	36·1
Bürdür	179,514	21,494	11·7	45·5
Bursa	693,894	70,265	10·0	48·9
Çanakkale	337,610	39,710	11·8	51·6
Çankiri	241,452	23,880	9·9	30·3
Çorum	446,389	34,547	7·6	24·5
Denizli	425,449	52,001	12·2	40·8
Diyarbakir	401,884	16,184	4·0	19·9
Edirne	276,479	33,113	12·0	47·7
Elâziğ	278,332	22,260	7·9	28·7
Erzurum	568,684	36,306	6·5	28·6
Erzincan	243,005	20,417	8·2	35·2
Eskişehir	368,827	45,443	12·2	57·9
Gaziantep	434,579	27,194	6·2	27·2
Giresun	381,453	25,760	6·8	26·0
Gümüshane	243,115	20,736	8·6	27·5
Hakkari	67,766	1,374	1·4	11·5
Hatay	441,209	36,299	8·1	33·5
Içel	444,523	48,360	10·0	44·3
Isparta	242,352	27,802	11·5	46·5
Istanbul	1,882,092	155,625	8·3	73·4
Izmir	1,063,490	112,959	10·6	56·0
Kars	543,600	49,011	9·0	29·9
Kastamonu	433,620	33,450	7·3	26·5
Kayseri	480,387	55,716	11·6	39·1
Kirklareli	241,146	33,034	13·6	56·8
Kirşehir	175,749	19,503	10·7	35·5
Kocaeli	297,463	26,610	9·0	49·6
Konya	982,422	100,510	10·1	39·9
Kütahya	367,753	28,106	7·6	31·8
Malatya	394,172	26,064	6·6	29·4
Manisa	657,104	64,871	9·8	42·3
Maraş	389,857	28,540	7·2	23·1
Mardin	353,411	16,157	4·5	14·3
Muğla	299,611	37,032	12·3	48·7
Muş	167,638	7,944	4·7	17·5

Table IV—continued

Province	Population (1960)	Elementary school (1959-60)	Percentage of total population attending primary schools	Literacy (Percentage of population 6 years of age and older)
Nevşehir	187,398	22,296	11·7	42·4
Niğde	322,917	31,801	9·9	32·0
Ordu	469,397	32,482	6·8	22·4
Rize	248,930	24,426	9·6	35·8
Sakarya	361,992	45,549	12·4	49·5
Samsun	654,602	40,738	6·2	31·0
Siirt	232,243	10,333	4·3	15·9
Sinop	249,730	22,430	8·8	29·4
Sivas	669,922	57,511	8·5	29·2
Tekirdağ	274,806	34,931	12·0	51·4
Tokat	437,590	36,826	8·4	28·8
Trabzon	532,999	37,102	6·9	29·1
Tunceli	140,068	12,161	8·5	29·0
Urfa	401,919	19,754	5·0	16·4
Uşak	184,733	23,519	12·4	38·9
Van	211,034	7,827	3·8	16·7
Yozgat	402,400	36,102	8·9	26·8
Zonguldak	569,059	44,759	7·9	36·8

ORTA AND *LISE* (1959-1960)

Province	Orta	Lise
1. Adana	10,567	2,027
2. Adiyaman	322	
3. Afyon	3,511	613
4. Ağri	611	147
5. Amasya	2,401	258
6. Ankara	20,082	6,866
7. Antalya	2,790	898
8. Artvin	2,125	269
9. Aydin	5,114	1,221
10. Balikesir	5,783	1,387
11. Bilecik	1,458	162
12. Bingöl	354	89
13. Bitlis	493	135
14. Bolu	2,860	501
15. Bürdür	1,584	242
16. Bursa	5,482	1,242
17. Çanakkale	2,700	429
18. Çankiri	1,282	219
19. Çorum	2,165	245
20. Denizli	4,700	906
21. Diyarbakir	672	
22. Edirne	1,896	410
23. Elâziğ	2,761	613
24. Erzincan	1,264	253

ORTA AND *LISE* (1959–1960)

Province	Orta	Lise
25. Erzurum	2,994	645
26. Eskişehir	5,444	1,243
27. Gaziantep	3,636	958
28. Giresun	2,368	298
29. Gümüshane	1,199	146
30. Hakkari	87	58
31. Hatay	1,654	886
32. Içel	5,521	1,134
33. Isparta	2,803	485
34. Istanbul	41,085	14,923
35. Izmir	14,930	3,672
36. Kars	2,858	
37. Kastamonu	1,940	369
38. Kayseri	5,106	997
39. Kirklareli	1,992	350
40. Kirşehir	1,649	200
41. Kocaeli	3,082	548
42. Konya	8,383	1,448
43. Kütahya	1,902	299
44. Malatya	4,012	735
45. Manisa	5,183	1,031
46. Maraş	2,486	580
47. Mardin	1,059	267
48. Muğla	2,790	239
49. Muş	403	133
50. Nevşehir	1,029	295
51. Nigde	2,599	555
52. Ordu	3,133	513
53. Rize	1,847	339
54. Sakarya	2,997	470
55. Samsun	5,028	855
56. Siirt	593	129
57. Sinop	1,254	196
58. Sivas	4,963	743
59. Tekirdağ	2,324	272
60. Tokat	3,643	400
61. Trabzon	4,167	977
62. Tunceli	1,243	171
63. Urfa	1,882	418
64. Uşak	1,881	326
65. Van	736	203
66. Yozgat	1,882	318
67. Zonguldak	4,680	998
Total	253,474	58,954

TABLE V

URBAN–RURAL DISTRIBUTION OF ELEMENTARY EDUCATION

Year	Urban Population	Elementary School Enrolments	Percentage of Population	Rural Population	Elementary School Enrolments	Percentage of Population
1955	6,927,343	666,247	9·6	17,137,420	1,296,749	7·5
1960	8,881,542	978,358	11·0	18,873,278	1,585,837	7·9
	(estimated population of cities 10,000 inhabitants and over)	(1959–60—includes private elementary schools)		(estimated population of places 10,000 and less)	(1959–60—includes private elementary schools)	
1962–63		1,219,786			2,179,820	

Sources: *Milli Egitim Istatistikleri Ilk Ogretim 1953–60*, p. 88. Jefferson Eastmond, *Türkiyede Okulların Gelişmesine Tesir Eden Faktörler (Facilitators of Good Schools, 1964)*, Ankara: Test ve Araştirma Bürosu, 1964, pp. 17–21.

TABLE VI

URBAN–RURAL PARENTAL BACKGROUND OF *LISE* STUDENTS
(percentages)

Parental Background	Public *Lises* N = 1063	Private *Lises* N = 1507	Minority *Lises* N = 932	Foreign *Lises* N = 1327	Total Students N = 4829	Total Students by Sex	
						Boys N = 3020	Girls N = 1819
Urban	60·5	81·7	89·0	95·0	82·0	76·0	92·5
Rural	39·5	18·3	11·0	5·0	18·0	24·0	7·5

TABLE VII

PARENTAL PLACE OF RESIDENCE
(percentages)

Location	Public *Lise* N = 1077	Private Turkish *Lise* N = 1554	Minority *Lise* N = 941	Foreign *Lise* N = 1342	Total N = 4914	Total Students Boys N = 3057	Girls N = 1851
This city or town	66·3	75·6	86·8	75·0	75·5	69·1	86·7
Another city or town in this vilayet	9·1	6·4	4·6	5·4	6·4	7·5	4·3
Nearby village in this vilayet	8·9	4·4	2·3	1·2	4·1	5·7	1·4
City or town outside this vilayet	9·6	11·5	3·8	17·6	11·3	14·1	6·6
Village outside this vilayet	6·0	2·1	2·4	·8	2·7	3·6	1·0

TABLE VIII

PERCENTAGE OF PRIMARY SCHOOL GRADUATES WHO ENTERED *ORTA* AND VOCATIONAL SCHOOLS

Year	Primary School Graduates		Entered *Orta* Schools (%)		Entered Vocational Schools (%)	
	Boys	Girls	Boys	Girls	Boys	Girls
1934–35	20,120	8,293	72·1	67	5·93	7·30
1935–36			72·1	67	5·93	7·30
1944–45	66,244	23,499	21·2	25	22·3	10·3
1945–46			21·2	25	22·3	10·3
1950–51	102,384	42,476	21·9	15·7	6·67	6·24
1951–52			21·9	15·7	6·67	6·24
1958–59	177,992 (193,847)	88,810[1] (95,825)[2]				
1959–60			42·6 (39·4)	27·2 (25·2)	4·0	6·5
1960–61[3]	226,280	111,474				
1961–62	115,336	32,259	50·2	28·8		

[1] Those who received diplomas.
[2] Those who enrolled in the fifth class.
[3] Enrolment in public primary schools.
Sources: Özalp, *op. cit.*, pp. 15–19. T. C. Milli Eğitim Bakanliği, *Mesleki ve Teknik Ögretim Müesseseriyle ilgili Rakamlar* (Ankara: Bengi Matbaasi, 1961), p. 18. The figures given by the various sources vary. According to those of the technical and vocational branch of the Ministry in 1959–60, the percentages of those who entered *orta* schools were for boys 45·1 per cent and for girls 24·7 per cent. The figures for the years after 1958 were computed from statistics of the Research and Measurement Bureau of the Ministry of Education.

TABLE IX

PERCENTAGES OF ORTA GRADUATES WHO ENTERED *LISES* AND TECHNICAL/VOCATIONAL SCHOOLS

Year	Orta School Graduates		Entered *Lises* (%)		Entered Vocational and Technical Schools (%)	
	Boys	Girls	Boys	Girls	Boys	Girls
1934–35	5,589	1,877				
1935–36			79·2	66·2	17·4	38·0
			(4,428)	(1,244)	(976)	(526)
1939–40	10,397	3,878				
1940–41			48·3	39·9	9·2	15·6
			(5,029)	(1,548)	(960)	(607)
1944–45	10,391	3,356				
1945–46			46·5	38·1	22·1	43·1
			(4,728)	(1,279)	(2,302)	(1,449)
1949–50	7,864	2,990				
1950–51			61·9	42·4	21·2	45·8
			(4,873)	(1,268)	(1,667)	(1,373)
1954–55	12,648	4,411	60·5	41·8	17·1	16·4
			(7,650)	(1,843)	(2,158)	(725)
1958–59	24,656	8,281	51·6	48·8	24·4	20·4
			(12,711)	(4,038)	(6,012)	(1,687)

Sources: Özalp, *op. cit.*, pp. 21–2; *Meslêki ve Teknik Öğretim, op. cit.*, p. 18.

TABLE X

DISTRIBUTION OF STUDENTS BY TYPE
OF SCHOOL
(Percentages enrolled in various types of school)

Year	Primary	*Orta*	*Lise*	Technical/ Vocational (middle and *lise* level)	Higher (post- *lise*)	Univers- ities only
1932–33	89·5	7·5	1·6	·5	·9	
1935–36	89·3	7·4	1·8	·6	·8	
1940–41	86·1	9·5	2·3	·8	1·2	
1945–46	89·2	5·6	1·8	2·1	1·3	
1948–49	89·3	5·0	1·5	2·6	1·6	
1961–62	84·5	8·5	2·2	2·9	1·9	1·2

Sources: Robinson, 'An Analysis of Turkish Education' (Ankara: Inter-national Bank for Reconstruction and Development, a working paper for the 1950 Economic Survey Mission to Turkey, 1950), p. 20. The figures for 1961–62 were taken from tabulations furnished by the Research and Measurement Bureau (mimeographed).

TABLE XI

PATERNAL OCCUPATION OF *LISE* STUDENTS
(percentages)

Occupation		Public (N = 1369)	Private Turkish (N = 1442)	Minority (N = 924)	Foreign (N = 1264)	Aggregate of Students in all *lises* (N = 4923)
Higher professional (doctors, engineers, scientists, university professors, etc.)	(1)	5·0	16·0	3·7	22·8	12·4
Professional and higher technical	(2)	6·6	9·4	10·8	11·5	9·4
Managerial and higher administrative	(3)	5·0	·8	1·2	7·7	5·7
Minor administrative	(4)	2·1	1·6	·4	·7	1·3
Clerical	(5)	20·2	16·6	4·0	16·2	15·2
Private traders, small business	(6)	13·5	23·7	32·0	29·9	24·1
Small farmers, fishermen, hunters, etc.	(7)	22·9	8·8	4·0	·9	9·9
Skilled workers and craftsmen	(8)	13·4	8·4	33·7	5·6	13·8
Semi-skilled workers	(9)	·6	·6	·5		·5
Unskilled	(10)	4·9	2·8	4·4	·2	3·2
Unidentified	(11)	5·5	4·0	5·2	·9	4·4

TABLE XII

PATERNAL OCCUPATIONS OF *LISE* STUDENTS AND OCCUPATIONS OF TURKISH MALE POPULATION

(percentages)

Occupations	Male population 15 years and over in 1960	Public	Private Turkish	Minority	Foreign
Professional, technical and related	1·6	11·6	25·4	14·5	34·3
Administrative, clerical and related	3·9	27·3	26·2	5·6	24·6
(a) Sales workers and related	4·0				
(b) Private traders, small business		13·5	23·7	32·0	29·9
Farmers, fishermen, hunters, forestry and related	62·3	22·9	8·8	4·0	·9
Workers in mine, quarry and related	·6				
Workers in transport and communications	2·7				
Craftsmen-production process workers	8·5	13·4	8·4	33·7	5·6
Unskilled workers	4·1	4·9	2·8	4·4	·2
Workers associated with 'services' (e.g., entertainment, sports and recreation)	3·8				
Unidentified and without occupation	8·5	5·5	4·0	5·2	·9
Total	100·0	99·1	99·3	99·4	96·4

Source: *1960 Genel Nüfus Sayimi*, Yayin No. 433, p. 20. The percentages in each category of schools were estimated from those on Table XI.

TABLE XIII

PARENTAL EDUCATION OF *LISE* STUDENTS
(percentages)

Level of Education (highest level of schooling)	Public		Private Turkish		Minority		Foreign		Aggregate of Students in all *lises*	
	Father (N=1370)	Mother (N=1389)	Father (N=1450)	Mother (N=1455)	Father (N=915)	Mother (N=920)	Father (N=1274)	Mother (N=1284)	Father (N=5031)	Mother (N=5072)
No schooling (never attended)	17.4	42.4	7.0	16.1	6.3	8.8	1.6	2.8	8.0	18.2
Attended but did not complete elementary school	15.8	15.5	9.4	9.5	25.1	19.5	4.0	3.4	12.0	11.0
Completed elementary school	18.6	20.6	10.8	16.0	16.7	22.6	4.7	11.0	12.0	16.7
Middle school (attended and/or completed)	13.4	10.4	13.1	20.2	21.2	26.4	10.7	28.0	13.3	20.0
Attended but did not complete *lise*	3.8	1.8	6.1	5.8	7.3	4.7	8.2	9.7	6.0	5.2
Completed *lise*	4.0	2.1	8.9	10.6	10.9	11.7	11.1	15.9	8.0	9.5
Vocational or technical school (attended and/or completed)	7.6	2.7	6.1	6.7	.4	.7	7.1	6.8	5.2	4.0
Higher institutions (Yüksek Okul) attended and/or completed	2.3	.5	5.2	2.9	2.1	.4	7.7	3.0	4.0	1.4
Attended but did not complete university	.7	.1	2.6	1.9	1.2	.5	3.5	3.7	2.0	1.4
Completed university	4.4	.4	21.0	4.2	3.3	.3	31.2	8.2	15.2	4.3
Another school	10.0	2.2	7.2	3.3	3.0	2.3	7.5	4.2	7.0	3.0
Don't know	2.0	1.3	2.5	2.7	2.3	2.0	2.7	3.2	2.3	2.0

285

TABLE XIV

PARENTAL EDUCATION OF *LISE* STUDENTS AND
EDUCATIONAL LEVEL OF ECONOMICALLY ACTIVE
TURKISH POPULATION 15–64 YEARS OF AGE (1960)
(Percentages)

Level of Education (highest school completed)	Turkish population 15–64 years of age		Aggregate of students of all *lises*	
	Male	Female	Father	Mother
Have not attended or completed elementary school	60·6	90·0	20·0	29·2
Completed elementary school	31·9	8·4	12·0	16·7
Completed secondary school (*orta* and *lise*)	4·4	·5	15·1	22·1
Completed vocational and/or technical school	1·4	·2	4·4	3·6
Completed university or equivalent higher institution	1·3	·2	18·8	5·4
Unknown level of schooling completed	·4	·7	—	—

Source: *1960 Genel Nüfus Sayimi*, Yayin No. 433, p. 32. The percentages
in each category were estimated from those on Table XIII and from other
tabulations of the data collected by the author.

TABLE XIV—*continued*

Public		Private Turkish		Minority		Foreign	
Father	Mother	Father	Mother	Father	Mother	Father	Mother
33·2	57·9	16·4	25·6	31·4	28·3	5·6	6·2
18·6	20·6	10·8	16·0	16·7	22·6	4·7	11·0
10·5	1·9	16·0	6·9	21·0	4·7	17·0	8·6
6·1	·6	4·7	1·5	·3	·0	6·0	1·5
6·2	·1	25·0	1·7	4·3	·0	37·3	2·6
—	—	—	—	—	—	—	—

TABLE XV

FATHER'S AND GRANDFATHER'S OCCUPATION, AND OCCUPATIONAL ASPIRATIONS AND EXPECTATIONS OF *LISE* STUDENTS

(percentages)

Occupation	Public				Private Turkish			
	F	GF	SOA	SOE	lF	GF	SOA	SOE
High professional (1)	5·0	2·4	52·4	19·3	16·0	6·7	46·8	23·8
Professional and high technical (2)	6·6	3·4	9·0	11·6	9·4	4·6	12·1	12·4
Managerial and high administrative (3)	5·0	5·5	1·5	1·7	8·0	11·7	1·6	1·9
Minor administrative (4)	2·1	·6	1·2	·1	1·6	1·0	1·2	·8
Clerical (5)	20·2	12·0	16·1	25·3	16·6	13·3	14·8	18·4
Trade and business (6)	13·5	12·7	1·1	3·9	23·7	18·2	4·0	7·6
Farmers, fishermen and hunters (7)	22·9	40·2	·4	1·8	8·8	19·2	·2	1·4
Skills and craftsmen (8)	13·4	7·5	2·3	2·7	8·4	3·9	4·0	2·7
Semi-skilled (9)	·6	·4	·2	·1	·6	·2	·1	·1
Unskilled (10)	4·9	2·1	·1	1·2	2·8	1·5	·3	3·0
Unidentified (11)	5·5	13·1	15·8	31·5	4·0	19·7	14·9	28·0

F = Father's occupation.
GF = Grandfather's occupation.
SOA = Student's occupational aspirations.
SOE = Student's occupational expectations.

TABLE XV—continued

	Minority				Foreign				Aggregate		
¹F	GF	SOA	SOE	¹F	GF	SOA	SOE	¹F	GF	SOA	SOE
3·7	2·8	45·2	19·4	22·8	10·9	48·3	28·9	12·4	5·9	48·4	23·1
10·8	5·7	8·2	9·1	11·5	5·9	10·4	11·6	9·4	4·8	10·1	11·4
1·2	1·1	·8	·1	7·7	10·1	2·6	1·9	5·7	7·6	1·6	1·5
·4	·4	·7	·1	·7	1·2	·4	·2	1·3	·8	·9	·5
4·0	3·4	18·7	21·2	16·2	14·8	14·5	17·8	15·2	11·5	15·8	20·6
32·0	24·6	1·7	5·2	29·9	25·5	3·2	4·5	24·1	19·7	2·6	5·4
4·0	7·0	·0	·0	·9	6·5	·1	·1	9·9	19·6	·2	·9
33·7	17·4	4·1	3·4	5·6	5·4	6·3	3·6	13·8	7·8	4·2	3·0
·5	1·1	·0	·1	—	·4	·0	·1	·5	·5	·1	·1
4·4	2·4	1·1	11·5	·2	·6	·5	4·0	3·2	1·6	·5	4·3
5·2	34·4	19·5	30·0	·9	18·6	13·7	27·4	4·4	20·3	15·7	29·2

F = Father's occupation.
GF = Grandfather's occupation.
SOA = Student's occupational aspirations.
SOE = Student's occupational expectations.

TABLE XVI

STUDENTS' REASONS FOR *LISE* VIS-A-VIS TECHNICAL/VOCATIONAL EDUCATION

(percentages)

Reasons	Public *Lises* (N = 1059)	Private Turkish *Lises* (N = 1536)	Minority *Lises* (N = 937)	Foreign *Lises* (N = 1324)	Total Number of Students (N = 4856)
Better job	6·3	7·3	12·7	5·4	7·6
Continue education in university	66·0	69·8	62·6	69·1	67·4
Broader general education	15·3	10·8	15·3	12·3	13·1
No ability for technical/vocational work	2·8	3·6	1·3	2·0	2·6
Suggested by parents or others	3·2	3·8	3·0	5·3	3·9
More respected by others	·5	·5	·6	·7	·6
Do not like technical/vocational work	1·8	·7	1·5	·5	1·0
Other reasons	3·5	2·7	1·7	3·1	2·8
Do not know or undecided	·6	·8	1·3	1·6	1·0
Totals	100·0	100·0	100·0	100·0	100·0

TABLE XVII

PROGRAMME OF STUDIES OF TURKISH *LISE*
(Effective since 1957–58)

Subject	First Class	Second Class Science	Second Class Literature	Third Class Science	Third Class Literature
Turkish language and literature	5	4	5	3	6
Psychology	—	2	2	—	—
Philosophy, Logic and Sociology	—	—	—	3	6
History	2	2	2	2	3
History of Art	—	—	2	—	1
Geography	2	2	2	1	2
Mathematics (Algebra, Geometry, Astronomy)	5	6	4	8	3
Natural Sciences (Biology, Botany, Zoology, Geology)	3	2	2	1	—
Physics	3	3	2	4	2
Chemistry	3	3	2	3	1
Foreign Languages (English, French, or German)	5	4	5	4	5
Physical Education	1	1	1	1	1
Military Education	1	1	1	1	1
Electives (Music, Drawing or Foreign Languages)	2	2	2	1	1
Total weekly periods	32	32	32	32	32

Source: M. Sitki Bilmen, *The Turkish Lise: Its Stable Characteristics and Curriculum* (Ankara: Maarif Basimevi, 1960), p. 18.

PROCEDURES IN *LISE* STUDY
CONDUCTED IN TURKEY
1962–63

1. Upon arrival in Turkey in the fall of 1962 permission was secured from the National Ministry of Education to visit schools and to administer a questionnaire to a sample of students in four types of *lise*, namely, (a) public *lises*, (b) private Turkish *lises*, (c) 'minority' *lises*, and (d) 'foreign' *lises*.

2. A list of all the *lises* in Turkey was secured from the Research and Measurement Bureau of the Ministry of Education. As a base for sampling an information blank was sent to the principals of all *lises* requesting current enrolment figures in each of the three *lise* classes.

3. The final sample included ninety-three *lises*: forty public (selected from a list of 130 such schools through a formula based on enrolments and location), thirty private Turkish, thirteen foreign-operated, and ten minority *lises*. Except for the public *lises*, these numbers represented *all* the schools listed under the respective categories. Another letter was sent to the principals of the selected schools requesting lists of names of all the students registered in the three classes. It was decided to take a sample of 6,000 students, 1,500 from each of the four types of *lises*, or 500 from each class. Since total enrolments in the minority and the foreign schools were less than 1,500 in each case, it was decided to include all students in the final sample. In the case of the private Turkish *lises* (total enrolment of about 6,000), 1,500 students were randomly selected from the lists. Selection was more difficult in the case of the public *lises* because of the large number of enrolments (about 88,232). Our problem was to give every student in a given class an equal probability of selection. To attain this, a formula was developed through the assistance of Mr. Jöel Tucker, an American consultant for A.I.D. attached to the Bureau of Statistics in Ankara. Our final sample included about 5,500 students.

4. In the meantime, a questionnaire was constructed and a pre-test was run on 200 students in two representative *lises:*

one in Ankara, a cosmopolitan centre, and another in Kırşehir, a provincial town. On the basis of the responses and intensive interviews with students, the instrument was refined further in terms of the criteria of validity and reliability.

5. The final questionnaire was then administered to the sampled students.

6. Of the total returns, 5,126 were cleared, the answers were coded, and the data were punched on IBM cards. The coding was done by the writer and a trained group of Turkish coders. There were four cards for each sampled unit, making a total of 20,504 punched cards. These cards were brought to the United States and processed at the University of Chicago.

GLOSSARY

Azinlik: minority.

Bash defterdar: literally 'head accountant'; formerly finance minister.

Bash Vekil: prime minister.

Darülfünun: in Ottoman, 'university'.

Darülmaarif: formerly a type of civil service school; also known as *Valide Mektebi* (School of the Valideh Sultanah).

Darülmuallim: formerly a men's teacher-training school.

Dere-beyi: provincial landlord, feudal chieftain.

Devlet: state; government.

Devshirme: literally 'act of gathering or collecting'; formerly the recruitment and selection of boys for service under the Sultan; also simply used to refer to the boys so selected.

Din: religion, faith (especially the Moslem religion).

Din ve Devlet: faith and state.

Dragoman: literally 'translator'; used to refer to certain high officials attached to the Sultan.

Efendi: master; a former title of respect used after a name, equivalent to 'Mister' or 'Esquire'; gentleman.

Egitim: education.

Egitmen: village teacher.

Enderun Mektebi: literally the 'inside school'; the name of the Ottoman Palace School.

Etatism: one of the basic six 'fundamental and unchanging principles' undergirding the political ideology of the Republican People's Party (1931) and later incorporated into the Turkish Constitution (1937); a translation of the Turkish word *devletchilik*, meaning 'statism'. It was defined as follows: 'to interest the State actively in matters where the general and vital interests of the nation are in question, especially in the economic field'. The assumption by the state of many of the economic activities of the country.

Evkaf: plural of *vakif*, meaning 'pious foundations'.

Ezan: in the Moslem religion, the call to prayer by a muezzin.

Ferman: command, decree; an edict issued by the Sultan.

Gâvur: infidel, non-believer, non-Moslem.

Gazi Egitim Enstitüsü: Gazi Pedagogical Institute (Ankara).

Genel Kültür: general culture; similar in meaning to the French *culture générale*.

Grand Vezir: in the Ottoman period, the chief minister of the state; something like a prime minister.

Güzide Sinif: literally, 'the chosen or select class'; the elite.

Hatti-i-Sherif: Noble Rescript.

Hatti Humayun: Illustrious Rescript.

Hakim: judge.

Harbiye: War Academy (College).

Hoja: a Moslem priest, a school teacher.

Hürriyet: freedom, liberty.

Ich oglan: formerly, 'inside boys' in the Palace School.

Idadi: same as *idadiye*; a preparatory secondary school the establishment of which was provided for in the 1869 Regulations for General Education; something like a junior high school.

Ilmiye: from 'ilm' meaning knowledge or science; those belonging to the hierarchy of Moslem learned men.

Imam: a religious leader; the religious functionary who leads Moslems in prayer.

Imam-hatib: prayer leader–preacher; with *okul* (school) it refers to an educational institution for the training of religious leaders.

Inkilâp *or* inkilâb: radical change; revolution; transformation; reform.

Iptidai: from *ibtida* meaning beginning; in the Ottoman language, a primary or elementary school.

Irade: command, decree.

Irfan: knowledge; culture; refinement.

Islahat: improvement; reforms.

Ish Adamlar: business people (men).

Ish Bankasi: Work Bank, Business Bank.

Istanbul Erkek Lisesi: Istanbul Boys' Lycée.

Janissaries: in the Ottoman period, the corps of soldiers recruited from non-Moslem groups, but converted to Mohammedanism; the military branch of the Ottoman state.

Kadi: a judge of the Islamic Holy Law (*Sheriat*); a Moslem judge.

Kalem: 'pen', office, bureau.

Kalemiye: from 'kalem'; formerly the 'men of the pen', i.e., officials or 'clerks' in the government service.

Kapi Kullari: literally, 'Slaves of the Gate'; formerly applied to the recruits (*devshirme*) who served the Sultan.

Kâtib: a scribe—an official.

Kaymakam: the governor of a sub-province (*kaza*), an administrative unit.

Kaza: unit of local government governed by a *Kaymakam*.

Kismet: destiny, fate, luck.

Kolej: college; used to refer to a type of public secondary school established in the 1950's, where the medium of instruction is English.

Köy Enstitüsü: village institute; a type of educational institution which was established in 1940 and continued functioning in its original form until 1950.

Küchük tüjjar: small merchant.

Laicism: one of the six basic principles underlying the political ideology of the Republican People's Party (1931) and later incorporated into the Constitution (1937); in Turkish *Lâiklik*, it signifies the ideology of 'secularism' and the secularization policies during the republican period.

Lâla: tutor, pedagogue.

Lise: the Turkish equivalent of the French word *lycée*; an upper secondary school (grades 9–11); something like the American senior high school.

Lokma: a syrupy sweet fritter.

Maarif Emine: an administrator who supervises schools.

Maarif memuru: educational official (officer).

Maarif müdürü: educational director.

Maarif Umumiye Nezareti: formerly Ministry of Public Education.

Maarifi adliye: justice education.

Maarifi Umumiye Nizamnamesi: Regulations for General Education.

Mejlisi Kebiri Maarif: Higher Education Council.

Medrese: formerly, a Moslem college where theology and religious law were the predominant subjects taught.

Medreseji: a supporter of the religious colleges (medrese).

Mekâtibi Umumiye Nezareti: formerly, Ministry of Public Schools.

Mekteb: school; used to refer to a religiously oriented type of school usually adjoined to a mosque.

Mektebi Irfan: literally, 'school of knowledge'; an academy established by Reshid Pasha.

Mektebi Maarifi Adlî: School for Justice Education.

Mektebi Sultanî: Imperial School; refers to the first lise established in the Ottoman Empire.

Memur: a government official, roughly equivalent to the English 'clerk'.

Meshrutiyet: in the nineteenth century, the system of government based on a new constitution; the era of constitutional government.

Millet: in modern Turkish, 'nation', 'people'; in the nineteenth century, a non-Moslem community of the Ottoman Empire, e.g., Greek Orthodox millet, Jewish millet, etc.

Milli Egitim Bakanligi: National Ministry of Education.

Milli egitim müdürü: national education director.

Molla: formerly, a high ranking judge; theological student.

Müdür: director; principal; one who directs or superintends; an administrator.

Müfti: also mufti; a Moslem jurist; a senior Moslem priest; a canon lawyer.

Muhasib: accountant, bookkeeper.

Muhtar: village headman.

Muhtelif gayeli: literally 'multi-purpose'; when used with *okul* (school), a sort of 'comprehensive school'.

Mülkiye: literally 'civil service'; also the school for civil servants established in the nineteenth century.

Mustakil ish yeri müdürü: private business executive or official.

Müsteshar: councillor, Secretary of State; Undersecretary.

Mutasarrif: formerly the governor of a sanjak (province).

Nahiye Müdürü: the official 'directing' or governing a nahiye i.e., a local administrative unit consisting of one or more villages.

Nizam-i Jedid: literally 'new order'; the title of an Imperial Rescript issued by Selim III in 1793.

Okumac yerleri: reading places.

Olgunluk: maturity, ripeness; used to refer to an examination taken at the completion of a *lise* course; something like the German *Abitur*.

Orta: middle, medium; shortened form of ortaokul (middle school).

Ortaokul(lar): middle school(s); a three-year (grades 6–8) secondary 'junior high' school.

Özel Türk: private Turkish.

Pasishah: ruler, sovereign, especially the Sultan of the Ottoman Empire.

Para: money; about a halfpenny.

Populism (in Turkish *halkchilik*): one of the fundamental principles of Turkish socio-political development and modernization. It was incorporated into the Turkish Constitution of 1937 and signified the idea that authority, sovereignty, power, etc. rest with the people. It also referred to a view of society based on equality, popular participation, individual freedom and 'economic sovereignty'.

Porte (also Sublime Porte): used to refer to the Ottoman or the Sultan's government and court.

Râya: subject; peasant.

Reis Efendi: formerly, head of central administration.

Rüshdiye: in Ottoman, a type of middle or 'upper elementary' school.

Serbest meslekler: free professions.

Sheriat (in English also written 'Sheria'): Islamic religious law.

Sheyhülislâm: formerly, the chief religious leader of the Empire.

Shura: council.

Siyasal Bilgiler Fakültesi: Faculty of Political Sciences (Ankara University).

Softa: fanatic, bigot; Moslem theological student.

Sübyan (also *sibyan*): in Ottoman, literally 'children', but used to refer to a type of primary school.

Sultanî: imperial; pertaining to the Sultan; after 1868 used to refer to a secondary academic school, used interchangeably with *lise*.

Tanzimat: literally 'reorganization'; used to refer to the social and political reform of the period 1839–76.

Tanzimatji: reformer; a person supporting the reforms of the Tanzimat period.

Tarikat: religious order or brotherhood.

Tash mekteb: literally, 'stone school'.

Tejvit: art of reading or reciting the Koran with proper rhythm.

Tedrisati Iptidai Kanunu: Provisory Primary Education Law.

Terjume Odasi: Translation Chamber.

Tevhidi Tedrisat Kanunu: Law of Unification of Education (Instruction).

Timar: military fief.

Tuba Agaji: a tree in Paradise supposed to have its roots in the sky and its leaves in the earth.

Tuba Agaji Nazariyesi: literally, 'theory of the tree in Paradise'; it was used to advocate the educational theory that educational reform should start at the top, i.e., the university and the *lises*, rather than at the bottom, i.e., the primary schools.

Tüjjar: merchant; used to refer to big or small business man.

Türchülük: concept of Turkism.

Türk Ojagi: Turkish Hearth (a national cultural movement).

Ulema: learned men; doctors of Islamic theology.

Ulumu Edebiye: literary sciences.

Vakif: pious foundation.

Vali: the governor of a Turkish province (vilayet), an administrative unit.

Varlik Vergisi: tax on property or possessions; capitation tax.

Vatan: motherland, one's native country.

Vekil: in Turkey only, 'Minister of State'.

Vekiller Okulu: ministers' school.

Vilâyet: a Turkish province governed by a Vali.

Yabanji: stranger; foreigner; foreign.

Yedek Subay: supplementary officer; reserve officer.

INDEX